Charlemagne's Cousins

ALLEN CABANISS, professor of history at the University of Mississippi, has written extensively on the history and theology of the Middle Ages. The author of two biographies, *Agobard of Lyons: Churchman and Critic* and *Amalarius of Metz*, he is also editor and translator of *Son of Charlemagne* and co-author of *Early Medieval Theology*.

Professor Cabaniss, who received his doctorate from the University of Chicago, is a fellow of the Royal Historical Society and a councilor of The Order of the Crown of Charlemagne.

Charlemagne's Cousins

CONTEMPORARY LIVES OF
ADALARD AND WALA

St. Paschasius Radbertus,
Abbot of Corbie

Translated, with Introduction and Notes, by
ALLEN CABANISS

SYRACUSE UNIVERSITY PRESS

Meis dilectissimis—

PAUL T. JONES, IV
W. RUTLAND CUNNINGHAM
IRVIN E. LUNGER
G. B. "BART" DeLASHMET
M. C. "CHOOKY" FALKNER
JOHN R. FARRELL
TERENCE S. TARR
FRANK W. HUNGER
JAMES L. GRAHAM
FLORIAN H. YOSTE, III
WILLIAM E. YOSTE
PAUL E. JONES, III

Quos duodecim omnes
adhuc amavi
etiam nunc amo
semper amabo
amicos carissimos

Acknowledgments

The annotations will indicate my great indebtedness to many predecessors in this area of study. The reference division of the library of the University of Mississippi has been of invaluable aid in securing interlibrary loans, microfilms, and Xerox copies without which this undertaking would have come to naught. It is with special gratitude that I record my thanks to the Committee on Faculty Research of the Graduate School of the University of Mississippi, Dean Lewis Nobles, chairman, for making a generous grant to enable me both to prepare and publish this work. My sister, Frances C. Stephens, has been of incalculable assistance in proofreading and indexing.

The persons named in my dedication are friends who have contributed beyond measure to my life. Some I have known for forty years or more. Others belong to these later days. To them I can never fully express my gratitude and devotion. Happily they are all still living: "semper sint in flore."

ALLEN CABANISS

University, Mississippi
May, 1967

Contents

Abbreviations

PL   J. P. Migne, *Patrologiae cursus completus: series latina*

MGH   *Monumenta Germaniae historica*

PLAC   *Poetae latini aevi carolini*

Adalard   The Life of Saint Adalard (*Vita sancti Adalhardi*), as here translated

Wala   The Life of Wala (*Vita Walae seu Epitaphium Arsenii*), as here translated

Charlemagne's Cousins

Introduction

THE AUTHOR

Only a brief account of the life of Paschasius Radbertus, author of the two *Vitae* here translated, is necessary. He and his work are quite well known and there is a recent biography, namely, Henri Peltier, *Pascase Radbert*.[1] The following will simply sketch the salient facts of his life so far as they are available.

Nothing is known about Radbertus' family or place and date of birth. It has reasonably been supposed that he was born between 785 and 795.[2] Reared by the nuns of St. Mary at Soissons, he was devoted to them and especially to their abbess Theodrada, sister of his heroes, Adalard and Wala. While still a child he received the tonsure (the monastic "haircut") in the presence of these women. At some early stage in his life, Radbertus abandoned his convent home and (as he said) "lost the tonsure, being for a long time an exile in the world, stained with many worldly activities."[3] What he meant, we do not know, but before 812 he went to Corbie to take monastic vows under Abbot Adalard, whose ardent disciple he became. There he also came to know Wala, Adalard's brother and successor as abbot. With these two, he was as it were a third.[4]

Until Adalard's death in 826, the life of Radbertus was chiefly concerned with the interior life of the monastery, with study, and with teaching, although in 822 he was one of those who went to participate in the establishment of the New Corvey monastery. It is

I

possible that some of his writing was done during the rule of Adalard, as will be indicated below in treating his publications. He was also one of the monks sent to the palace to secure the election of Wala to succeed Adalard. From that time until Wala's death in 836, Radbertus was affected, along with his hero, by political events in Frankland. Much material relating to his manner of life during this period appears in his books, especially in the *Vita Walae*.

Before 846 he became abbot of Corbie, which he governed for about ten years. Internal difficulties in the monastery or his own desire to return to study caused him to abdicate his position about 852. Thereafter he spent some time at St. Riquier, but his latter years belonged to Corbie, where he wrote the bulk of his works. He died on April 2, in the year 865 or earlier.[5]

Radbertus' earliest treatise was part of a commentary on the Gospel according to St. Matthew,[6] but ultimate completion of the entire work took many years. Books I–IV were written before 826 and dedicated to Guntbald, a monk of St. Riquier. Books V–VIII were written while he was abbot of Corbie and dedicated to all brothers of St. Riquier. The remainder, Books IX–XII, was finished after his resignation. Sometime after 826 and before 833 he wrote one book, *De fide*, dedicated to Warinus, abbot and archimandrite of New Corvey. This is preceded by a bit of verse with the acrostic "Radbertus levita." [7] (He chose never to be advanced beyond the order of deacon.) A little later Radbertus honored Abbot Warinus with another book, *De spe*,[8] and still later after retirement a third one, *De caritate*.[9] The two on faith and hope are alluded to by Engelmodus of Soissons in his poem to Radbertus.[10]

Upon the death of Adalard and election of Wala, Radbertus composed his *Vita sancti Adalhardi* and the *Ecloga* [11] with which it concludes. During Wala's 831–33 exile, Radbertus published his most famous treatise, *De corpore et sanguine Domini*,[12] the first systematic study of Eucharistic doctrine, containing an early elaboration of the dogma of transubstantiation. It was dedicated to his former student, Placidius, and was also accompanied by acrostic verses. Much later, about 844, it was reissued with additional verses and offered as a Christmas or Easter gift to King Charles the Bald. This book evoked heated debate even at Corbie, where a fellow monk, Ratramnus, controverted it with a work bearing the same title.[13] As partial answer to some of the discussion, Radbertus in his old age prepared a letter on the subject to Frudegard, a monk of New Corvey.[14]

About 845 Radbertus returned to exposition of Scripture with his commentary on Lamentations in five books.[15] It was addressed to Odilmannus Severus, a fellow monk and one of the interlocutors in the *Vita Walae*. This work is sometimes deemed Radbertus' last. Possibly so, but the second book of the *Vita Walae* is probably later. *De partu Virginis*,[16] in two books, came after 846. They were written for his friend Emma, abbess of St. Mary at Soissons succeeding her mother Theodrada. While still abbot, Radbertus wrote about the martyrdom of Saints Rufinus and Valerius.[17] After his departure from office he compiled three books in exposition of Psalm 45 (Vulgate, Psalm 44),[18] dedicated to the nuns of Soissons.

The first book of the *Epitaphium Arsenii* or *Vita Walae*[19] was written not too long after Wala's death in 836 and before Radbertus himself was made abbot. The second book came perhaps fifteen or more years later, after Radbertus had ceased to be abbot. His Marian works cannot be dated with any assurance. They are the treatise *De nativitate sanctae Mariae*[20] and four homilies on the Assumption of the Blessed Virgin.[21] Other writings there probably were, but they are no longer extant.

Radbertus' fame rests on his Eucharistic discussion of the body and blood of Christ, but it is worth observing that the bulk of his work was scriptural commentary. Much of his writing contains not only important autobiographical data covering the span of his life but also intimate details of the life of the time.

THE SUBJECTS

Adalard and Wala were half-brothers, sons of Bernard, who was a natural son of Charles Martel.[22] Thus they were nephews of King Pepin and first cousins of Emperor Charlemagne. Adalard was born about 752 of Bernard's first wife, a Frankish woman.

Wala, the second son, was born about 773 of Bernard's second wife, a Saxon woman. There were three later children of the Saxon wife: Gundrada, born about 775; Bernarius, born about 776; and Theodrada, born after 776.[23] Another well-known cousin was St. William of Gellone, count of Toulouse and father of the still more famous (or notorious) Bernard, count of Barcelona.[24]

Trained in worldly wisdom at the palace school in the days of King Pepin, Adalard was a slightly younger fellow student of the future emperor.[25] In 770 or 771, about the beginning of his reign, Charles had, at the urging of his mother, married a daughter of Desiderius, king of the Lombards. But after a year he repudiated her (perhaps, but not certainly, because of her failure to produce offspring [26]) and married Hildegard, a Swabian noblewoman.[27] The action produced a crisis in the life of young Adalard. He could not be persuaded to recognize the divorce or do loyal service to the new queen. Despite efforts to appease him, he decided to abandon the court. So it was that at the age of twenty he applied for admission to the monastery at Corbie.[28]

The abbot and prior may have been suspicious, for it appears that he was allowed at first only to take a series of yearly vows.[29] His initial assignment was the humble one of gardener, and it is presumed that the hand of his cousin Charles was responsible for that lowly office.[30] But Adalard became a devoted monk. Because of his family connection and reputation, however, kinsmen and friends visited him more frequently than he thought fitting. Weighing the matter carefully, he decided to leave Corbie. In 775, therefore, he went to Monte Cassino, where he was allowed to remain only a short while. Royal envoys were sent to return him to Frankland and to Corbie.[31] Shortly thereafter he was designated as co-abbot, and in due course he succeeded his elder colleague Mordramnus.[32]

As the abbot of a great monastery and member of the royal family, he could not avoid administrative duties imposed upon him by virtue of office and by the dynamic Charles. In 809 he was sent to Rome with Bishop Bernarius of Worms to inquire of Pope Leo III about a definition of the doctrine of the procession of the Holy Spirit.[33] But apparently he had already been employed earlier to advise Charles's son, King Pepin of Italy. Indeed the *Vita* states that Italy had been "entrusted to him that in a useful and honorable manner he might mold with justice and discretion the realm and its king, the younger [34] Pepin, into the status of a commonwealth devoted to cultivation of religion." [35] It is not likely that he spent continuous time there, for it was said of him that only he could "year after year cross and recross the Alps without hazard of blindness." [36]

At King Pepin's death and the accession of his very young son Bernard, Adalard was again summoned from monastic life to serve as protector of the Italian state until the youthful king should reach his majority.[37] By now his virtues and abilities were so highly esteemed that the pope quipped as he greeted him, "O Frank, you know that if I shall find you other than I believe you to be, it is no longer needful for any Frank to come hither whom I ought to believe." [38] It was probably during this interval that the warring cities of Spoleto and Benevento were effectually reconciled as also were the Greeks of southern Italy and the neighboring islands.[39] His peacemaking facility may, however, have been the product of a much earlier stay in Italy, for the *Translatio sancti Viti* states that he had once sought to live the life of a hermit near Benevento.[40]

About this period his brother Wala made his first appearance on the historical scene. In the spring of 811 he was one of the Frankish counts who confirmed a treaty of peace between Charles and the Danish King Hemming.[41] In the same year he was one of the Frankish counts who witnessed the last will and testament of the great emperor.[42] A year later, when young King Bernard of Italy had reached his majority, Count Wala was ordered to go to the peninsula with him to participate in a campaign against Moslem raiders from North Africa and Spain.[43]

Like his older brother, Wala, too, had been trained at court,[44] but while still a youth he incurred the temporary disfavor of his cousin Charles. It has been supposed that he was in some way involved with the 792 conspiracy of Charles's son, Pepin the Hunchback.[45] Whatever the reason, he was banished from court for a while and compelled to live under the surveillance of some of the loyal magnates.[46] It is further presumed that it was during this first exile (?) that he married a daughter of William, count of Toulouse.[47] Although her name is not given in any of the sources (she may have been Rothlindis), the fact that he was a brother-in-law (as well as first cousin once removed) of Count Bernard of Barcelona is established.[48]

After an interval of unknown duration, Wala was restored to royal favor, indeed to high favor. Both his *Vita* and that of his brother state that he was elevated to a station second only to the emperor.[49] The position involved not only stewardship of the Carolingian household but also administration of justice, counsel for Charles, and indeed leadership of an army in battle.[50] It was undoubtedly in the latter capacity that he entered Italy in 812 to assist young King Bernard and thus to be near his elder brother Adalard. By this time and until Charles's death, Adalard and his brothers and sisters, as a closely knit family circle,[51] exercised a strong and enviable, perhaps inordinate, influence on their imperial cousin's court. Despite earlier divergences of opinion, Charles had not only been completely reconciled with them, but he also relied heavily and confidently upon them, especially upon the three brothers, Adalard, Wala, and Bernarius.[52]

The sister Gundrada, "in constant attendance on her brothers . . . was friendly to the king." [53] Alcuin, who called her Eulalia, looked upon her as a peculiar intercessor with Charles and as an example of goodness for the women of the palace.[54] He probably discussed the current Spanish heresy of adoptionism with her; he dedicated to her a treatise on the soul's power of reason.[55] The "Irish exile," in a poem to Charles, sent greetings to Gundrada, "fair of face and manners." [56] The youngest of the family, Theodrada (for whom Charles may have named one of his daughters), had, like her brother Wala, once been married. But later, by 810, she was abbess of the convent of St. Mary in Soissons,[57] where she was succeeded in 846 by her daughter Emma. She was indeed the benefactress of her brothers' biographer, Paschasius Radbertus.[58] She seems not to have been as deeply embroiled in the political affairs of the time as the older children,[59] yet her position implies great authority and influence in public matters.

The death of the great Charles brought a temporary eclipse to the fortunes of this illustrious family. For some unknown reason, the grim, unsmiling Louis the Pious distrusted his kinsmen and sought as quickly as possible to remove them from proximity to the palace. Sources favorable to the family state only that pestilent and envious men advised the new emperor to rid himself of his father's councilors.[60] Count Wala, in particular, was greatly feared. Some even supposed that he might conspire against the emperor, but instead he quickly submitted. It is significant that most of the older magnates waited for Wala's reaction and only then did homage.[61] Adalard was apparently the first to feel the weight of Louis's disfavor. Hurriedly leaving Italy and its youthful King Bernard upon hearing of his cousin's death, he had returned rather pointedly not to the court but to the abbey of Corbie, from which he had been on leave for four or five years. Very soon, without an accuser, without a conference, hearing, or trial, he was summoned to court, stripped of every possession, office, and dignity, and banished to the monastery of St. Filibert on the island of Noirmoutier (Hermoutier) in the mouth of the Loire.[62]

With the fall of Adalard came the fall of his half-brothers and sisters. Bernarius, who had been professed at Lérins, but who had been living at Corbie, was ordered to return to Lérins.[63] (Later, just on the eve of his restoration, he appeared at Fleury.[64]) Gundrada was banished to the convent of St. Radegunda at Poitiers,[65] where fifteen years later Louis's second wife, Empress Judith, would be compelled to take the veil. But, "as if blameless" (a curious nuance), Theodrada was left in her position at Soissons.[66] And, finally, Count Wala, now a widower, laid aside the baldric of a soldier,[67] laid aside the warfare of the world,[68] and made profession of monastic life at Corbie, where his brother's successor, another Adalard, was then abbot.

The next seven years were tragic and disturbing for Louis the Pious and for his empire. But for the subjects of the *Vitae*, they were peaceful and quiet. Wala's *Vita* relates how diligently he applied himself to monastic obedience, humility, and discipline, so that whether he had entered willingly or not, he became indeed a true monk.[69] Similarly Adalard's *Vita* relates how the elder brother became a beloved figure at Noirmoutier despite the fact that he was in reality a prisoner and initially treated as such.[70]

In 821, however, at the October diet in Thionville, Louis the Pious granted clemency to a number of political enemies and ordered Adalard's release from Noirmoutier. Bernarius, his brother, at that time in Fleury, was also allowed to return to the monastery of Corbie.[71] The leave-taking from St. Filibert was an emotional experience as also was the reception at court. The emperor and representatives from Corbie urged Adalard to resume his station as abbot. Although thin and gaunt with ascetic privation, indeed ill with fever and nearing the age of seventy, he acquiesced and for a brief interval enjoyed peace and rest.[72] But not long, for early in 822 he was summoned to court by the emperor,[73] who sought a more effective reconciliation with him and also, according to the source, with Wala.[74] Or one may perhaps assume that Wala simply accompanied his aged brother to the palace to assist him because of his physical infirmities.

In the meanwhile, during Adalard's banishment and Wala's monastic confinement, the political situation in Frankland had undergone a change. The earlier years of Louis's reign had been characterized by replacement of the older advisers of Charlemagne with a grim and serious group of the new emperor's intimates. Many of them, however, had died by 821. The rebellion of his nephew, King Bernard of Italy, had been ruthlessly crushed, but the very cruelty of its suppression had provoked an unfavorable reaction. The death of the good Empress Irmingard cast gloom over the palace. Louis even considered abdication and admission into a monastic community. Dissuaded, he married Judith in 818.

Gradually there emerged two parties to struggle for domination of the emperor's spirit: one, a court party which would ultimately have Judith as its center; and the other, a baronial party which would ultimately rally around the three sons of the late Empress Irmingard. Motives were mixed, of course, and members of the parties changed sides on occasions. Many factors entered the situation: the old strife over church lands sequestered by Charles Martel, the rather curious prominence and influence of Jews in Frankland, the contemptuous treatment of certain clergymen called chaplains, Louis's seizure of Italy from the descendants of his nephew, and the rearrangement of Charlemagne's plans for division of the empire, to mention only the more immediate ones.[75]

The amnesty of 821 may, therefore, have been the result of baronial pressure on Louis to reverse his course. On the other hand, it may have been Louis's effort to bolster his own plans by gaining support of such of his father's councilors as were still living. In any event, during the August diet of 822, held at Attigny, Louis made overtures to the baronial party. The symbolic expression of his apparent acquiescence was his dramatic penance for maltreatment inflicted upon King Bernard of Italy. That was followed by consideration of other demands of the clerical segment of the baronial party. Gestures were made respecting restoration of church lands, better training of clergy, and removal of the evils of simony and neglect. Although implementation of these reforms was slow and in most instances not forthcoming, Abbot Adalard declared that not since the reign of King Pepin (Louis's grandfather) had he seen such lofty and glorious attention given to the progress of the commonwealth.[76] His circle of friends agreed that a new order had been born for Frankland and that a new dawn of justice was rising.[77] How mistaken they were is another story, but at least the old Carolingian councilors seem to have been satisfied and completely reconciled with the emperor.[78]

The few remaining years of Adalard's life were filled with activity despite his advanced age.[79] He worked indefatigably in his own monastery at Corbie [80] and found time to write a treatise on government for the guidance of Louis the Pious.[81] He faithfully attended the imperial court on necessary occasions. He and Chancellor Helisachar,[82] sometimes with, sometimes without Wala, acted in some instances as intermediaries for those who wished to approach the emperor. Bishop Agobard of Lyons was one such person, but the experiences were so humiliating that he suspected them of misrepresenting him or withholding information from Louis.[83] Adalard's major concern, however, was directed toward completion of the Saxon monastery of New Corvey.

The establishment of a daughter-monastery in Saxony had long been an interest of Abbot Adalard. Even before he had gone to Italy to serve as regent between the death of King Pepin and the majority of young King Bernard, he had initiated the project by securing appropriate lands for the new foundation.[84] But owing to his absence, work had languished. Then came his exile to Noirmoutier. His namesake, Adalard the younger, who served as abbot of Corbie during the interval of banishment, goaded no doubt by

Wala, who had just been professed,[85] secured permission from Louis and Bishop Hadumar (in whose diocese the new monastery was to be erected) to inaugurate the work. But aridity of the soil, poverty of the community, a rapidly increasing number of monks there, and the constant drain on revenues of the mother-monastery caused grave problems.[86]

On his return to favor the senior Adalard took immediate steps to aid New Corvey and then approached the emperor for permission to find a better location for the monastery. Louis agreed to the request and Adalard and Wala undertook a journey to Saxony.[87] In August, 822, a suitable site was procured, and by the latter part of September removal from the old site was effected.[88] In the year following, Adalard and others formally organized the daughter-community and gave it some regulations.[89] It may have been at this time that the aged and saintly abbot named the place on the Weser "Corbie" for his monastery at Corbie on the Somme.[90] For the sake of clarity it is usually denominated "New Corvey." The establishment of a cloister of nuns at Herford was in some manner associated with the founding of New Corvey, but it requires no discussion here.[91]

The part played by Wala in the aforementioned activities is of profound interest. First, as indicated above, he was the one who prodded the younger Adalard into action.[92] Secondly, he was the one who skillfully persuaded Theodradus to relinquish his ancestral heritage as a site for New Corvey: "no other mortal could have done that." [93] Thirdly, he was the one whose earlier military fame was sufficient to deter Saxon bandits from plundering lands of the new monastery.[94] Fourthly, he was the one whom the people of the region loved and admired, while ignoring Abbot Adalard.[95] And, fifthly, he was the one whom the monks of New Corvey desired as their superior at the death of Adalard.[96] It would appear, therefore, that Wala's part was of highest significance.

But involvement in the affairs of Corbie and New Corvey did not exhaust the energies of the dynamic Wala. In the autumn of 822 the forty-nine-year-old monk was commissioned by Emperor Louis to assist his son Lothair in governing Italy.[97] His *Vita* states that he was Lothair's protector and indeed deputy of the realm,[98] and it records two remarkable instances of his efforts to enforce justice.[99] It was also probably during this stay in Italy that Wala

procured for his abbey of Corbie a copy of the Roman antiphonary. In 832, when the great liturgiologist Amalarius was visiting
Rome to seek a copy, Pope Gregory IV replied, "I do not have an
antiphonary to send to my son, the Lord Emperor. When Wala
was here on a special mission, he took the ones which we did have
with him on his return to Frankland." [100] This remark has a
faintly amusing quality, as though the pope had no particular interest in the matter and wondered why people in Frankland were
so concerned. It indicates also that the spread of the peculiarly
Roman rite was not at the instigation of the pope, but of the
"northern barbarians." One cannot but wonder why the Roman
See did not have a number of copies on hand.

Wala's work in Italy was not of continuous duration, for there
are indications that he returned to Frankland at intervals in order
to transact business there. It was perhaps sometime in 823 that, as
noted above, Bishop Agobard visited him and others at court and
then directed a communication to them.[101] It was possibly Wala
who about 824 sent word to Agobard that ugly rumors were being
circulated about the bishop as a notorious troublemaker. And it
was probably he to whom Agobard in late 824 or early 825 directed in reply his treatise, *On the Management of Church Properties*.[102] In any case, when his work with Lothair in Italy was accomplished, Wala returned in 825 to Frankland,[103] doubtless
bringing with him the Roman antiphonary books for use in the
monastery at Corbie.[104]

It may be that Wala's return was in part prompted by the fail-
ing health of his brother, Abbot Adalard. On the third day before
Christmas, 825, the old man fell ill with a "violent, raging fever." [105] He dragged himself to the offices of prayer, but to his
sons in religion it was obvious that their venerable and holy abbot
was dying. One of his former monks, Hildeman, who had been
made bishop of Beauvais, was sent for to keep watch with him during the remaining days and death.[106] After a vision of Christ
present with him, he died on January 2, 826, about three o'clock in
the afternoon.[107] With Bishop Hildeman performing the obsequies, he was buried in the monastery chapel among four of his
predecessors in office.[108] According to his biographer, "the defense of all Europe has suddenly perished." [109]

Shortly after Adalard's death, the brothers of the abbey sought to elect Wala as abbot and sent a delegation (including Paschasius Radbertus) to ask Louis the Pious for congé d'élire.[110] For some reason Wala had earlier gone into hiding at New Corvey. Although Adalard had already designated Warinus as his successor at the daughter-monastery, the brothers there also tried to secure Wala for the place.[111] So Wala returned to Corbie. At court an effort was made (with imperial approval) to dissuade the brothers of Corbie from electing Wala,[112] but they were successful in securing the emperor's permission and so Wala became Adalard's successor.[113]

For a while he followed his late brother in attachment to the imperial household. In a letter addressed to him and Archchaplain Hilduin in 826, Bishop Agobard observed that Wala was "always" at court as one of the very few godly advisers of Louis the Pious, but, as earlier, of no assistance to Agobard.[114] Wala also took special interest in the Danish mission of Ansgar, a monk of both Corbie and New Corvey.[115] Some of his monks marveled that he had time for God with his varied and innumerable involvements.[116] Often amid crowds of dignitaries, present everywhere and moving restlessly far and wide, both host and guest at many important banquets, absorbed in the fluctuating course of events, he was indeed a true courtier.[117]

But he did not neglect monastic duties and responsibilities. For "this then was his business and the reason for his business; this was his leisure and labor; this was his fasting and vigil; this was the constant care and anxiety of his mind; namely, that he might never cease what he had once undertaken in the soldiery of Christ." [118] He was both true monk and true abbot.[119]

Within the next few years, however, Wala was affected by the worsening condition of the Carolingian realm. Party lines were becoming much sharper and partisan bickering more acute. Desperate efforts were made in 828 and 829 to remedy the situation, but events were moving rapidly toward a violent climax. The intrigues of Count Bernard of Barcelona and Empress Judith were notorious and provocative.[120] Wala, ceaselessly active, was convinced that a judgment of God was imminent. He had pleaded with his kinsman Bernard, but to no avail.[121] Despite a severe infirmity in the summer of 829, Wala received a constant stream of visitors seeking

counsel.[122] His reply was for them to return to the palace to investigate, surreptitiously if necessary, in order to determine the
truth.[123] Wala's reaction indicates an ambivalence, as though he
realized that drastic procedure was requisite, yet sought if possible
to spare Louis the Pious.[124] But open revolt could not be denied.
About this time he wrote a small book no longer extant unless incorporated into parts of his *Vita*.[125]

At the diet of Compiègne in May, 830, an aristocratic conspiracy, involving magnates of both clerical and lay orders as well
as the three elder sons of Louis, succeeded in forcing Judith to take
the veil at St. Radegunda in Poitiers [126] (where Wala's sister Gundrada had also spent some time in banishment); in tonsuring her
brothers; in blinding Heribert, brother of Bernard of Barcelona
(who had escaped to Spain); [127] and in bringing pressure on Louis
the Pious to abdicate.[128] Wala was a reluctant accomplice in all
these actions,[129] but he supposed that they were necessary for the
good of the emperor and empire, for the good of Christianity and
the common welfare.[130]

The revolution was of short duration. By the autumn diet at
Nijmegen, Louis was back in power; his wife was returned to
court; Lothair was deprived of his title as coemperor.[131] Punitive
action was then launched against the rebellious barons, both lay
and clerical. Wala suffered exile: first, in 831, to a high mountain-
ous region near Lake Leman; [132] secondly (after Judith's return to
court), to Noirmoutier where his brother Adalard had once
suffered confinement; [133] thirdly, early in 833, to Germany (precise location not known); [134] and lastly, to his own monastery at
Corbie, but shorn of rank, office, and honors.[135]

In the meanwhile, another large-scale revolt was brewing [136]
and Wala soon became embroiled in it. In 833 he was about sixty
years old and wearied with the harassments of his exile. But emissaries from Pope Gregory IV were urging him to enter the contest
once more.[137] An even greater pressure was the approach of
troops from the three brothers threatening to take him violently.[138] Wala, therefore, yielded, hoping to serve as mediator between the opposing forces,[139] though the undertaking was fraught
with peril.[140]

The story of the confrontation in late June, 833, has been re-

counted many times, and Wala's *Vita* presents a particularly intimate and moving eyewitness record of it,[141] as well as of the diet
of Compiègne in mid-November.[142] Louis was compelled to strip
himself of the imperial dignity; Judith was imprisoned at Tortona;
Lothair was elevated to the title of emperor.[143] Pope Gregory IV
returned to Italy thoroughly disillusioned, and Wala returned sorrowfully to Corbie.[144]

During the winter of 833–34 sentiment again changed and on
March 1, 834, Louis was once more reinstated.[145] Reprisals began.
Fearing them, Wala fled to Italy to the monastery of St. Columban
at Bobbio, where the brothers quickly elected him abbot.[146]
There he lived nobly and peacefully the remaining two years of his
life except for a brief visit as emissary of Lothair to the council of
Thionville in May, 836.[147] On August 31 of the same year he died
at Bobbio,[148] called by one partisan of Louis the Pious, "a disloyal
one"; [149] by another, one of those "by whose departure Frankland
was deprived of her nobility, emasculated of her strength . . . ,
annulled of her wisdom"; [150] and by his own disciples, "a senator
of senators." [151]

THE BOOKS AND THEIR VALUE

There is no question about the purpose of the two *Vitae*. They
are primarily personal tributes to the memory of beloved fathers in
God and as such documents prepared for edification of posterity.
In the case of Adalard, Paschasius Radbertus stated, "I seek to
adorn the grave with letters, so that the odor of your virtues may
. . . be fragrant far and wide for future times"; [152] and again, "I
weave over the grave a garment of letters so that the holy name
may be preserved for future ages." [153] In the case of Wala, he
stated that he was urged to "depict as a memorial for the ages a
representation of the character of our Arsenius." [154] Because of its
brevity the *Life of Adalard* is usually recognized as the more conventional saint's life. The *Life of Wala*, on the other hand, being
twice as long as the former, has more of the nature of true biography.[155] In both the author clearly intends his work to provide
patterns of life to be imitated.

Both *Vitae* have a certain literary preciosity. That of Adalard, for instance, contains a chapter devoted to an incident recorded in Cicero's *De inventione rhetorica*, II, 1, relating how the artist Zeuxis proceeded when he was employed by the people of Crotona to do a likeness of one Helena.[156] Near the end of the *Vita* there is another chapter recounting the story of Orpheus' descent to the lower world.[157] Both chapters are obviously unnecessary, since they add nothing to the *Vita*. The author apparently introduced them to provide embellishment. To a great degree also the concluding "Eclogue of Two Nuns" served the same purpose.[158] The description of Adalard's appearance is merely an adaptation of passages from the Song of Songs, indicating a similar artificiality.[159]

The preciosity of the *Life of Wala* is present in a somewhat less obvious manner, but it is there nonetheless. The form, for example, is dialogue, in itself hardly customary for biography. The employment of pseudonyms is another mannered feature of style. To characterize Wala, extensive phrases are dipped from the Acts of St. Sebastian.[160] Long passages from the comedies of Terence are woven into the text.[161] Several pages incorporate a lengthy passage from Job.[162] As in the earlier *Vita*, these are illustrations of the writer's learning, facility, and skill; they contribute to our knowledge of Radbertus, but not particularly of his two subjects.

Both *Lives* contain occasional intimations of mild humor.[163] Both make use of plays on words and alliteration.[164] The *Vita Walae* has a trace of prose rhyme.[165] Both employ many of the same quotations from or allusions to classical authors and the Bible.[166] Although both conclude with conventional visions at the death of the heroes,[167] they are remarkably free from the usual miracle stories. The earlier one may be presumed to have been written as a funeral eulogy to be read publicly;[168] the latter, perhaps as a conference or discussion in which the hero is defended against carping criticism. Yet the style of both, as heretofore indicated, was intended to be relatively entertaining or at least not dull.

It is not entirely proper to dismiss the *Vita Adalhardi* as of no historical worth. Although it was intended primarily for edification, it contains a considerable amount of important historical information. Since the purpose of the *Vita Walae* was to correct mistaken ideas about its protagonist, it necessarily contains much more material of historical nature. Radbertus was, it is true, far more notable as theologian than as historian, a fact which may account for the discursive quality of his writing. He was indeed aware of his defective chronology,[169] and he halted between characterizing his *Life of Wala* as *fabula* or as *historia*.[170] But his goal, at least in the *Vita Walae*, was to relate (1) what he had observed as an eyewitness, (2) what he had heard, and (3) what he had deduced by mental processes.[171] The first two objectives are stated in terms of quotations from Terence, but the third in his own addition. The expressed intention is worthy of both theologian and historian.

The *Vita Adalhardi* appears to have been based on observation and oral reports, as doubtless modified by deduction from data supplied by those two sources. In the *Vita Walae*, however, it may be added that there is evidence of employment of documents, perhaps as many as four: first, a booklet written by Wala himself making suggestions for improvement of the state;[172] secondly, a compilation of patristic citations for papal authority;[173] thirdly, a series of communications between Louis the Pious and his three elder sons on the eve of the second revolt;[174] and fourthly, an account of Wala's last days ordered by Queen Irmingard.[175] At least one document is cited in the *Vita Adalhardi*, a letter by Adalard to Lothair.[176] None of these, by the way, is still extant.

There are some historical details in both *Vitae* which may be known from other sources, but which are either confirmed by these *Vitae* or given with greater precision, notably, of course, the ancestral and family kinships of the two protagonists.[177] Of special interest is the shifting relation of the two, now tense, now intimate, with their imperial cousin Charlemagne and his successor.[178] There are also important data, such as the age of Adalard at his monastic profession,[179] which permits an approximate estimation of his date of birth; and such as the high regard in which Wala was held by former military foes,[180] which may in part account for his eminence in the Carolingian world. The *Vita Adalhardi* apparently gives a firm basis for considering Desiderata (Désirée) to have been the name of Charlemagne's first wife;[181] as the *Vita Walae* records, for whatever the information is worth, the last words of its hero.[182]

Both works have as their chief historical value observation of life in a ninth-century monastery, expressions of attitudes toward conditions of the times, and unusually vivid pictures of contemporary figures. There is a delightful story of the cellarer of Corbie roughly chiding Abbot Adalard for feeding guests so well that nothing remained for the brothers. To Adalard's bland reply, "The Lord will provide," the rude cellarer exclaimed, "You always promise that, but what you dispose of indiscriminately will not be provided right now!" [183] Generally, however, the brothers respected their abbot's need for some moments alone without responsibilities.[184]

The warm feeling he evoked is illustrated by an appealing little incident which occurred when, after seven years, he was allowed to leave Noirmoutier to return to Corbie. The brothers were weeping and kissing him farewell. But one brother, Ragnardus, was so moved that he could not bear to be present for the leave-taking. Adalard missed him and asked for him. Ragnardus was found in his cell, sobbing with heartbreak. Begging the messengers not to betray his emotional outburst, he agreed to go down to the beach where Adalard was embarking. The latter hastened down from the ship to embrace Ragnardus, who then cried out, "Oh my father, I would rather bury you dead here than to have you abandon me." The brothers and servants thereupon burst forth into loud sobs. Even the biographer waxed poetic as he ended the account:

> At last the sails are lifted;
> oars are rowed;
> everyone gives a groan.
> On shore they watch him
> as long as they could see him.
> But one spirit of love glowed in them
> and they could not restrain him.[185]

The *Vita Walae*, being longer, has more incidents similar to the preceding. Wala's leadership (and perhaps impulsiveness) is illustrated by a story from the days of his novitiate. A river nearby was overflowing. The brothers were ordered to take measures to prevent further inundation. Wala decided to enter the stream clad in his tunic only and urged others to do the same. Many followed him, but when report reached the abbot, the latter wisely ordered them out of the river because of the bitter cold.[186] Wala also took special care of poor guests, cleaning their dirty shoes, their stinking clothes, and festering sores.[187] In winter he made the fires for the brothers. Often so blackened with smoke and soot, he appeared to be a phantom flitting from fireplace to fireplace.[188] He sought to wear particularly rough shoes, but the abbot discreetly forbade him to do so.[189] When he had to travel about after he became abbot, he never permitted provision to be made for covering against rain. Although drenched, he lay down at night in deep furrows of the fields with only a saddle for headrest. "Nothing else did we have except what we had above and below in the daytime. This was the only mattress for a bed, a sufficiently honorable vanity!"[190]

Both *Vitae* present evidence not only of their protagonists' spiritual offices, prayers, and tears but also of their administration of the monastic communities. Adalard often rescued households from the crushing burden of poverty, placing destitute widows and aged men on various lands of the monastery where they could be carefully tended. Orphans and cripples were similarly treated, "so that everyone might possess the properties of this abbey as his own patrimony." He himself acted on occasions as physician and nurse and taught others how to perform those duties.[191] Wala was especially diligent in supervision of the monks under him. He persuaded, commanded, censured, and taught.[192] One brother, too weak for such discipline, tried to escape, to be (as Wala no doubt supposed) "rebarbarized." But soldiers were summoned to guard all entrances and exits. Fearfully the erring brother returned, but Wala wept like the father receiving the prodigal son. The author observed, "Even I bellowed when I saw them weeping, . . . as if we had received him from the dead."[193]

There is no need to single out in these biographies particular expressions of attitudes toward the conditions that prevailed at the time of writing. They should be obvious to any reader. And in a sense it is probably unnecessary to indicate the vivid portraits they present of contemporaries. Yet, since two of those personalities are of intense interest in their own right, namely, Count Bernard of Barcelona and Empress Judith, it is worthwhile to note the characterizations in the *Vita Walae*. Distorted though they are, they are fascinating and picturesque. Both can be corrected from other sources. Bernard has already had a modern biographer,[194] but Judith still awaits hers.[195]

The language of Radbertus fairly tumbles over itself to show how evil those two appeared to him. Bernard was an accursed wallower in hog pools of filth, a wild boar on a rampage of destruction. He had violated the imperial bedchamber, broken treaties, practiced tyranny. In his revelry and debauchery he turned night into day and day into night.[196] He was a monster—seditious, blind, mad, immoral, and shameless.[197] An adulterer and the impious enemy of religion, he exerted his influence by practicing the art of sorcery.[198] Not one good word does this vicious creature receive from Radbertus.

The portrait of Judith is almost as unflattering. She was indeed the very personification of adultery, who dominated every thought, word, and action of Emperor Louis.[199] She was the real wielder of the scepter and by her nod she swayed everything. She demanded fawning adulation and attention. Only those who satisfied her whims received reward.[200] The veil she was once forced to undertake she despised and trampled under foot. Then, motivated by lust for vengeance, she pursued Wala relentlessly like the Visigothic Queen Brunhilda who persecuted St. Columban so mercilessly.[201] Like the earlier queen, she was guilty of irreligion and intolerant of any critic. She was filled with guile and fraud.[202] It was no doubt well for Paschasius Radbertus that both Bernard and Judith were long since dead when he wrote.[203] But however one-sided, the passages describing these two are the most vivid and exciting in the *Vita Walae*.

It remains now to consider a few of the artistic qualities of the two *Vitae*, for although they are, as indicated above, historical, they are primarily literary products. The author was indeed quite consciously striving to make them such and at least once refers to himself as "an artist albeit unworthy." [204] Earlier he had remarked, "I do not weave eloquence of counterfeit art, but I wrap it carefully in a clean winding cloth of purity." [205]

In addition to the literary devices already cited, there is frequent use of rhetorical questions, apostrophes, and the almost "purple" overwriting of the gift of tears possessed by both Adalard and Wala.[206] In the *Vita Adalhardi* occur chapters on the mystical meaning of numbers [207] and of the location of New Corvey,[208] as well as discussions of rhetorical rules.[209] The occasional employment of an allusive word or phrase, such as "the wave-wandering wheels of the world," [210] indicates a literary sensitivity. But proof of the literary aspiration of the *Vita Adalhardi* is the "Eclogue of Two Nuns" with which it closes and with which it is, at least in part, summarized. One might add also the very large number of quotations from the Song of Songs: thirty (or thirty-five, counting repetitions) verses are cited, coming from each chapter of that biblical romance.[211] These are quite aptly and effectively embodied in the warp and woof of the text. Of classical authors there are no less than five passages from Vergil (*Eclogues* and *Georgics*, but not the *Aeneid*), two from Cicero, and one each from Horace and Plato. From Christian authors there are two from St. Jerome and one each from St. Ambrose and Venantius Fortunatus. And the foregoing count is no doubt incomplete. These citations are especially interesting in view of Radbertus' apparent disapproval of employing pagan literature in Christian writing, but more will be said of this below in connection with the *Vita Walae*.

The *Vita Walae* confronts us at the outset with its form, that of a dialogue. There are five interlocutors in Book I (Paschasius, Adeodatus, Severus, Chremes, and Allabigus) and three in Book II (Paschasius, Adeodatus, and Theophrastus), all presumably monks of Corbie. This "literary device . . . was," according to M. L. W. Laistner, "unique at that date," [212] a statement that is not entirely accurate, for there are extant simple question-and-answer booklets prepared for instructional purposes.[213]

A question nevertheless arises about the source of Radbertus' usage. A glimpse at his citations of authors will suggest a possibility. Of Christian writers he quotes or alludes to one passage each from Boethius, St. Ambrose, St. Jerome, the Venerable Bede, the *Acta Thomae*, and the *Acta sancti Sebastiani*, two from Ausonius, and three from St. Benedict's *Rule*. Of pagan writers he cites one passage each from Ennius, Cato's *Distichs*, Horace, Statius, and Lucan, and three from Cicero, eight from Vergil, three from Seneca, and seventeen from Terence. Although the foregoing count is surely incomplete, it is sufficient to indicate heavy reliance on

Terence. (One is reminded of the tenth-century nun of Gander-sheim, Hrotsvitha, and her reflection of Terentian influence.) Sixty-seven lines are quoted by Radbertus, coming from all six extant plays of the Roman comic writer.[214] It is worth noting also that the name of one of the interlocutors, Chremes, is a Terentian name. The Roman playwright is referred to in the *Vita Walae* by name and also by the designation *comicus* (the comic writer). All the passages are neatly woven into the texture of Radbertus' composition, indicating once again his consummate skill. Incidentally they occur only in Book I. It is safe, therefore, to assert that the form of the *Vita Walae* is a result of Terentian influence and a close study of the playwright.[215] Thus the lie is given to Radbertus' disparagement of classical literature.

The pseudonyms in the *Vita Walae* are another device derived from literary sources. Only superficially and legalistically could they be deemed efforts to mask identities, for they are quite transparent to any student of the period. They must have been even more so to contemporaries. Indeed only one is still doubtful.[216] Appropriate nicknames were characteristic of the palace academy of Charlemagne, perhaps a result of Alcuin's playfulness, some derived from classical, some from Christian antiquity. So, too, in Radbertus' work.

Despite his knowledge and employment of Vergil, Radbertus apparently had some animus against him. Addressing his interlocutor Adeodatus, he cited a passage as being from "your Vergil." "This verse," he wrote, "although given high praise in your Vergil, appears much earlier in Horace. . . . It is obvious that in a great many places your ingenious and able Vergil derived praise from the sentiments of others and from many fragments of the philosophers, and as a beggar has prepared foolish entertainment for boys." [217] Unfortunately for Radbertus' literary criticism the passage in question does not appear in Vergil. Our author was confused: it was repeated not in Vergil, but in the much later poet Ausonius. Not once, but twice did he make the same mistake, for in a later statement to Severus he referred another Ausonian quotation to "your aforementioned poet." [218] The great preference for Terence is a strange one, but typical of the Middle Ages.

BIBLIOGRAPHICAL NOTES

The basis of the following translations is Dom Jacques Mabillon's text as given in Migne, PL, cxx, 1507–1556C (*Vita sancti
Adalhardi;* columns 1553A–1556C are the *Ecloga duarum sanc-
timonialium*) and 1559D–1650B (*Epitaphium Arsenii seu Vita
venerabilis Walae*), carefully compared with G. H. Pertz's selections *Ex vita Adalhardi* in MGH, Scriptores, II, 524–32; Ludwig
Traube's critical edition of Radbertus' *Ecloga* in MGH, PLAC,
III, 38–51; and Ernst Dümmler's very fine critical edition of
Epitaphium Arsenii in *Philosophische und historische Abhandlungen der königlichen Akademie der Wissenschaften zu Berlin*, II
(1900), 1–98.

There has apparently been no other translation into a vernacu-
lar language. The following is as literal as possible considering the
requirements of English syntax and idiom. Punctuation and division into paragraphs are those of the translator. Identification of citations and allusions are also those of the translator assisted by references in the editions mentioned above and commentaries noted
below. Even so it has been impossible to trace numerous passages
which have the earmarks of being quotations. With few excep-
tions, no effort has been made to annotate the *Ecloga duarum sanc-
timonialium* since Traube has done that adequately.

Information about citations and MSS is presented by Ernst
Dümmler in *Gesellschaft für ältere deutsche Geschichtskunde Ar-
chiv* (Hanover), IV, 301–305, and XXVII, 291. Bernard Simson
has quite ingeniously recognized the quotation from Ausonius in
"Zum Gedicht de viro bono," *Rheinisches Museum für Philologie*,
XLI, 638f. Max Manitius, *Geschichte der lateinischen Literatur des
Mittelalters*, I (Munich: Beck, 1911), 401–11, is an established
and reliable source of all kinds of information.

The *Vita Adalhardi* has attracted very little attention, although
there was a tenth-century epitome made of it under the initiative of
Gerard of Corbie (PL, cxlvii, 1045D–1064B) and a book of St.
Adalard's miracles ascribed to the same Gerard (PL, cxlvii,
1063C–1072D). The *Vita Walae* has, on the other hand, evoked

three very important treatments in modern times. Out of the nineteenth century come Louis Auguste Himly, *Wala et Louis le débonnaire* (Paris: Firmin Didot Frères, 1849), and Carl Rodenberg, *Die Vita Walae als historische Quelle* (Göttingen: University Press, 1877). The latest and by far the best is Lorenz Weinrich, *Wala—Graf, Mönch und Rebell* (Lübeck and Hamburg: Matthiesen, 1963), Vol. 386 of *Historische Studien,* an excellent and substantial study. The life of Paschasius Radbertus has been compiled fairly recently by Henri Peltier, *Pascase Radbert* (Amiens: Duthoit, 1938).

For overall purposes of chronology, historical details, and much else, Bernard Simson, *Jahrbücher des fränkischen Reichs unter Ludwig dem Frommen,* 2 vols. (Leipzig: Duncker und Humblot, 1874, 1876), and Johann Friedrich Böhmer, Engelbert Mühlbacher, Johann Lechner, *Die Regesten des Kaiserreichs unter den Karolingern* 751–918 (Innsbruck: Verlag der Wagner'schen Universitäts-Buchhandlung, 1908), must not be neglected. In spite of their age, they are indispensable.

Chapter divisions occur in the editions, but I have taken the liberty of introducing division into paragraphs. For ease in citation I have also numbered each paragraph within a chapter. The parts of the "Eclogue" at the end of the *Life of Adalard,* I have designated by letters in parentheses; and similarly the introductions to the two books of the *Life of Wala,* by numbers within parentheses.

The Life of Saint Adalard

by PASCHASIUS RADBERTUS

Chapter 1:1. It is a prize of achievement to emulate certain very learned men who, with pious affection of mind, dutifully and piteously wept at the funerals of those beloved in Christ and who, as they wept, also pursued them with much praise. As blessed Ambrose said in his work on Valentinian, "Although what you grieve to write may increase sorrow, yet we are greatly refreshed by memory of him whom we have lost and whom we lament. While we write and direct our mind toward him and fix our attention on him, he seems to us to live again in speech" [1] and to make his way gently but completely into the marrow of our mind.

1:2. But it is an undertaking for posterity that we commit to writing the examples of their virtues. We pay our debt of charity to our neighbors, and we do not deny to our sons the examples of fathers whom they ought to emulate. We know that they have not perished after death, but by dying they have been transformed in blessedness and they have arrived at the deathless joys of supreme felicity. So they should by no means be entirely blotted out of memory, especially those whose removal hence by death was not a cessation, but a transmutation to the better. Nor should one say, as in Scripture certain faithless ones madly state, "The time of our life is petty and loathsome, nor is there refreshment at the end of a man, and there is no one known to have returned from the dead." [2]

Nor should one say that we were born from nothing and after this life we will be as though we had not been. It is true and it must be stressed that Christ rose from the dead and by dying conquered death. Similarly all who die in Christ may be found no longer dead, no, but alive and blessed in Christ. God is the God of the living and not of the dying,[3] because all they who are in Him are found alive in Him who lives. Hence it is that the Scripture usually says that they are sleeping.[4]

Chapter 2. It is, therefore, as I said, most fitting to emulate holy men such as the aforesaid Ambrose and blessed Jerome and other imitable holy men, who produced eloquent funeral orations for their dear ones. If I cannot attain the heights of their eloquence, you know nonetheless that material for such speech is not lacking. By writing I seek to recall him whom the whole world proclaims as holy and admirable. We have seen him and enjoyed the love of his intimate acquaintance. So, although we are unworthy and unlearned, we cannot be entirely silent. While we no longer see him with our eyes, we should at least attend him with the service of our mind.

Chapter 3. While I begin to think about him, I am inwardly affected by two contrary emotions, namely, grief and joy.[5] The Apostle forbids us to mourn in such a situation, but my and our sudden desolation prevents us from rejoicing. Taxed with both of these tributes derived from piety, it is fitting rather to rejoice, even to rejoice beyond measure, with hope of the everlasting promise concerning so great an advocate. There is not the least doubt that he has already passed through the happy contests nor that he has found rest in Christ, there in blessedness forever to remain. Overcome I am by love's lament rather than by idle despair, yet I do not contend that I should be spared. The Apostle does not forbid weeping, only that we sorrow not for the sleeping as others do who have no hope.[6] It is one thing to sorrow with despair and another to mourn and grieve that we have come hither because of sin, that in a measure we seem scarcely to be anything. So to bathe with tears the tomb of dear ones ought to be an expression of due piety, not of error.

Chapter 4:1. With this piety, therefore, albeit in a sluggish mind, I recall you, O father Adalard, most beloved of men, adornment of old age, image of holiness, model of virtues. With the bonds of love I recall you. Scarcely can I restrain myself between both emotions. I know that the Lord Jesus Christ wept for dead Lazarus whom He loved, and not only wept but was also disturbed in spirit.[7] I am driven to weep sorely, since I am deprived of such a great oracle of heaven. Nature itself teaches us that we ought not to forget our dear ones. To these faculties, then, we can commend them: esteem may be held firmly in mind even if sight of the flesh is taken away; and love which not long since had influenced the mind will not die while he whom we love lives better.

4:2. So, my dearest of ancients, after the manner of the multitude, I bestrew your sepulcher with flowers. But I also seek to adorn the grave with letters, so that the odor of your virtues may not be shut up in a tomb, but may be fragrant far and wide for future times. Unlike certain ones I do not think that children drawn from here and there should be assembled at your tomb to feign your praises in song and by lugubrious notes to incite the hearts of listeners to weeping and moaning. But not to abdicate the rights of truth by sloth and torpor, I will entrust them to faithful letters, and thus refreshed by your encouragement, I will remember you through the ages. You will never be away from my mind if I begin to spell out your name and praises. Reliable is my conscience that whatever I shall say will be far less than your rightful praise. I blush very little to persuade such things of you. Your present absence,[8] still bitter to me, generates new tears in me, while your absent presence [9] may cause rejoicing that you have already arrived at long-promised joys.

Chapter 5:1. Please do not say to the one who weeps, "You ought to rejoice rather than weep over me, O sons of the dear ones. For you know that I have escaped the mockeries of the world and come to the fount of eternal life. If you love me, you will rejoice exceedingly because I already enjoy the vesture of immortality and I am satisfied with gazing on the glory of the majesty." I know, my father, I know that you have laid aside fleshly garments and that you already enjoy the heavenly vision. But I am overcome and drenched with pious love; I weep for your present absence.[10] Everything I see seems sad to me and I sigh knowing that you are absent.[11] To employ the words of Fortunatus:

As a loving lamb driven from the breast of its mother
Wanders sorrowful and anxious in grassy fields:
Now it flees to the plains, beating the air with its bleatings;
Now it returns to the folds. Without the mother nothing is
    pleasant.[12]

5:2. Thus from your words, O father, I prompt myself while I am absent. Would that the day of your departure have not dawned, for a worse one there could not have been for me, nor could a more savage one dawn upon your followers. Under bitter sorrow I do not find a measure by which to determine what to do or to perform. Since the Apostle forbids,[13] I dare not weep much. Although reluctant, I am persuaded by the glory of your splendor to rejoice. For you, my father, the winter has passed and the rain has ceased.[14] The wedding of the Lamb has come; you enjoy delights in the midst of paradise; your voice has sounded in my ears; and the voice of the turtledove is heard,[15] saying, "As we have heard, O sons, so have we seen in the city of the Lord. We have indeed heard glorious things, but we discern even more powerful attributes in the city of the Lord of virtues." [16] It is, therefore, "of virtues," not of vices, because God founded it on a perpetual foundation forever. I know that you are indeed already singing such matters, but grieving I sigh and anxious I groan, now for a long time separated from your company. And because it is later, the world proclaims you as a man of virtue, although we neither touch nor see you.

Chapter 6:1. I know that you do not wish to accept these praises, because you now have them written in heaven. There you made your storehouse and there always was the dwelling place of your mind. Although I will present what I am pondering, I congratulate you because you are enjoying what you have loved. I am happy for your sake, but I grieve for my sake deprived so soon of nourishment. Overcome, therefore, by your joys, I do not refuse to give thanks to God. Indeed I do give thanks that we have had such a one as you are. Because we have first lacked you, I am overcome by true emotion that you have adopted comrades in your partnership in paradise.

6:2. So, my father, look, I pray, through the lattices, through the windows,[17] look with the Lord's permission upon the sons of the vow. I know the charity you have received from the Lord and the faith and hope with which you have been fastened firm, like an anchor to the Lord. I am sure that your triple rope is so strong that it can never be loosened. You marvel not only at the clouds and stars under your feet but also at the high plain of heaven, while you are clothed in snowy habit. I beg you not to delay your mercy upon the humble ones whom not long since you summoned to the field of battle against such matters. Strong as death, my father, was your love.[18] By no enemy were you conquered; by no contest overcome. Courageously you spurned the delights of the world. We believe that you are undoubtedly crowned with the glory of one in triumph. Come, O daughters of Jerusalem, and see [19] the diadem with which our ancient has been crowned with eternal solemnity! With what golden habiliments he has been clothed! Consider how, while still a youth, he overcame the malignant foe; how, while still a boy, he crushed the world under foot.

Chapter 7. Of royal stock he was,[20] nephew of great King Pepin, first cousin of Charles Augustus, trained in all prudence of the world amid young recruits of the palace, brought up by teachers along with the prince of the land. Yet he chose to become a friend of justice and truth rather than consent to unlawful proceedings, even when diverted by many blandishments. The following is an illustration. Emperor Charles repudiated Desiderata, daughter of Desiderius, king of the Italians.[21] Only a short time earlier, at the urging of certain Franks, he had sought her in marriage. Although our blessed ancient was still a young recruit in the palace, he could by no means be persuaded to associate with the new queen in any loyal service as long as the former one was still living. In every way possible he condemned such a marriage. As a boy, already noted for his blessed quality, he mourned that some of the Franks would be thereby perjured and that the king would be involved in unlawful marriage, since his proper wife had been driven away without any reason. Kindled by this excessive zeal, he chose to abandon the world while still a boy rather than to be involved in such matters. He did so to show his kinsman that, although he could not successfully prevent, he would by leaving indicate disapproval. No less than John was he prepared to die for

justice, as with equal exertion he reprehended the unlawful bold-
ness of the king and despised a marriage of this kind.[22] Nor did he
deem the laws of kinship to require assent to lust, but only the laws
of Christ which he set forth, not tolerating himself to violate them.
A man free in mind, he wished to bear the ignominy of the cross
with Christ, to confound whatever powers there were, if only he
might be adopted in the Kingdom as a son of the King.

Chapter 8:1. Despising therefore the riches of Pharaoh's kingdom,[23] he arrived at length as a monk (like Moses in the desert) [24]
to enjoy the solace of God. No longer shod with the world, he
could see the heavenly vision on the mount.[25] Stripped of all such
things and sanctified by God's grace, he became a disciple of the
Savior. He had read, "Unless one renounces everything he possesses, he cannot be my disciple." [26] Nor was he unaware that it is
easier for a camel to pass through a needle's eye than for a rich man
to enter the kingdom of heaven.[27] He also laid aside the burdens of
the little colt to run more easily the narrow and strait way of
God's commandments.[28] With such matters laid aside, he longed
like David's stag [29] for the fountain of Corbie, no, rather, of Christ
in that place.

8:2. When he had dwelt there a short while, the disciple of
humility suddenly became the teacher of virtues. He who only yesterday appeared to be a servant was revealed as a leader of others
and a guide of his fellow soldiers in Christ. For, O good Jesus, you
chose him for yourself when he was a raw recruit and a child. He
had not chosen you, but you had chosen him, had even chosen him
ahead of time, anticipated by your grace. You chose him fully
when he was twenty years old, when unhappy human age is too
frail and most inclined toward sin. That was the age when all your
recruits from twenty years and upward were enrolled by prophecy
in the book of life, when they were departing from the land of
Egypt.[30] Again all of this age were numbered by Joshua. Thereafter those who could advance to the wars were reckoned in the
heavenly guild.[31] These only could pitch tents in the Lord's camp,
these only advance to the wars.

8:3. It is truly marvelous to be victorious at a time when he was
diverted by various blandishments; to triumph although pressed by
many arguments. Twenty is calculated as five four times or reck-

oned as four five times. When they were thus assembled, it was determined that they only would be most disposed to the wars who had grown to the age of the Old and New Testament and who had been brought up in its wisdom. The strength of these is most appropriate for carrying on war. It should warn them to conquer themselves first, for at such time the enemy employs great faculties for deceiving to the extent that he is in the flesh.

Chapter 9:1. At that time, therefore, O Christ, when in age a youth, in mind a nobleman, he cast down the allurements of the world. He laid aside the weapons of King Saul, so that the monstrous deceiver of souls might be laid low by one stone only,[32] namely, by you whom he cherished in his heart. Thenceforward he chose to carry you with him in his heart of hearts, with you as author to struggle against spiritual forces of wickedness in heavenly places.[33] What more? Having thus approached the field of combat, he arrived at the monastery.[34] Knocking with a yearly vow, he entered at last the gates of justice through which only the just enter.[35] With increase of grace he came thereafter to the gate which alone leads certain ones to life.[36] He trod the narrow and strait way which belongs to a few,[37] so that with enlarged spirit he might run the way of God's commandments with talent of keenest art.[38]

9:2. For a long time he so flourished in the midst of monastic discipline that he was present more in heavenly than in earthly affairs. The fathers, induced by some kind of disposition (perhaps by royal order), made him the gardener. A good athlete of Christ, he rejoiced as if amid the delights of Paradise and by obedience he was made happy in spirit. He knew that the Lord had been buried in a cave of this kind and that He had appeared to Mary as a gardener.[39] He knew that He arose in the same such place and that angelic visions had therein appeared.[40] So, digging up treasure in the garden of the spirit, he anointed the body of Jesus with manifold odor.

9:3. What then do you think he said as he associated with such a duty? If I am not mistaken, he said (perhaps not with voice, but with mental disposition), he said, "Let my beloved come into his garden planted with virtue, and let him eat fruits of his fruit trees." [41] He had in his mind different herbs of virtues. Consequently he did not hesitate to say that He may eat the fruits of His fruit trees, of His fruit trees because he congratulated not himself but the Lord's grace if he bore anything good in his mind. Let others cherish labors in the field more than virtues of the spirit protected by obedience. Adalard did not neglect such things but consecrated his soul to the Lord as a garden of delights. He remembered what He said to him, "Put me as a seal upon your heart." [42] Encompassed by this fortification he delighted in the Lord's spiritual conversation with him more than in matters of temporal importance. His beloved, Christ, had come down to visit the garden of his spirit.[43] He came down as to a garden of spice and there He grazed on delights of virtues.[44] The garden of delights is moreover called Paradise, because it is understood as the mind of man and because Eden is interpreted as "garden of delights." [45] Certain ones have also called it "flowering." Christ had, therefore, come down to it to gather the lilies of charity and to see the Punic apples that have sprouted.[46]

Chapter 10. The spirit of a good man is, as I have observed, a garden of delights filled with virtues and hence Paradise. There myrrh is reaped, that is, mortification of the members with spices of virtues; the rose reddened with the blood of martyrdom is gathered; fruit trees of the valleys glisten, besprinkled with heavenly disciplines; Punic apples are sprouting because of the fragrance of good deeds; apart from it the blazing ardor of God's love lies concealed therein. If you wish to behold, brother, it was there that our ancient was entirely lovable and sweet, there that he was adapted to every expression of purity. Does it not seem that honey and milk drip from his tongue? [47] With his speech he made his way so gently that he ever rendered his hearers drunk with holiness, made everyone united with him by reason of excessive sweetness. What else were his lips but a dripping honeycomb? [48] Or as I said above, what else but an instrument of the Holy Spirit? Otherwise human wisdom could not comprehend what he was saying. Full of the gift of holiness his words dripped with heavenly prophecy.

Chapter 11:1. For a long, long while he was moved by the Holy Spirit. He is said to have been mindful of the precept given to Abraham, "Go out of the land and away from your kin and out of the house of your father, and come into a land which I will point out to you." [49] He debated such matters with himself. While meditating he decided that he had not yet fulfilled this precept in earnest. Although he had mentally abandoned the soil of his birth, he reflected that he was still bodily present in it. If, in accordance with the precept of the Gospel, he had already abandoned father and mother and kindred to be deemed a worthy disciple of God,[50] he was still being troubled even more because of his family.

11.2. Since it was one of considerable reputation, kinsmen and friends kept visiting him and calling on him more often than the man's peaceful spirit would have required. For this reason it came to pass that another Elijah slipped away in flight, not from a Jezebel, but from desire of the flesh. The serious soldier of Christ sought by escape and flight to find himself more fully. He who might have been sustained by many flattering indulgences became a sojourner and a pilgrim, like Christ having nowhere to lay his head. Thus, putting himself to flight in order to find himself, he came by the strength of the Word to Monte Cassino, not wishing to learn about the country nor to boast about himself. He supposed that he wished only to understand himself and that as long as he stayed within the boundaries of his own country he would not be separated from vices. Lest he should again be bound up in new nets of the devil, he went out beyond, walking rapidly as if in some manner he might be able himself to learn thoroughly by recital of the truth, "I live, yet no longer I, but Christ lives in me." [51]

Chapter 12. So he came to Monte Cassino where the fount and origin of all religion was supposed to be. He was received by the abbot of the monastery, but by a disposition of God's judgment he was allowed to remain there for only a little while. In that place a certain anchorite is said by God's Spirit to have declared openly to him who he was, whence he was, and for what purpose he had come. He foretold that after a short interval the king's envoys would come to seek him and return him to his own place. Hearing this, he was deeply disturbed that lack of success would follow his vows. So, taking the abbot aside, he gave all his possessions to him. Then he asked and begged permission to flee if he could and also for his name never again to be heard for a long, long time.

Chapter 13:1. But God quickly anticipated their plans. Since they were acting too slowly, he was overtaken by envoys who seized him and with no delay led him back to his country. What do you suppose? How bitter was his spirit, how sad, that he should return against his will to the boundary of his own country and the sweet fields of his own soil! [52] Let our fellow monks who rest unconcerned while besmeared with soot of shadows hear about a man of this kind. Let them hear who draw after themselves flocks of worldlings. Let them hear that it is not safe for them to be besmeared with fondness for kinsmen. Christ did not know his mother and he was unaware of his brothers, in order to show true brotherhood of mind. "If anyone," He says, "will do the will of my Father who is in heaven, he is my brother, sister, and mother." [53] He recalled a disciple from the duty of burial, not permitting him to bury his father with the obligation due the flesh. "Let the dead bury their own dead," He says, "but you follow me." [54] Our holy ancient knew all that and it was for that reason that he was making haste to flee from the midst of his compatriots. He remembered that Jesus did not perform signs in His own country, nor is a prophet without honor except on his own soil.[55]

13:2. When despoiled of the honor of the world, Adalard made haste to get away from the bonds of dear ones so that he might appropriate to himself true honor of mind and, as I shall indicate later, live an angelic life on earth. He believed that he would not be able to become a true pauper as long as he remained in the midst of his kinsmen who flourished with honor of the realm and glittered with abundance of riches. Shattering therefore the claims of his famous name, he who was formerly wealthy sought to become poor without ambition. But as he set an example for despising what was his own, he became more distinguished in poverty, more brilliant in flight, more sublime in humble wretchedness. If I may employ the words of blessed Jerome, some may be richer as monks than they would have been as worldlings.[56] They may possess riches under the poor Christ which they did not have under the opulent but deceiving devil. The church may long for them as rich men whom the world formerly held as beggars. But our Adalard, trampling down all worldly matters, conquered (in figure), crushed under his feet all worldly affairs.

Chapter 14. While he was sitting as a quiet victor in the lofty citadel of mind, a new order of battle was in the providence of God begun. For not long after he had returned, it came to pass that, with consent of the abbot of the monastery, he was made an equal. It was as if another Augustine was chosen as successor while his predecessor was still living. The latter, however, was elected bishop, while the former was designated abbot. Yet both were found as perfect stewards of God. Like a servant of the aforesaid father Augustine, this blessed one was an outstanding imitator of the former's works, penetrating in character, ready of will, rich in eloquence, flowing with sweetness in greeting, impressing a hearer with such enjoyment that you could believe his tongue nothing other than a pen of the Holy Spirit. Tears graced his preaching; his groaning softened hardness of heart. The "latter rain" [57] of tears was poured out of him so that minds might more fruitfully take in seed to produce fruit and so that he might soften the heart of his hearers with love of charity by a feeling of this kind.

Chapter 15. His voice, full of the grace of verdure and all constancy, seemed stronger. Gleaming in countenance, he was believed full of the richness of the Holy Spirit. According to a statement of Horace, which is acclaimed with great praise, he was "strong, and in himself complete, polished and rounded." [58] Strong he certainly was in faith, solid in constancy and virtue, so much so that he seemed to tremble at nothing, to be hesitant at nothing, even though the entire world, terror stricken, might be falling into ruin. If he were sometimes driven by a blast of terror, he subdued it alternately by hope and reason. Worldly fear, however, could never stab him. "Polished and rounded" he was in himself, no, rather in God, because he was not only adapted to virtues and morals but also suitable in all matters and worthy of love. He sought to be all things to all men and to bring advantage to all. [59] Noble in blood, he was even more noble in morals; full of God's wisdom, but not lacking in work; handsome of face, but more handsome in faith and holiness; rich in offspring, but richer in nurture, since he was born as a descendant of the offspring of heaven.

Chapter 16:1. He was wholly clothed with the new man and, so far as lawful for mortals, recreated by God in the profoundest degree. His cavalry was a chariot of virtues, the wheels of which chariot were prudence, justice, fortitude, and temperance. [60] Prudence was so great in him that a fountain of counsel seemed to trickle from his mind. He discerned at one and the same time things past, present, and future, so that of each one he foresaw what should be done or followed by God's counsel. How much he pursued justice Frankland is witness as well as the realms submitted to him for counsel. In particular is Italy a witness. It was entrusted to him that in a useful and honorable manner he might mold with justice and discretion the realm and its king, the younger Pepin,[61] into the status of a commonwealth devoted to cultivation of religion. There he merited such great praise for his love of virtue that by certain ones he was heralded as not a man but an angel. All acknowledged that he never looked upon outward appearance.

16:2. Contrary to a popular proverb, the bulwark of his spirit was not dashed to pieces by a golden fist.[62] Alone, they said, he could cross the river of greedy Acheron[63] and year after year cross and recross the Alps without hazard of blindness. When he was present the loftiness of the proud openly trembled, the humility of the gentle boasted. At his accession he put down every tyrannical power, powers who like evil robbers were plundering[64] people the more daringly as they were aided by permission of a lawful master. They were also laying waste all the land with infamous violence. First, he restored peace to them; thereafter the holy judge restored to each his own[65] rights. So great was the virtuous wisdom resting upon him that instead of the magistrate's rod he employed a judge's word. He made no delay in defining for each the justice that belonged to him. Each one, therefore, fulfilled his own duty and none trespassed upon the rights of another. He was a true treasury of the poor, patrimony of widows, father of orphans, comforter of the grieving, arm of the infirm, and scourge of the proud. Yet by his character he put down everyone from artificial arrogance of mind and broke no one inwardly, except him whom he deemed incorrigible.

Chapter 17. So it was that he reached the boundaries of the Romans, strong in virtue, yet mild and gentle. There he was received by Lord Leo, at that time the apostolic pontiff. No Frank had ever been received with such an expression of friendliness. Some of ours relate that the pope said humorously to him, "O Frank, you know that if I shall find you other than I believe you to be, it is no longer needful for any Frank to come hither whom I ought to believe." It was thereby clear how much weight the man had whose emptying of the faith of the Franks would recommend that no family should be believed or of what strength he was.

Chapter 18. How great he was they prove by adducing many fulfilled promises. Letters bear witness which he recently [66] directed to Emperor Lothair about the faith which should be maintained among men. In part he wrote thus, "O prince, you know that good faith has often prevailed amid bloodshed and clash of savage arms even among pagans. You know that this is so in order that each may commit himself more profoundly to vows of faith. How much stronger should be the agreement of a Christian pledged in truth? May no one deceive you, O emperor, for when faith is violated against anyone, man is not despised, but God the witness and my truth." On the basis of such statements it is clear beyond doubt that it would be easier to violate chains of iron than for the faithful promises of this man to be stained. In his whole heart nothing shone but the fountain of truth and marvelous simplicity. If you examine him carefully, you would find in him a spirit stamped with Christ. In no way, therefore, could he be corrupted.

Chapter 19. His spirit was as the garden of Paradise, enclosed with the wall of faith,[67] planted with all kinds of virtues. He imitated the humility of this one, the tenderness of that one. He pursued still another's mode of frugality and modest habit of dress. He had the patience of that one and the meekness of this one. Yet he frequently spoke to me with sighs and with the mouth of piety, "Upon whom will I rest my words if not upon the humble and peaceful and tremulous?" [68] You know, good Jesus, how he unrolled such things for himself with unremitting disposition of mind. He had it in himself clearly and fittingly to persuade men to holiness. All your precepts entrusted to him he held in mind. With words of your commandments before his eyes, he deliberated with himself. With single consideration of mind he meditated on the lives of the saints. Their examples of virtue he ruminated zealously, that from all these he might gather one perfect man, full of God and adorned with the duty of religion.

Chapter 20:1. Tully, the king of Latin eloquence, writes in the second book of *Invention in Rhetorical Art* that when the people of Crotona flourished with wealth, when they were thus deemed blessed, and when they sought to adorn the temple of their religion in a splendid manner with pictures, they summoned a certain Zeuxis [69] who apparently excelled all other painters in skill. At great cost they invited him to paint the likeness of a certain Helena which would through the ages endure as a marvelous work. He thereupon inquired what beautiful virgins they had. Immediately they led the artist into the gymnasium and showed him many youths of great merit. Then they boasted only [70] the most honorable victories in gymnastic exercise. When he had marveled at the fine forms and bodies of the youths there, they said to him, "The sisters of these youths are the virgins among us. Their great merit you can conjecture from these."

20:2. "Bring them to me," he said, "so that from them I may paint the most beautiful features and transfer to one likeness what you think you seek." When they had complied, the painter chose five whose fine form he judged to be beautiful. He did not believe that everything they thought lovely could be found in one body. Nature has not completely polished anything perfect in all its parts in a single example; it would not have anything to bestow upon others if it granted everything to one.

Chapter 21. If our ancient also entered the gymnasium of this life after he had been purified in the font of baptism, after he had renounced the world, how did he with pure intent of mind gaze upon different ones paying attention to different things? Some he saw sweating for honors of the world and joys of the present life, others for luxury and lust of the flesh. Some he saw pursuing justice, as well as others peering toward the future life. From all those he chose them whom he could understand as the five virgins who ceaselessly trim their lamps with holy oil of charity and prepare to go forth to meet the bridegroom and bride.[71] With watchful spirit he imitated them lest a thief coming in the night might kidnap the sleeping one.[72] From the gymnastic song of saints he heard how worthy of honor were the victories. From all these he formed again in himself one likeness of Christ. In one God and Man, Christ Jesus, he found all things that are of the loveliness and comeliness of eternal life more than what he could understand. The perfect which nature has forbidden in all parts of the church, grace has yielded that God may be all in all.[73] From all through all he performed amply that he might now find Christ in all. For this reason he was called by some *Antonius* (as the letters of Master Albinus state);[74] but by others, as noted above, *Aurelius Augustinus*. He did one thing characteristic of Gregory, but another of blessed Silvester.

Chapter 22. My conscience is witness that I often wondered why he would accept so much in return to expend for use of those in need or of his own monks, until I examined the life of blessed Silvester.[75] In this respect Adalard imitated the latter's life, namely, that he would always rather be found as a pauper borrowing than as a rich man. To those depending on him he often observed, "O, you want to know, do you, whether you will appear greedy or liberal? Know then that if you fear that you have given more to anyone than was fitting, you will be exposed as greedy; but if less, it is assuredly a sign of liberality. I therefore warn you, my son, that if you neglect, you will appear as a culprit to pay out more of our own than to pay out less."

Chapter 23:1. Supreme Virtue knows that more often than not he paid out so liberally that he himself seemed to be a pauper and his own monks at the same time appeared to be in need. But happy and rejoicing he exulted in the Lord, saying, "Would that in a small way we may share Christ's poverty!" Never did it occur to him that it would be possible for matters to come to this. Christ, however, continually quickened the petty-minded ones to learn to pay out their own liberally and to rely on God's largess. There was one occasion on which every bit of cheese in the monastery had been set out for guests and none remained for the brothers. The cellarer, with a certain attitude of mind and a threatening tone of voice, asked, "What are you seeking with the outlay of such a huge quantity? You are leaving nothing for the brothers to eat?"

23:2. With a sweet expression and a smile, Adalard replied, "The Lord will provide." [76]

23:3. "You always promise that," continued the cellarer, "but what you dispose of indiscriminately will not be provided right now!"

23:4. In the meantime, while they were chatting, two wagons

came up in front of the gate, one bearing a load of fish, the other full of cheeses. When the blessed father heard about that, he happily called for the cellarer. "Look, brother," he said, "you have betrayed what you feared. But look, improvident sloth is refuted."

23:5. Then the cellarer, who was of simple mind and seeing that he was betrayed by kindness, said, "My father, give as much as you will. Never again will I say, 'The Lord will not provide,' but I will say that truly as much as you wish will be given."

Chapter 24. So great a man with such a prudent disposition could not be unaware of what, to whom, and how much he might give away. This was his sole vice, if I may use such terminology. Let us consider what he usually said: "If I had so little to give that in sharing with two indigents neither would receive much help, it would seem to me preferable to give all to one (if he is suitable) rather than share almost nothing with both or leave them both entirely empty." So to one he weighed out the gift of benevolence and to another the gift of piety. See, O hard of heart, see the bowels of pity. Although this one could not be generous to all, yet by his compassionate disposition he was affected by the griefs, penuries, and varied misfortunes of all as if they were his own.

Chapter 25. So great a man he was that of himself he could truthfully declare, "I am wounded with love." [77] If he had not been wounded by love, he would not have repeatedly bemoaned the misfortunes of all. He wept indeed every day once or twice at least, at matins and at vespers. This perpetual fire in him did not fail from the altar of his spirit, but burned perennially with devotion. There he became a sweet holocaust to the Lord; there victims were immolated, especially in the middle of the night, for he was ever watchful in prayers. There he burned every fat of the flesh and allurements of desire with a blaze of devouring flame. All the vitals within and the head with the feet, that is, the beginning of life and its end, he burned as a sacrifice to the Lord.[78] He bathed everything first with tears so it would burn more purely to the Lord. Never have I found a man in whom there was so great a fountain of tears and such profound sighing. You might suppose that inwardly everything released in tears was shattering the breast with deep sobs. When he was beating himself with blows thick and fast to elicit a richer shower of tears, it seemed as if thunders were resounding in him. We may rightly call them thunders, because you, good Jesus, were within to bedew the seeds of virtues with tears and to cleanse with a fount of sprinkling the fruit of the full field which you had blessed.

Chapter 26:1. Sometimes when I in my smallness inquired about the origin of this kind of mourning and the grace of such great weeping, he replied, "I wail, my son, I wail not as if I would please myself to weep in humiliation or that I may gaze upon the sacraments of heaven. No, I mourn myself, considering what I am. I mourn not because I wish to bewail myself, but I wail because I know that I should be bewailed." O the profound humility of the man and the high genius of his mind! For you express those sentiments, not because you knew that you were such, but to invite me, whom perchance you did know to be such, to bewail albeit later and to soften a stony heart with your tears. You wept because you had entered the holy of holies and you could no longer continue what you were discerning. For hope that is disquieted distresses the soul. With your mind's eye you were peering at that heavenly country where the hymn-singing choirs were proclaiming the praises of God. You were enjoying that blessed, happy harmony [79] of heaven where with ceaseless voice musical instruments re-echo for joy of jubilation.

26:2. What is even greater, you have made your very soul a habitation of the Holy Spirit. [80] When the same Spirit flew upward a little higher that you might search after Him, you wept for excessive love and you spoke thus, "My soul became liquid as He spoke to me, if indeed He has spoken and gone away. He has gone away so that the mind greedy to enjoy may flame upward more happily and when it has found the flame of love it may hold it more firmly." In the moment of death, my father, the holy disposition did not depart from your mouth. You then said, "My soul has thirsted for the living God. When will I come and appear before God's face?" [81] You were already longing to enter the place of the wonderful tabernacle; already the voice of exultation was in your ears and the voice of confession was in your mouth. Already the sound of banqueting was being heard; already you had in some manner entered among those whose dwelling place is that of all who rejoice. Even as you were lamenting, all those things were present before your eyes. Full of love you had fainted as you said, "I adjure you, O daughter of Jerusalem, if you have found my beloved, that you may announce to him that I am fainting with love." [82]

26:3. The pious reader [83] will understand that if he withdraws himself occasionally from such meditations for certain businesses at hand, it was as if going away from the saints he hastened more quickly to return. Yet constantly finding himself complete, he was present complete as if in the daytime he had nothing else in his hands. Soon tears were present, soon groaning, and every expression of devotion. In that place the mind was renewed and every sense of the body was constantly dying to the world.

Chapter 27. When he entered upon God's office, which he was accustomed to say with pleasant spirit, he laid aside all plans and temporal matters at the door and went in to be present to God and himself completely and entirely. If you had observed him, you would have seen him suddenly enter the more secret matters of the mind and look with fearsome countenance upon something I know not what. He dipped his tongue like a pen in the fountain of the Holy Spirit that he might be pure enough to sing the praises of God. Amid praises he discerned some kind of music and sometimes wept beyond measure. And why indeed is it amazing? I have heard a certain bishop making the following comment about him at court when the king and councilors were giving attention to some business and when the crowd in usual fashion was making noise on all sides. In the midst of them he sat mourning as if he had come there to a contest of weeping. While dwelling there he was thus secretly attending the King of heaven.

Chapter 28. Amid hazards of the world, busy here and there about affairs of the church, he nonetheless did not abandon the ordinances of the *Rule*. In place of reading he gave his time to tears, and for the remaining offices he served the Lord with joy of mind. On a journey his companions and associates knew that he did not wish to be approached. They walked, therefore, at a distance from him so that he could busy himself with God alone. For the time had already come for him to adore the Father not in the mountain, nor in Jerusalem nor (if I may so state) in any particular place, but in spirit and in truth.[84] He had made his own soul a temple of the Holy Spirit [85] and a habitation of truth. Everywhere he was entirely with himself and entirely with God, and he walked anxiously with him.

Chapter 29. Always was he found cheerful, kindly, joyous. To all men was he patient, tolerant, friendly. A son of peace he was and a chain of charity, so that brotherly hearts might cling mutually together. Spoleto and Benevento learned this. Formerly they strove ceaselessly against each other with hostile sword. But the blessed man approached and entered Benevento to effect reconciliation. While there he restored such peace between them that to this day they cling together, bound and confederate with each other in the peace of Christ. Not only between them, but also among the Greeks and all the islands of the sea, he earned a great reward of love and fame of virtue. In this discord he pondered carefully that both were Christians and brothers. They could not be pleasing to God when bloodied with slaughter and preys of their own capabilities. For the Apostle says, "Everyone who hates his brother is a murderer and we know that no murderer has eternal life remaining in him." [86] The holy father cast himself between them and restored to fullest degree the peace of Christ which the devil had violated. An extraordinary zealot for justice, he seemed tireless in a matter of this kind.

Chapter 30:1. When Emperor Charles had made an end of his life [87] and his offspring Louis Augustus had succeeded to the realm, the devil's envy acted in the latter and truth suffered violence in the usual craftiness of wicked men. It was nothing new, for among evil ones truth is always treated as hostile and justice is rent by the crimes of the foolish. Already, according to Plato's statement, the old depravity of perverse men was deploring the blessed happiness of commonwealths, if students of wisdom were ruling them or if their rulers were studying wisdom.[88] Incited by guile and envy, they supposed that, if they could remove Daniel from the king's side,[89] justice would lose its status, since it had no longer a protector and wickedness, destroyed by its own frauds, would regain a place of dominance. For, O God, observer of all souls, you who had sown a plan in this one's heart, you knew that he would yield to the commands of king and church. You knew that he would not do this except out of common zeal for all good things. You knew that freedom, relieved of the tyranny of more powerful ones, might wage war more readily for the Lord and that the praises of all churches might rightfully be more devoutly rendered to the Lord. But God, who always summons His own up higher,[90] sought to approve this man more openly and to show how great he was in adversity.

30:2. Since by God's grace he had already secured for himself by life and manners the seven beatitudes of the Gospel,[91] so he might by his works fulfil the remaining eighth.[92] "Blessed are those," says the Gospel, "who endure persecution for justice, for theirs is the kingdom of heaven." [93] He suffered from the arrogance of evildoers; he was charged with defrauding humanity. This was he who for love of justice and truth had publicly kept nothing for himself, but in every manner delivered himself even to death. Never had he hidden truth out of fear, never had he allowed a lie to have an opportunity. Wretched ones whom the greed and cruel worthlessness of ignorant men harassed, he mercifully covered with the purity of truth. When the blindness of wicked men concealed webs of spiders more craftily than they could conceal fish nets, he refused to appear before them, lest the shame of depravity be more fully revealed and justice withdrawn. Sentence was therefore passed upon him without an accuser, without a conference, without even a hearing or a trial. Stripped of present possessions, divested of office, defiled in the estimation of the crowd, he went into exile for the good of the commonwealth.[94]

30:3. But how blind and foolish was the cunning of perverse men! They supposed that on account of thirst for office they could besmirch and stain the reputation of good men's virtue. For they are tortured by the glory of another the more they fail to achieve that by which he is held worthy of the honor of eminent name. But "if God is for us, who is against us?" [95] So they lied in order to befoul the splendor and felicity of those who lifted skyward the fortifications of their abilities. There thieves do not break through nor steal.[96] After God no one has anything more precious than himself. He who guards himself by working well must possess himself and God completely. Never could he be false advocate to empty himself of his own honor and abilities (than which nothing was richer) if someone outside himself would not cast himself away.

Chapter 31:1. The most priceless kind of possession is splendor of virtue, than which nothing weightier is gained, nothing sweeter to love is discerned, nothing happier possessed. This treasure our ancient strove by working to gain for himself, by seeking happily found, by possessing bore with him wherever he went. However much he had been occupied with affairs of the world, intent in the same degree upon his possession he restored here and there more richly and so gained heaven for himself. Once you were shameless in knowledge of the profits of lust, but Christ's soldier was not bound by your bonds nor was he blackened by your darkness. Defending the lofty citadel of charity, he subdued the world under his feet by his banquet of liberality. Wherever he was led not by the jealousy of envious men, but by the Spirit of God, he went willingly as if invited to a great feast.

31:2. Tell me, I beg, O wretched passion for the world, why you were seized by its vain joys? Why did you embrace external goods and indulgence of the moment instead of eternal delights of life? Never could you make yours what the nature of things makes foreign to you. If you seek to satisfy nature, know that it requires little. If nothing could be sufficient for indulgence of cupidity, O passion, O wretched presumption of mortals and heedless imitator of the virtues, why is it that you would be submerged in such great billows? Why are you preoccupied in misfortunes of eternal death? Why do you heedlessly overstep yourself, since you would lose the whole if you could take anything from it? We know that you have always waged war against justice and truth, yet you are still tormented with the bruise. You bloodied the world with the first fratricide in Abel. Through all time since you have butchered with the sword of iniquity thousands of saints. Even more criminally you sold the Lord for the price of cupidity. Thenceforth still conquering, you will be conquered, you who are already trodden upon by the feet of the saints.

31:3. Unfortunate one, why do you not listen to the complaints of saints under God's altar crying against you, "Avenge our blood, O Lord"? [97] Do you think that because you did not spill this one's blood you will be pardoned? Iniquity has lied to itself. Do you not hear the Lord speaking, "Vengeance is mine and I will repay"? [98] Although you shortsightedly supposed that you had exiled our ancient from seats of the land, his Lord used that for a crown. In usual manner your blind evil has turned to another's good. Gold is again put in a furnace; it is proved by fire of trial; it is beaten and polished; and lo, a beautiful vessel, formed in honor, shines in splendor. But while someone present surveys the outcome of such matters, he thinks perhaps as Vergil thought, "Nor does anyone of the gods care about mortal affairs." [99]

31:4. Sometimes the just man perishes in his justice. He is slain by deceit of slanderers and some depraved man arrogates for himself the praise of wisdom. Yet the outcome of the affair has approved the end of both matters.

Chapter 32:1. In the meanwhile our ancient, although superior in wisdom, was sent to the island of Herus as if he were one of the baseborn. Deprived of every human honor,[100] he was sent there, but on all sides he was sustained by a heavenly bulwark. At that time the happy chariot, joined in kinship in the manner of Ezekiel,[101] was dissolved. Over them Jesus [102] was guarding, suitably girded with the breastplate of virtues. There had been five begotten of one man. The august emperor had employed the familiar counsel of three of them. Along with the stable square he had ruled the empire of the Franks [103] thus fully organized for increase of the commonwealth. About these horses Habakkuk had not unfittingly sung to the Lord, "You who mount upon your horses, horsemanship is your salvation." [104]

32:2. Their course was indeed unequal, but an equal mind was borne to the palm in the beginning. Henceforward the Holy Spirit guarded over them, and with equal vow one purpose was consummated in them. At first they seemed to run as horses of different colors but harmonious in will alone. Afterward, as blessed Jerome says, the same ones in this work draw one yoke of the chariot with equal neck and purpose.[105] They did not wait for blows of the whip but they flamed at Christ's urging and for the army they became masters and leaders of holiness. Our holy ancient was the oldest, already devoted to the Lord in age and grace, maturest in counsel, surpassing the others in sanctity. Then came Wala, most eminent of men, who later succeeded him as abbot of the monks. At that time first among the first and a man more lovable than all others, he clung to the king with immeasurable friendship, for which he was elevated to great dignity of superintendence. In senate he was most celebrated and in military service strongest in discretion. Such great praise pursued him in every phase of life that for a long time he was reputed to be able to do by love more than some could do by their ambitions or others by their tyranny. He was indeed a guardian of justice, an adornment of honor, and a just oppressor of oppressors.

Chapter 33:1. To these the sister Gundrada clung fast, in constant attendance on her brothers, differing in sex, but similar in virtues. Although the virgin, most noble of nobles, was friendly to the king, and although she dwelled amid wanton heats of the palace and charms of the youths, even amid caresses of delights and blandishments of passion, yet she alone was worthy to bring back the palm of modesty. She was able to cross over foulness of the flesh by an unharmed path. She bore with her a scepter of chastity, for she believed it would be richer for her to maintain integrity of the flesh than to violate the rosy flowers of modesty. Chastity is a virtue by which she happily merited to be crowned, as the eloquent Tertullian describes, "The flower of morals, honor of the body, adornment of sex, integrity of blood, loyalty to one's family, foundation of health, precedent of a good mind in all respects . . . ," and "Albeit rare, nor easily perfected, and scarcely perpetual. . . . ." [106] Christ's handmaid elected, amid all perils to chastity, to seek out a field for this kind of struggle, and she deserved to obtain the triumph of decency.

33:2. The other two were our Bernarius and his sister consecrated to God, Theodrada. She had married but had later hurriedly grasped the second grade of chastity. They now sat at home with Mary at the feet of Jesus: [107] she governing the life of the nuns at Soissons, he observing Christ's discipleship with us. Yet both hastened to run toward the prize of heavenly calling.[108]

Chapter 34. In this sweet fivefold number, I observe the musical sound repeated and re-echoing in part as well as the quantities of their harmony sounding in concert together. If you note the men first and then the two sisters, it will be a Greek diapason and a proportion of one and a half quantity, for the three together surpass the double by a half of itself. One, namely, our blessed ancient, sings harmoniously between two men and two women; thus they express the honey-flowing concord of musical art and the pyramid of geometrical training. But what Adalard the ancient did amid the four for them to sing well together, that indeed the same one towering above summons them to burn with love of heavenly country in the manner of a four-tongued fire. If you look upon them as guides in business of the commonweal, three will again be disposed like Martha to public duties [109] and two at the feet of Jesus intent so as to hear the word. Even so our father, the ancient, is the middle one who between both lives, active and contemplative, walked in measured and moderate manner. Finally if you look once more at them carefully there are three who chose the triumph of continence and two who at first practiced chaste marriage but at last drew the equal yoke of monastic discipline. Clothed therefore in all doubles they are in all things proclaimed harmonious, concordant, and equally swift.[110] I contemplate them, each one indeed, as one with Benjamin among the patriarchs clothed with five robes,[111] but by our Jesus bedecked more gloriously afterward with simple nuptial dress. I contemplate also the talents entrusted to them, but in all these I read one reward beyond measure.

Chapter 35:1. In these and all matters they strove eagerly in turn for each other. But the wind of envy came and scattered far from each other those in whom the glory of the entire realm especially flourished. The purpose was that they might be manifest as approved and that those to whom they went might be sustained by their virtues. Yet Corbie, long praised by many, was then grieving and weeping when it was deprived of so great a patron. For its consolation, however, it was deemed worthy, by the Lord's provision, to receive Wala as Christ's recruit. He was a very eminent man, a noble among nobles. Later, after his brother's decease, Corbie rejoiced and exulted to have him as abbot in Christ's place.

35:2. O providence of God, O providence of the eye prepared to run through all the earth [112] "reaching from end to end strongly and disposing all things sweetly"! [113] How incomprehensible are all your works and judgments, you who use human blindness as an incalculable counsel of light! At times you flog the sons whom you are preparing to crown. So it was, my almighty Father, that our Bernarius was sent back to Lérins.[114] But your Wala was received by Corbie as a recruit. Laying aside the baldric of soldiery to put you on as a whole will of holiness, he eagerly grasped his first military service of paradise to consummate the measure of Christ in himself. As if blameless, Theodrada was left under holy profession at Soissons. On the other hand, Gundrada was sent to St. Radegunda (formerly a queen) so that anyone with whom she had in part communicated when she flourished amid hazards of the palace, might emulate the tokens of her virtues, and so that she, praying to God day and night with her, might by supplication receive consolation for herself and her own.

Chapter 36. When they withdrew from the palace as if in disgrace, our ancient went forth as if summoned to a banquet, strong in faith, keen of mind, conscious of purity. He gave thanks that he would be found worthy to suffer contumely for the truth.[115] Now bestowing a kiss on a weeping brother, now visiting a sister with the fondness and exhortation of holy ones, persuading his friends to fortitude of mind, showing the magnates of the palace an example of virtue, he demonstrated to all the marvelous constancy of his mind. It is related that two archbishops, weeping as they departed from him, spoke thus to the august emperor who had questioned them, "What are you thinking of, O emperor? Do you seek to vindicate yourself by disgracing this man and by exiling him to some random part of earth? We declare that you could never make a greater joy for him than this. For now a heaven-approved suffering is granted him, especially today when he is glad to receive an excess of food, that is, his original freedom in Christ. You should know also that never happier, never more joyful has he seemed to us at any other time. He rests on holy hope; he quails at no confrontation with the one who smites him; and no grief pierces him." When the emperor heard that, he was covered with shame. He was pained that he had done [nothing] to check what there already was by way of embarrassment.[116]

Chapter 37. But Christ's holy servant spoke to Caesar as if to those imputing it to him as reproach, "Do not, my brothers, do not pay attention as though what is done to us were in man's power. Even if one should choose something other than what had once been proffered by God, it could not be declined until it had first been completely fulfilled and no disposition can be fulfilled unless he agrees. I warn you, therefore, beloved, pay attention to God to fulfil his will in us, although I would not have desired it through his hand, just as Job accomplished whatever was ready regardless of how many things there were.[117] Otherwise, when what has been prearranged has been completed, we will be recalled not because it will be that one's will, but whenever God will by his nod graciously decree. In the meanwhile, spare, I beg, the prince granted to us by God, for he is not exercising his own will but— now and then—the will of our Lord against whom we have sinned. As blessed David said, if the Lord arouses him against us, pray suppliantly that the sacrifice of our humility may be fragrant,[118] and that He may receive His penitents in all things. So may His will be done." See what great and immovable patience clung to him! How great his teaching and how great the bowels of pity! Amid all these disturbances and amid the voices of grief and tears, he was a comforter and persuader of virtues.

Chapter 38. He was a mirror of holiness and a pleader at law amid all the conflicting complaints. Who would have a stony heart [119] and not weep? Who would be cut from granite and not mourn? Who could restrain himself with iron eyes from grieving? For at that hour all with one voice were crying in lamentation, "It is the worst kind of blindness and ill advice that the fount of counsel is carried away in exile. That will not be recovered, nor will another Frank be like him so great an advocate of charity and truth. It is clearly the worst fault and crafty guile of venom. See what very evil time is upon us when just and good men are dishonored and when there is no one to forbid. What do you think will happen to us? The opponent of perversity is taken away and what further opportunity for justice will there be? What soundness of counsel, especially when everyone seeks his own? No one takes counsel for the commonweal, but each for himself and only in an evil fashion. Counsel is sold for gifts. They pursue payments, they look for their own gain."

Chapter 39. In such complaining words the hearts of all are compelled to mourn tearfully. They were unaware that it came to pass by God's hidden judgment so that when the evils were accomplished our ancient would not see. In the meanwhile the penalty of sin raged freely against certain ones. As if that which he desired might be lacking to him, he was, by God's disposition, expelled from human orbit. When he was forbidden to look on the soil of earth, he became like John an investigator of the heavenly country [120] because he fed on heavenly sacraments. What do you think? Could God have forgotten that He might delay him from such a task against his will? But now perhaps the long-desired vow is granted him, as if God had first vexed him with laborious honor, so that He might later terminate it by the gift of care. Or as if, accustomed to angelic conversation, he might wash away with a flood of tears the stains of dust soiling him amid the hazards of the world. The fact is doubtless believed that in seven years [121] (a number devoted to this purpose) he might be led by the Holy Spirit as in some manner to deserve completely the sevenfold grace of the Spirit.[122] Otherwise so great a reputation for virtue would not have been conferred except by divine will. Already famous and belonging to almost all parts of Europe, it was thus arranged that he might illuminate also the soil of Aquitaine to its limits. It was indeed that he, who flourished everywhere with a name of holiness, might be returned to all even more famous and might, with God's help, everywhere abound more richly in the rewards of merit.

Chapter 40. Suitable witnesses of this kind of thing are his defenders, the holy brothers, among whom the blessed one lived an angelic life (or so it seemed to them) through the seven-year period. These brothers he moved with a holy flame of devotion toward what is God's. So great was the virtue of charity in him that he could make his way gently in all men and with his own love for them strengthen them more fully in God's cause. God's supreme strength tempered certain harsh misfortunes for him, as it made the midst of the furnace a blowing wind of dew for the three children.[123] He was not struck with blasts nor buffeted by the force of winds, for he was grounded in Christ's love. I could ask with the Apostle, who might separate him from Christ's love? [124] Tribulation or persecution or famine or nakedness or sword? Truly, as I shall indicate more precisely, neither death nor life nor things present nor things future nor any other creature could separate him from the love of God that is in Christ Jesus. For his feet were grounded upon the rock and therefore he could not be shaken.[125]

Chapter 41. At first he seemed to pass the time among those blessed men as if under guard. But when they recognized him they began to burn with great love for him. They began to revere and exalt him in very great measure, not because of his honorable and royal lineage, but because of the beauty of his life and pattern of his wisdom, as well as for the loftiness of his virtues. Even the abbot of that place and all his holy colleagues revered him with deference as an abbot. They began to treat all their affairs in accordance with his suggestions and to obey him in all matters, as once he revealed to me in conversation. You, O God, Father incomprehensible, were disposing all these arrangements by your command so that your devoted servant might at length obtain long-sought leisure and that your devoted soldiers might be sustained by his counsel.

Chapter 42. There he soon had time for the heavenly sabbath in endless enjoyment. There he tasted how sweet the Lord is.[126] How measureless were the praises and thanksgiving that re-echoed from his mouth in that place, there is no one who can fully declare. For him that place was a fortunate habitation like Paradise from which the first man was expelled by the serpent's envy.[127] Marvelous to fullest measure was the order: the latter was covered with confusion when he was thrust out,[128] but the former brought back glories to that place as though by his own persuasion, for he was already enjoying angelic association. It was with him as a certain poet says,

How safe the rest and the life unaware of disappointment,
Rich in various treasures, and leisure in broad estates.[129]

And thus was he made exceedingly joyous and happy amid caressing leisures of holiness, as if in the midst of the pleasant place of flower-bearing Paradise. There is no doubt that he was pruned off thus to exile by hatred of truth as blessed John was, according to the statement of the presbyter Venerable Bede.[130]

Chapter 43. Everywhere we may discern the wave-wandering wheels of the world and the camps of Babylon and Jerusalem clashing together with mixed emotions, first weapons and then flight being taken alternately hither and thither. So it was, my Father, almighty God, that your sweating athlete bewailed only the peril of this life. Drenched with grief he groaned and lamented, he asked and begged that you spare the blindness of his enemies. The aged father both saw and foresaw in this time that the wretched life of humankind was brought to nought by luxuries; that Jezebel was declaring herself a prophetess and was seducing God's servants to commit fornication and to eat things offered to idols, to follow the gluttony of the belly, and to be crowned by lust.[131] It would seem monstrous if gluttony might reign without lust or lust without gluttony.[132] Alas, how wretched the condition of the belly! Clinging with kinship for such parts, it is closed at both ends and it is clothed with hollow honor by contempt for evil felicity. If I may employ a poetic expression, I warn you "who pick the flowers and strawberries growing on the ground," flee hence, for a serpent lies hidden in these enjoyments.[133] Yet our ancient ceased not to weep for them whom, like certain birds, night awakens and day blinds with greed for getting rich. While they gaze not on God's providence but on their own ambitions, they imagine that license or impunity in crime is entirely fortunate. In the meantime, by enormity of their shamefulness, they accumulate benefits for the heavenly man, so much so that he might think every joy present for him, while he victoriously discharged the temptation of envious ones. Whenever he turned, he went about growing and making progress.

Chapter 44. He rejoiced that God's will might be fulfilled in him, because he was prepared to be wholly subject to God. Amid other patient words, he said about seeking exile that he wished to emulate the simplicity of sheep and like a hare not to be concerned with change of place. "The sheep," he said, "is shorn of its fleece without jealous envy to clothe others with warmth. The nakedness of another is warmed by the stripping of its clothing. So also if there is in my experience any useful matter, I wish anyone to receive it freely without profit to me. If, moreover, I am put to flight hither and yon like a hare by instigation of a waylayer, I neither abandon with sorrow the place of quiet where a short while ago I had settled, nor hold with love the place to which I am driven. Our life is in heaven.[134] We, therefore, savor those things that are above and not those things on earth.[135] We are dead with Christ and our life is hidden with Him in heaven; and when Christ our life shall appear, we shall then also appear with Him in glory." [136] With these and like words he strengthened the spirit of the brothers on the rock that is Christ.[137] Thus placed outside the world amid waves of the sea, they might be more profoundly confirmed in heaven by hope, which we have as an anchor.[138]

Chapter 45. Throughout the seven-year period his fatherly authority and virtuous distinction had encompassed much of the foregoing. With the Lord's consent it came to pass that he soon made an end of his exile and that he was restored even more famous to his own honors. I say, "to his own," because they rightfully befitted him and demonstrated by his merits the highest function of fatherhood. In another respect he, whom meritorious honor and wisdom properly adorned, should be restored to honors. He had not, of course, lost that by which he could be deemed worthy of reverence, but in the estimation of the multitude he had been deprived of honor and so as far as possible it had to be restored by the scythes of dignities. He whom heavenly grace illuminated could not be dishonored, as well considered truth makes clear. Undue honor may grow splendid on the highest seats, but it disgraces rather than adorns the foolish. If he were not lifted up to high office, his disgrace would be less evident. As a tumor stands out on top of the skin, a certain one observes, so an unworthy prelate can be seen. But our ancient was everywhere revered by everyone, not so much for the meritorious honors conferred by others, but for his very own. He was deemed worthy of honor by all. Dignity cannot change evil ones, although it displays them to the view of many, but it rather makes them more contemptible, indeed more unworthy. Our ancient was possessed by such great loftiness that he seemed to be honored not alone by degree of sublimity. He was sustained by great counsel and so even among the obscure he seemed exceedingly honorable.[139]

Chapter 46. When the time was completed, he was at length with greatest deference recalled to resume his former dignity.[140] Far and wide everyone exulted and almost everyone was congratulatory. Voices of happiness hither and yon were lifted upward to heaven. Monasteries of monks manifested joy; clergy of the churches sprang with delight; the masses everywhere laughed gladly and pleasantly. The concourse of people in common festivity was such as if an extraordinary person were restored by a proclamation from heaven.

Chapter 47:1. But when the brothers with whom he had spent the interval heard of his departure from them, they began immediately to be sad and sorrowful. Yet in a certain degree they were glad. Overcome with tears of love, they could scarcely let him go. Ragnardus, venerable in virtue and afterward abbot,[141] glowed with peculiar spirit of mind, shedding tears with grieving spirit, yet at the same time happy while weeping. He was happy because the lover of truth would receive a place of valued merit, but he mourned because he was deprived of the presence of so great a man. The day came when the holy worshiper of God was on the point of departing. All the brothers with burning mind were washing his path and footprints with tears. They were kissing them and bidding him goodbye. The aforesaid man of God, however, remained at home and betook himself to a bedchamber of tears. He did not wish to see leaving him whom he wished to remain longer with him and for whom he was prepared even to die.

47:2. But our ancient asked especially for him and waited for him. He was found in his obscure place weeping, sobbing, and sighing. When he had been summoned to bid our ancient farewell and was told that the latter would not leave until he came, he begged the messengers not to betray that he was there weeping aloud. When the charitable old man heard all this, he quickly stepped down from the ship to embrace the brother whom he knew to be holy. The holy old man approached and began with a loud voice to cry out, "What, O fortunate father, have you sought here? Why do you wish to show yourself to me? As God is witness, I would rather bury you dead here than to have you abandon me and live away." Then all the brothers and servants follow him with loud sobs. Finally the sails are hoisted; the oars are rowed; everyone gives a groan. On the shore they watch him as long as they could see him. But one spirit of love glowed in them and they could not restrain him.

Chapter 48. Gaunt with long privation of body, his flesh weakened but not his heart, he came at last to the palace. There he was received ostentatiously on every hand. The question naturally arose how the royal highness pleased him, for they were afraid to incur future hazard for injury to such a great man. The blessed ancient observed that they were meditating such matters with shame.

He therefore rushed into their midst and soothed the shamefast mind of the king with adequate affability. He persuaded him to forget this deed and reckon all things to be God's judgment.

Chapter 49. At the prince's urging he was constrained to take back his own monastery of holy life. His own sons in religion importuned him that they might deserve to receive him once again. As the long-awaited one approached to clasp them time and again in holy embraces, a fever hostile to health vexed him so that two dispositions wounded the minds of each. The sadness of compassion and the fervor of happiness were fighting in each because they saw the savagely worn limbs of the dear man for whom, as strong as they were, they might endure even loss of life. But first the magnitude of his joy overwhelmed everyone, then the outpouring of his tears. Together with mixed emotions they lifted happy praises skyward, for in him no one hesitated to approach the Lord. Everyone thus received him with joy and wished for him joy. And the kindly man graciously conversed with them all.

Chapter 50. For a short period he rested sweetly in that place, enjoying the duty of love. Soon, however, receiving a magnificent invitation from the august emperor, he returned to the palace. When he entered shining with rays of virtue, the stars grow dim, as a certain one says, because a Titan is approaching.[142] But there also naked foolishness appeared, covered by a pall of gloom. Excessive folly came into being, misleading to great absurdity the senate of the people. When they had been deluded by too much envy, it led them into vanity, treated them plausibly (as it seemed) to the greatest degree during this period. The dire captivity of many of them was related, especially of those who were of royal lineage. In one person freedom was restored to all wherever they were detained, except those whom death had earlier deprived of life. The tonsure imposed on many by savage fury now passed over to a crown, and they voluntarily gave to God what a short time ago they had unwillingly received as if in ignominy.

Chapter 51. What more? The glorious emperor himself underwent public penance for some of his misdeeds and became the humblest of all.[143] With kingly exaltation he became his own worst convicter, so that those who had been offended in transgression might be healed by the royal satisfaction. There is no doubt

that all contemplated his willingness and perceived his unwilling-
ness.[144] If the declarer of truth had not returned, it would not
have been apparent by what sluggish spirit they were oppressed. So
the mature old age of their blindness took care that the wound was
treated in persuasion by the healthful antidote of Christ.

Chapter 52. Adalard was zealous that the virtues of justice and
wisdom might receive their thrones, so that anyone at all might
preserve what had been entrusted to him and that to each his
own [145] rights might be dispensed. He checked novelties of words
and daring presumptions, according to the Apostle, as a plague in
everyone.[146] Everything that he could not find in the law of charity he deemed hostile to God and repudiated it as though it were
poison. With these and similar proclamations he shone brighter and
brighter as gold proved by fire. To everyone he became tenfold
more honored. In the mouth of everyone his name re-echoed over
and over again. Everyone tried to embrace him with their arms. He
was cherished by all as a father. To magistrates of the churches [147]
he was a humble son, although of counsel and prudence he was a
renowned conveyor. With his tireless labor for all to be found perfect and worthy by God, it seems that at last a new order of
Franks was being reborn and the dawn of justice was rising from
the east.[148] On its part the prone level surface of rage had already
fallen silent and, as Vergil says, "the breezes of windy roar had
fallen." [149] As the same Vergil says again (if I may alter the quotation slightly), the virgin of desire had returned. Saturnian realms
had come back, because the offspring of a good mind had already
shone from high heaven.[150]

Chapter 53. Everyone about him was enlightened to a great degree with zeal for reparation. Enjoying highest leisure, he wished
only to strip himself of those cares in order to be attentive to himself and God. But the holy brothers in no wise allowed that, although he offered them the great excuse of his old age. But more
mature by so much age, he only seemed more appropriate for those
striving toward the peaks of virtue. He was flourishing abundantly
with vigor of the Holy Spirit and with continuing briskness of un-
exhausted flesh. Even more than steady youths could pursue, he
took pains to be wearied with toils and vigils.

Chapter 54. Who was ever so ardent as he? Who was ever so

cruel a judge of another as he was of himself? He had need of correction, of course, but never except of himself was he harsher. By his brothers and sons he was often publicly reproached for being so earnest with himself, since he was observed by all. "I have a care for myself and I shall see to your servant lest wearied by hunger and toils he perish." For a while after this he hid himself away. But not long afterward he resumed fasting and toils such that youthful members could scarcely endure to witness the frugalities and vigils with which he treated himself. He was nevertheless always full of the grace of verdure, always sufficiently ruddy despite discernible thinness. He was handsome of countenance and pleasing in appearance. No sluggish passion wrinkled his face and forehead, but mature cheerfulness conspired to make him entirely seemly and fitting. Holy whiteness adorned him with snowy luster, but like a lily above rosy garments, like tops of palm trees, the hair of his head gleamed above his skin. As it is written in Canticles, our ancient was "white and ruddy, chosen among thousands." [151] Thus in him human nature might be censured, because it is corrupted with vices before it is adult.

Chapter 55. If I should seek to praise the mass of his body covered with much luster, whatever I say would be too poor. He shone all the more beautifully because he sprang forth, found again by Christ, adorned with splendor of virtues as a lily among rosy colors. No doubt all flesh is hay and all its glory is the flower of hay,[152] but Christ's virtue, which always flourished in him, remains forever. Yet I will be incapable even if I should wish to describe the form of his nobility from boyhood (called in Greek *characterismos*).[153] Even if his appearance is considered according to the eloquence of rhetorical art, that is, whether it could be proved as becoming of praise, so much more is that preferred in him which came from flesh to spirit. Many descriptions have been bestowed on his appearance according to the aforesaid art and from them he is best known. According to rhetoricians, a perfect man's quality is considered in respect of name, country, family, position, lot, body, education, customs, food. Then one considers if he administers affairs well and by what family custom he is held. Lastly, consideration is made of disposition of mind, profession, situation, dress, countenance, gait, speech, mood. When such matters about Adalard have been examined, our ancient was pleasing to look upon and he flourished with many tokens of virtue. So there are prominent evidences of praise of him in artistic celebration.

Chapter 56. In the foregoing catalog one rightly inquires first about his name and whether he was a wise man. But if he was educated in heavenly mastery rather than in artistic eloquence, how was he not wise? Wisdom is the knowledge of human and divine matters together with zeal for living well. There is no doubt that he could properly be called a true philosopher and certainly a wise man, who through God's grace prudently pursued the things of God and energetically managed the things of men. He himself was always at hand expending every endeavor of his life in these two precepts. By nation he was of the highest stock of the Franks, but as reborn in Christ, in whom he dwelt by the Spirit, he appeared to all as entirely of the tribe of heaven. Although in flesh he was born here, there is no doubt that his fatherland was the heavenly Jerusalem,[154] as the Apostle said, through Him who made us to sit now by hope [155] in heavenly places.[156] By stock most noble of nobles he sprang from the family of Franks, but at length by Christ's grace [157] he was adopted by God as a son. Although he might seem great in royal prestige, he was made greater by sublimity of endless life. His life marks out by what lot he would be increased when he abandoned everything, according to the statement, the poor man reigned by possessing God. So, as we believe, as we desire, the joys of life serve him while he is established [158] over many things.

Chapter 57. Distinction of manner makes clear how handsome he was in body. A statement from the Canticle of Canticles is not unworthily adapted to him,[159] "His head is of the best gold; his hair indeed as the peaks of palm trees," for daily he took care to ascend upward to God. "His eyes are as doves above streams of water which are flowing with milk," because his guileless face was wholly intent on Christ's teaching, from which we as little children were nourished with milk, not mixed with the gall of desires, but bathed with true innocence of mind. Moreover, "his cheeks are as beds of spices which were planted by paint-sellers," namely, adorned by holy teachers with every flower of doctrine and vegetable of virtue. "His hands are beautifully wrought," molding the

appearance of holiness and quickly pressing with spherical movement to every good; "full of hyacinths," glistening in the likeness
of heaven, laying up treasure in heaven, filled with many rewards.
"His belly is ebony," studded with ranks of virtues. "His throat is
very sweet," because of the honeycomb of eloquence; "and he is
wholly desirable" with credibility of manners and extraordinary
charity. We therefore seek you, father, while you graze among the
lilies.[160] We seek him whom our soul loves. On the bed night after
night we seek you with tears.[161] Let your voice sound in our
ears, I pray. Your voice is sweet and your face handsome. We
cannot fail to love you as father, you whom we believe will appear
for us.

Chapter 58:1. To turn now to education, he was like Moses
learned in all wisdom [162] of the present life as if a son of the king.
Thereafter he was conducted to Sinai into the presence of his
Lord. With Him he entered enjoyment of continuous intimacy.
His life is witness to the manner with which he was adorned, a life
redolent of tokens of highest merit, a life proclaimed aloud with
great publicity. That nourishment, which philosophers define as
fruition of work completed, achievement of promised rest, was the
Lord whom he esteemed, loved, desired. The grades of these virtues are as follows. First, a frame of mind is established. Then, for
some reason, the same affection undergoes a momentary change of
spirit or body. Thereafter, from that which is affected, it turns itself into zeal to obtain its own effect. Zeal directed toward something habitual and ardent is occupation of the mind with great
will.

58:2. The quality of the matter acquired is put on when we
fully obtain what is perfect, as it is written, "May your priests be
clothed with justice and may your holy ones exult." [163] Happy indeed is the cloak of virtue with which each is clothed, and he guards
his own vesture so as not to walk around naked. One clothed with
the wedding garment is not cast outside.[164] If our first parent had
only kept it in Paradise, he would not have been found naked when
his eyes were opened.[165] Or, as it is written, as one was going
down, robbers stripped him, beat him, and abandoned him.[166] But
our ancient was bedecked with flowers, was covered again with
such a habit. We believe that he already heard Christ saying to

him, "He will walk with me in white, for he is worthy, and I will not erase his name from the book of life." [167] An extraordinary abbot he was, clothed in such a habit. He exerted himself so that in place of food for sustenance he might enjoy Christ with whom he was clothed.

Chapter 59:1. It now remains, according to the previous outline, to inquire how he administered his own property. But how shall I say he administered it if he did not retain it for himself? He had done what he had heard from the Lord, "If you wish to be perfect, go, sell all that you have, and give to the poor. . . . Then come, follow me." [168] The holy brothers, whose counsel and allegiance he employed, are suitable witnesses about the manner in which he administered affairs of his church. It was through them that he arranged everything so that it would be sufficient for all, but neither superfluous nor totally lacking. Everything was to yield to the praise of God in humane fashion. He bestowed upon the brothers healthful matters of the present life and cut off what was injurious and superfluous, administering, however, to guests in great abundance.

59:2. From yoke of servitude he often preserved a household unharmed. Distributing destitute widows from this kind of household and single men throughout different villas, he continuously furnished them contributions. He also arranged a hospital for orphans and cripples as well as for guests in those same places as occasion arose, so that everyone might possess properties of this church as his own patrimony. I have God as witness that he himself, acting as physician, often taught the attendants this duty, so that they might devise in an orderly manner how to prepare something for them to eat and so that the health of these might not suffer in food of this kind. No one was so generous to the king from our riches, so that God might be glorified in all things as bestower of everything. He judged it more blessed by far to give than to receive.[169] As much as he could himself, he chose always to walk in the middle between poverty and riches for the sake of others, so that those who have might learn how to be as though they were ones who did not have. He also reckoned it just that all servants of the church thus think of him as father, lest puffed up they might contend that he was lord. Above all, he professed to be a patron and director of their virtues, so that he might also be master, or rather (albeit discreetly) a most cruel persecutor of their vices.

Chapter 60. According to the standard of habit to which he was accustomed, he was acquainted with the measure of the holy oracle wherein manna was concealed in a golden urn together with the golden altar of incense and Aaron's rod that budded.[170] It was twenty cubits in length, twenty in width, and twenty in height.[171] Completed on every side with a twin ten, its perpetual square could be sustained by love of God and one's neighbor. There is no doubt but that the Lord would be his foundation within the measure to which he was entitled. Divine contemplation alone knew how our ancient acted in his own domestic manner.

Chapter 61. In affection he was allured by the stimuli of all good things that by duty as by little torches he was inflamed far beyond the brotherly bowels of charity. In the art in which he was learned, it was clear that he was found fertile in skilled counsel. He was, it is said, an investigator with a thousand eyes of prudence, also a very skilled disputant in the virtues, and indeed a very holy establisher of the liberal arts. In him you could prove that statement of blessed Anthony that perception will find skill and that he who is sound in perception does not need skill.[172] What now shall I say of situation? As I have already observed, he glistened as an outstanding representative of royal stock. What shall I lavish on the other situation, that he was more properly adoptive or disowned? He was a son of Bernard, brother of great King Pepin, but no one denies that he was an adoptive son of God.

Chapter 62. In respect of the sacred dress Adalard wore, Christ is proved to have been his long tunic. His monastic clothing, however, was scarcely adequate. He wore it to fortify his body against the cold rather than as something befitting his honor. Some people have said playfully that it was indeed a breastplate against the cold. It was of leather like a breastplate, a warm poultice about the bowels. In countenance he was sweet and in stature like a palm tree. He was beautiful and seemly in appearance as if nourished by the delights of Paradise. How beautiful were his steps and how splendid his feet as he preached the Gospel! [173] Surely he was more unburdened than those stags, more ornate in shoes than the prince's daughter.[174]

Chapter 63. How fluent was his speech, how full of meaning, how sweet to hear when it flowed! His letters were directed to a great many people. The words of all who testify are that they never heard anyone speaking more richly or expressively. More melodious in voice than a swan,[175] he caressed the listener, but sweeter than honey was the melody to the palate of the heart. His narrative was clear, brief, and lucid, the kind of speech which orators extol with highest praise, nothing obscure or doubtful in meaning. Proceeding with plain step in periods, his honey-flowing meaning came to a close with rich finish. The sound of the declaration was an exposition of style so that comprehension of the words might be more aptly formed by the voice. Each quality of the parts was restored to its own meaning, having all members of the narrative distinct point by point and thus easy to be retained. It was indeed most suitable for persuading or dissuading. He always moved his hearers to more avid attention, to a desire warmer than fire. He shattered sluggishness and aroused those who were deteriorating. If such eloquence were granted to me, I might more satisfactorily fulfil what I have attempted. But excuse must be made for my ignorance, pardon granted for my promise, for no one's pen may disclose this matter better than his. As his life was more excellent, so his speech was superior. But since the wave of genius is denied me, I can only wish to fulfil the law of charity.

Chapter 64. It remains now to suggest what kind of person he was in mood. Yet with what quality of skill shall I unfold the disposition of his spirit, who in all the business of life was always impressed with one mental flame? Longing earnestly to be dissolved and to be with Christ,[176] he wore himself with labors. Although he professed otherwise, he felt inwardly that he had to continue in flesh for our sakes. So with complete effort of life he worked amply to be useful to everyone. He was always occupied with a thousand charitable affairs. He was the counsel of the entire fatherland, the father of all those in want. With mouth and hands, with every conceivable ability, he was servant of all for the liberty of Christ.

Chapter 65. Since he was always aflame with ardor, he came to the boundaries of Saxony. There a very small cell was being constructed by a holy man of the same name, Adalard. The cost was being borne by the mother-monastery for several reasons. His son, who was of the household, had been nursed there. The blessed man had served in his place while he was an exile on the island of Herus, a citizen of the world and of paradise. The devout father and most holy ancient, seeing that the work, a duty of piety, was already begun, approached the king and asked permission to seek another place for construction. Where it was proved to be neither profitable nor fitting.[177] The august emperor rejoiced greatly when he heard this and wished to lavish many gifts upon him. Although Adalard would never agree for anyone to make gifts to him, the emperor wished nonetheless to maintain him as anyone might have wished or at least as much as Adalard might have wished, even if very modestly. For Adalard always conformed to that statement of the Apostle that "it is more blessed to give than to receive." [178] When authority had been granted by the king to build wherever he would, he chose for his monks an exceedingly pleasant and suitable location. Afterward the king, for the love of almighty God, conferred many benefits.

Chapter 66. The place was situated on the bank of the Weser for those going toward the rising of the sun from Fons Patris.[179] Set in the level ground of the valley, it was in the shape of the [Greek] letter *delta*. It had the aforesaid hollow toward the rising of the sun, and a mountain stretched in front near the river. From the south another mountain emerged from the river bottom and reached toward the setting of the sun. From the north still another stretches with equal distance from the region until they are connected with each other, leaving a path in the middle. A valley was thus created in the middle expressing (as well as I remember) the [Greek] character *delta* in this manner. There was justice in the arrangement, for the teacher of truth, trained in the divine will, chose such a place where he might nourish, define, and mark Christ's disciples with his own character in that place.

Chapter 67:1. In all geometrical figures nothing is more complete and perfect than a triangle. This number only is arithmetically the foundation of width and surface. Whoever will carefully inspect this figure will discover nothing more marvelous in these skills. In our learning nothing is greater or better than the Trinity, the true God. Nothing at all formed without this number is perfect, that is, without beginning and end and without a middle between beginning and end.

67:2. This figure is therefore the originator of latitude since all other surfaces are released in it. It is subject to no beginning; it takes no start from a latitude other than itself; it is therefore unrolled in itself. If it should be elevated upward, it is obligated to inflame those dwelling therein with the fire of charity. Because its beginning is made from its own latitude, it illustrates that the broad commandment of God cannot be accomplished at all except by a broadened heart. Because it resolves all surfaces in itself, it signifies clearly that all the remaining virtues are finished by its latitude. Charity is perfected only by worshiping the Trinity in Unity, so that true perfection may be an indivisible unity in these three. It suffices for me to say these things to show how prudent and wise Adalard was and with how much ardor of charity he burned. He prepared for his disciples such a place to dwell in, well supplied with water, as if a lesser Egypt and another Paradise of the Lord for those coming from Fons Patris toward the rising of the sun. I spoke truly of Fons Patris, because reborn in Christ they are believed thereafter to cross over not only toward the rising of the sun but even beyond the sun. This place the blessed father called *Corbie* [180] from the name of the other, as a sign for the future by whom it was first founded.

Chapter 68:1. Who, my dearest father, may be adequate to relate your prudent teaching? As often as I recall you clearly, I marvel how circumspect you were in all things. I recall your teachings with which you nourished and built up the tender ones respecting faith and charity [181] (between which you also placed hope), concerning manners and every teaching of life. Amid solicitude and business you accomplished what was offered to them by whomever they ought to have received. You commended to them to be greedy in nothing for worldly things and to accept nothing by which others might be vexed. If they were heirs of the property of a liberal donor, they should consider carefully that by chance they to whom the inheritance belonged might not afterward become destitute. In all places where he was in charge, it was his anxious and holy consideration to receive nothing dishonorable. He desired moreover that no one for the sake of mercy be repressed later by penance. He said that many—not only rulers of the churches, but also those who had renounced the world and who were spending their time for God in that place—would be deceived for this reason, namely, that they abounded in too many possessions, so many indeed that they who ought to have died to the world were compelled to serve the world.

68:2. "How could it be profitable," he asked, "for future heirs to be despoiled of their properties and for them again to be enslaved to secular affairs? It is fitting for us in the present time to be subject to the commonweal, since diminished by our greed it obviously cannot subsist of itself. So we unhappy ones who ought to be free in Christ have become, albeit unwittingly, slaves of a disgraceful servitude. When therefore the opportunity comes, we carry the soldiery of the world as if for God's sake, since the Apostle says, 'No one fighting for God involves himself in secular matter.' [182] It is not exacted of us to retain necessary things only, but to possess even superflous things, as they say. Insofar, then, as we seek to be expansive in possession, we are straitened in every good work. Be content, my little ones, in Christ's poverty without which no one is rich. You know that the poor in spirit are blessed and to them the kingdom of heaven is promised.[183] Do not be willing, my brothers, to lose eternal possessions for the sake of property and by pursuing avarice. Be what Christ's eternal calling wanted you to be. Thus, by sharing Christ's poverty, we may merit to be rich with Him endlessly."

Chapter 69. Daily Adalard strengthened and confirmed them with this kind of exhortation. In that place, therefore, with God's active cooperation, he built a foundation not only of the monastery but also of the heavenly fatherland. What do you think then, with what great joy his spirit was affected, with what great happiness, when almighty God's love burned so warmly in them that every region might bless God through them? Exulting and rejoicing hither and yon, he ever returned to us, because for holy love and spiritual joy he could scarcely restrain himself that through him Christ might be glorified by many. Watering and grazing us with heavenly pasturage, planting and enlarging us in Christ, he caused us to produce much fruit for God. In every respect he showed himself as acting in Christ's place, outstripping everyone in humility.

Chapter 70. Mightily influenced by a spirit of jubilation, he sought a field of entrance. According to blessed Augustine in the book where he speaks of the quantity of the soul,[184] this entrance is one of seven, namely, the sixth virtue of perfection. The fifth degree is tranquility; the sixth, entrance; the seventh, contemplation. These qualities can most suitably be accomplished while a soul goes forward and while it is busy in itself with itself. With daily ardent desire toward God, he approached Him, saying, "My soul has thirsted for the strong living God. When shall I come and appear before God's face?"[185] When, indeed, since ceaselessly contemplating in clear light he clings to Him on whom even angels long to gaze?[186] Now our ancient has happily arrived, giving thanks that he has merited. Now he understands and comprehends with supreme spirit of liveliness.

Chapter 71. What shall I say other than the statement of Elisha, "My father, my father, the chariot of Israel and charioteer of virtues!"[187] Behold how suddenly desolate you are leaving us! With tearful voice, therefore, we look for you and in our innermost heart we search every morning for your honey-flowing manners. Never is the pupil of our eye still nor is it comforted unless it foretold that you would be better for us when present with it. We recall from what breasts you gave us milk; how great an oracle of God we enjoyed in you; with what great oars of wings we were borne along; with what bowels of charity we were nourished. Even if we were of stone, your pious conversation might soften us. You became all things for us all, so that you might make us gain for Christ. But if you turned yourself to the special concern of certain ones, you gave in a moment counsel of life to one, while you smothered another with kisses. Grasping the hand of one, you stroked that of another with marvelous fondness, and so you were one to all and complete to each.

Chapter 72. Although you might always hold the names of the brothers written in the bowels of holy solicitude, even so a special number of them carefully inscribed was almost never out of hand. You would inspect all unremittingly and deal anxiously with the morals of each one with you. You strove in judgment about each one with you so that afterward you would not undergo any loss of sheep committed to you. Knowing what was suitable for each, you could demonstrate to all what was fitting for the salvation of each.

Your discernment, insofar as can be said, in no respect deviated from its purpose. Ease of completion was made ready for each and accomplishment was made suitable for all. Throughout the week you left none ungreeted with intimate disposition. Except when it was palpably impossible, you daily instructed anyone, providing healthful things for everyone and denying to none immediate necessities. For that reason, O daughters of Jerusalem,[188] bewail this our ancient, take up lament. Bewail him "who clothed us with the scarlet" of charity woven entirely "of delights," [189] who furnished worship with adornment of virtue. Put on sackcloth and mourn bitterly, for he who consoled us and nursed us in his bosom has been taken away. Mourning my soul will mourn and tears shall be in my voice [190] as long as I do not look upon him whom my soul loves.[191] Do you not think, O father, that the time will come when in some manner I will be permitted to look upon your face, upon the likeness of your countenance?

Chapter 73:1. But now, my soul, what shall we do next? Now we are situated amid fields of roses and we have descried the pleasantness of virtues more richly bedewed from the font of the Holy Spirit. But now it is imperative that we unfold the end, his death. We must give glory to God that we have had such a man with us; we must weep that we have now lost him; we must express praise because he has at length arrived at the joys of the blessed. The more delightful it is for us to be busy with what we have loved, so much the more serious it is to endure his absence, which we always see as present. While we are besprinkled with mist, everything we see is sorrowful. Our eyes are darkened; we are overwhelmed with sobbing; our fingers tremble; our head reels; tears are pouring forth. There is a wish to weep with a holy disposition of love. The more copiously we hammer these matters for consolation, the more gloriously we are affected by love. But by loving we are also oppressed with grief.

73:2. So, O my dearest father, I will quickly pass over the pages of your death in which for a long time vigorous apathy [192] has assaulted me as I lingered. Ability to grieve drops indeed for a while, but shortly afterward we are comforted by the attainment with which you are now happy and joyful. Before the pen begins to strike the hour of your departure, return, O Shunamite, return,[193] I pray, that for a little while we may look upon you. Then may the reed of the tongue receive the spirit, and we shall more lightly cross over the bitter courses of reading. Return, return, my most beloved. What shall we see in you, except how you are arrayed as the brilliance of a camp? Once more at least, we beg, return to us, that we all may see you as we had you before and how great you are now. You have gone up, we know, through the desert as the dawn arising, beautiful as the moon, chosen as the sun, terrible in God, like an army of camps in array.[194]

Chapter 74. What can seem more frightening to human sight than the appearance of your countenance in the hour when you granted me pardon? You had ordered us, O father, as we prayed to sit on the ground, so that with uplifted eyes we could more clearly see yours and similarly you see ours. Never have I been granted anything more orderly from a teacher. Never have I seen anything more flaming or more frightening than your eyes. To explain the meaning more precisely, you spoke to us thus, "Behold, I am going to render account for the sheep entrusted to me. When you, O flock committed to me, are about to receive sentence for your obedience or disobedience, remember that I, who am now present with you, am going before you in that tremendous judgment. I will present what I have won from the money of the talents or explain how I spent it.[195] In the meanwhile, if there is anything wherein I was excessive toward you knowingly or unwittingly, wilfully or unwillingly, be kind, just as I in Christ's stead remit according to what is proper, if there is anything that is mine to indulge."

Chapter 75. When such matters had been put in order, his spirit departed full of warmth. It was as if he was already about to be judge over his own, to instruct himself to render account of his stewardship; it was as if he were then in the heavenly places about to fight against the spiritual forces of wickedness.[196] He had always handled himself as if at the moment of death. So then as he was about to go against the legions, he disposed the sharp edge of his mind to put to flight the wantonness of his life if he could without harassment. But because the one challenging with ten is said to have conquered twenty thousand, he always besought the Lord for those things which are of peace. "Lord, put me next to you," he said, "and so let the hand of anyone fight against me. Otherwise I will not flee the swarms of wicked men, because you alone are found free among the dead. The collector of taxes comes to you, but in you is not found anything that is his. Make me therefore cling more firmly to you that through you I shall also be free of all evil in your body."

Chapter 76. While he was thus chiding himself completely, he found in himself some things as if not yet exhausted. These he gave command to set forth in the presence of certain brothers, of whom I was one, albeit unworthy. Of these he asked if he should rightly be frightened to go to judgment. Hearing this, we reckoned that, according to divine Scripture, such matters which he had bewailed for a long, long time pertained to him no more. How minutely he explained how such matters continued in him! How harsh he was to himself in punishing himself for the deeds of others as if they were his own! While warning and instructing each one by one, he directed that after his death they should assemble among themselves for elections in peace, piety, and righteousness according to God's will. He also expounded his faith before certain of us, as well as all his teaching, so that he might the more firmly confide it to our hearts. Hence it was that we, though absent, are drenched with grief, but we are also joyful because we can recall such events of our father. By one we are impressed, to another we are exposed. We lament his loss because of his maturity of morals, firmness of faith, fullness of hope, pure foundation of charity, deepest humility in Christ, and richest generosity in all things. I do not grieve like the Savior over wretched Jerusalem,[197] but I mourn that in the death of one almost all virtues lie dead. I grieve not because he has failed us by going away, but because we have failed to see him whom we can scarcely or never remember without tears.

Chapter 77. Who with dry eyes will remember him from whom almost every adornment of honor has been removed? Or who does not grieve that the defense of all Europe has suddenly perished? Or who, without mental anguish, can recite the brightness of his eloquent letters, letters which (if you should hearken to the crowd) the sweet-dripping man spread abroad? If that barbarous tongue called Germanic [198] was spoken, it excelled in clarity of expression; but if Latin, the spirit was not beyond the greed of sweetness. O you all so dear to me, you who know what good the presence of so great a man held, you who are crossing through the way, attend and see if there is any sorrow like the sorrow of us all.[199] How suddenly the Lord has harvested us like grapes! And deprived of beauty we have become dirty. Mildew has taken possession of us, for rosy adornment has been turned to ashes.

Chapter 78. Like Simeon,[200] the old man had prepared himself to meet the Savior's birth with lamps lighted.[201] He was happy with the King of kings in his arms, the Lord Jesus Christ, who came from His own chamber.[202] But a violent, raging fever struck him on the third day before the Lord's birthday,[203] while in the middle of the night, according to custom, he was weeping in the basilica. Enduring thus to vigils, he with the brothers consecrated the Victim of joy to the Lord in his heart. There are many witnesses that the higher the voice in which the choirs sang, the more fully he wept in joy. Dragging himself along to the lauds of matins, he became no less feverishly sick with love of Christ, as it is written in Canticles, "Support me with flowers, press me with apples, for I am sick with love." [204] Although he was daily oppressed more and more with various ailments, he never relaxed his spirit, always intent upon God. With foresight, therefore, he arranged everything as if to bring nothing evil in the body. He so established and ordained each workshop that nothing might be found imperfect at his end. He desired especially that the holy day might be celebrated with due honors. While this was being accomplished, he began to be more and more violently burdened with fever. Yet daily he went to the oratory of blessed Martin, whom he had always in life loved with abundant love. There he heard Masses and received Holy Communion until the last day of life led him out of the gloom of this night.

Chapter 79. Bishop Hildeman, a blessed man, whom Adalard had nurtured as a monk and whom through the king's grant Beauvais had elevated to great honor, heard that the holy father was ill. He therefore came and kept diligent watch until he made an end of living. He also buried him with his own hands together with all the brothers. When he approached, the holy father rejoiced with great cheerfulness. He was made so happy that he scarcely restrained himself, exulting with excessive joy. He gave measureless thanks to God for encouraging him with his arrival, saying, "O God, establisher and ruler of all things, I give you thanks that I have not been deprived of my desire."

Chapter 80. The holy bishop was questioned by us whether Adalard should be anointed with the oil of blessing as appointed by the holy Apostle.[205] We also asked Adalard whether he desired it, although we knew without doubt that he was not burdened by the weight of sins. Hearing us, he directed his eyes toward heaven, clasped his hands, and begged for it to be administered. What do you suppose the holy mind was doing? With what tears was he then filled! His eyes were fastened on God; his hands were stretched toward heaven; and he invoked the Holy Spirit thus, "Now dismiss your servant, Lord, in peace, according to your word,[206] for I have received all the sacraments of your mystery. Now what remains except for me to come to you? [207] Yet not as I will but as you will, only let your will be done." [208] For a long time he had thirsted to come to the fountain. So, as if with joking voice, he had often said, full of the gravity of faith, "Hence shall I go and come to my God. Happy shall I come, happy shall I die, happy will I cross over the gaping pitfalls of this life. I am about to reach the joys eternal for so long a time promised to me."

Chapter 81:1. With these and similar words Christ's soldier armed himself with care until he entered with voice of confession and praise the place of the marvelous tabernacle. There was found a multitudinous army celebrating high festival. There our ancient dances exultantly and sings, "Night has passed away and day is at hand." [209] With each passing day, still burning with fever, he commended himself thus to God with measureless praise. But suddenly one day as the holy bishop approached him while he was alone, he cried out insistently, "Run hither quickly, O bishop, and kiss the feet of our Lord Jesus Christ, for look, he is present!" When the bishop heard, he trembled violently, not knowing where to go or what to do. Prudently, however, he checked himself silently and remained quiet.

81:2. When the octave day of Christ's birth had come,[210] he began more eagerly to insist that he be permitted to depart when those days had been celebrated. It was as if in some manner he sought at length to reach the festival which night does not interrupt nor malady destroy. So when midnight had passed, he arose and addressed the brothers, "O my sons in the Lord, exceedingly dear to me, know that today I shall go hence. It has been granted to me soon to go and to see (may it be so) and to appear in my Redeemer's presence. The course of my struggle is finished. It remains only that I do not know that I shall be accepted for the reward of my calling." But we believe, O father, that eye has not seen nor ear heard nor has it penetrated the heart of man,[211] otherwise the labor of faith is vain. If one can truthfully say with the Apostle, "I have finished the course, I have kept the faith. For the rest," what else can be said other than "there is laid up for me the crown of uprightness which the just Judge will reward me in that day"?[212]

Chapter 82. When morning had come and some of our monks had been summoned, the father began to urge that they finish matins more speedily. When the office had been ended, his tongue fell silent in praise of the heavenly Christ. Then, as all the holy brothers assembled, he received Holy Communion at the first hour of the day. They began with tuneful praise to commend him to the Lord and lingered in his funeral obsequies until the ninth hour. At that time, when Christ died on the cross,[213] Adalard surrendered his spirit. Thus judgment was granted by Him whose cross he had borne in life, by Him whom he had followed. Even at the moment of his death, he followed His footsteps. So he came to Him whom he had longed for, yearned for, desired with all his heart. What grief there was in that hour! How extraordinary were the laments of the monks! With one voice their singing lifted up on high, but the sobbing of all fell downward and broke each heart. As someone has said,[214] it was a holy experience to rejoice with so great a man and it was a holy experience to weep at his departure. Even if one were born of flint, would he not weep in the hour when God's eminent shepherd left and sought the heavens? He was, O good Jesus, one whom of all I found the complete and only abbot, whom of all I found seeking the welfare of another more than of his own. As a mother loves her only son, so he loved most tenderly, inviting all to take the solider matters.

Chapter 83:1. Behold, O men, and see, all people: Mother Corbie, beehive of monks, weeping, weeping, and saying, "My illustrious one has been taken from me. There is no one of all my dear ones who may comfort me. The Lord has accomplished His fury against me. He has done what He intended. He has therefore achieved what He commanded in ancient days, 'Earth you are and to earth you will return.' "[215]

83:2. The one most dear to me has gone away; he has departed. The virgin of Israel has returned to her own cities and now walks gloriously upon the waters of redemption.[216] To me he was the dearest of longings, the one converting my soul [217] and the guardian of my life. Rising for us at the beginning of vigils, he poured out his heart as water [218] in the presence of the Lord, but now the Lord had made us desolate for a while. We are weakened with grief for him. We therefore put our face in the dust, trusting in the mercy of the Lord that we may perchance hope to arrive there where our holy patron has already arrived. Until that is done, until the longed-for day has come, may my tongue cleave to my throat, if I do not remember you,[219] father Adalard, if I put you not at the beginning of my recollections. May my right hand forget me, if I do not unfold your name and praise. I believe, O dearest and most beloved, that maternal love could perish before we could cease loving you. Even if she forgets her own, we will never forget you. But while the ages remain and night divides its lot with day, the fame of your most holy life will be proclaimed. We will never be without your praise. But draw us after you, we beg, and we will run in the odor of your perfumes. For better are your breasts than wine; your fragrances, than the best pefumes. The upright ones love you. So we ask to arrive where you are grazing, where you are lying.[220] We know that it is in the south.

Chapter 84. We do not grieve the death of a spouse in the underworld as the fables relate that the Thracian bard did.[221] But we lift up the name of the father beyond the stars where you have ascended in state. That one was fortunate who was reputedly able to gaze upon the shining fountains of good and who could burst asunder the bonds of heavy earth. But even more fortunate are we who can direct so many holy prayers after you, O father. The aforesaid bard pretended that by weeping in mournful melody he could make the forests run after his spouse, could make the streams stand motionless, could make the hind expose her flanks undaunted to savage lions, could make the hare no longer fear the dog already pacified by song. When his ardor burned with inmost glow of body and everything which he had conquered could not soothe his mind, he went meekly to the god in search of his spouse. Not finding her there, he entered the houses of the underworld. There, accompanying his caressing songs with resounding lyre, he drained whatever he could from the foremost fountains of the muses. At his notes the goddess of the shades lamented and said, "At last we, the judge, are overcome and we therefore grant to the husband his wife redeemed by a song." According to the poetic account, he gave forth lamentations. How great the threnodies twin love had aroused! With what powerful prayers he had begged the favor! The nether world had been stunned by his new songs. The goddesses who were avengers of crime were quickly sorrow stricken and were soon drenched with tears.

Chapter 85:1. But, most beloved father, we do not suggest such fancies, for we know that apart from Christ no one has returned from the underworld. We seek to make clear what blessing love may effect. Love is its own greatest law, so by imitation we seek you as if through law, because all life was your law of life. May we therefore merit to approach you, yes, you, as if Christ, to whom we believe that you have come. We pray that, moved by our prayers, God may hear and that you will be happily bestowed on us, no, rather that we may be bestowed on you, because we seek you as one who has been given to paradise. We believe that you have already been crowned from the head of Amana, from the peak of Senir, from the den of lions, from the mountains of leopards.[222] All those you have indeed conquered in triumph. You have been made sweet and seemly amid the delights of paradise. On you there is no stain. You are embraced by the right hand of Christ. Sleeping the sleep of peace, you press the left hand under your head.[223] In His presence you have become as one who has found peace. Your couch is flowery according to the quality of reward because you are situated in Christ's peace. The beams of your house are of cedar and your ceiling of cypress.[224]

85:2. O father so favorable to us, we rejoice and wish you joy according to what we understand. With the house turned upside down, the drachma which was lost has been found in you.[225] It was lost when it was surrounded by the gloom of night, but with lamps aglow it is again fortunately found in you. So, in the meanwhile, when we can do nothing else, we sit around weeping over the rights of your sepulcher. Above it we scatter the flowers of prayer. Above it we read the good name which you have acquired

better than many riches.[226] Some of us pluck for you pale violets
and dazzling white lilies, others narcissuses and flowering roses.
Still others scatter sweet-smelling thyme. They gather marsh lilies
and stain them with soft blueberries.[227] Certain ones intermingle
sweet odors, but others bedew it with a salty fountain of tears. I
weave over the grave a garment of letters so that the holy name
may be preserved for future ages. I do not weave eloquence of
counterfeit art, but I wrap it carefully in a clean winding cloth of
purity. If anyone desires to know this man more fully or how
strongly he conquered the world by faith, let him read where a
new name is inscribed for him and the name of the city of new
Jerusalem.[228] When he has understood with what adornment the
city glistens, he will attribute all this to him, for in that place and
manner the city as well as its possessor is supposed to have been
made by God.

Chapter 86. But rejoice and be happy, O virgin of faith, O fortunate Corbie named for the old one, because you have been
worthy to have had and enjoyed such a patron in Christ. O eminent mother of religion, embrace, I beg, this man whom you have
trained soberly and discreetly as a novice in heavenly manners.
Emulate him who afterward increased you with many honors.
Since he was your councilor, why are you consumed with grief, O
virgin daughter of the most high God? Behold, for you as an heir
he left a brother who will still sweat for you with many labors.
Wipe away your tears, I beg. For when all parts of the earth have
sent their outstanding men, you will send to meet me out of your
midst this ancient. When the neighboring monasteries, St. Vaast
and St. Riquier, shall have given from every side men of noble religion, you will also give to God with equal vow a man most
worthy. You will not be fruitless since amid the others you gave
birth from the dust of the earth to Adalard from the Lord. No,
joyous and singing you will come bearing at least a few forces. Be
therefore comforted and act more hardily when Amalek meets you
in the way, for another Joshua is already with you as leader.[229]
Going on before he fights with valor in the battle line. Support
Wala, therefore, for he already contends at the head amid greatest
numbers. Attend Adalard also in the mountain already stretching
forth his palms on high to the Lord. The former fights, the latter

prays; the former presses the foe, the latter conquers. For the former, O mother most dear to me, is a "lover of the brothers and of the people of Israel." The latter, "who prays much" [230] for his own, is always full of charity; he will be a continual intercessor for the citizens. So, O Lord, according to the word of blessed Ambrose, no one has what is lacking to others more than he desires for himself.[231] After death may you not separate us from Adalard whom in this life we have held most dear. Cause us to be with him where you are, that we may enjoy perpetual sight of him with you in Christ, of him whom because of you we have loved as very, very dear, even though he is now dead in the peace of Christ.

Chapter 87. The body of the most beloved ancient was fittingly buried in the basilica of the blessed Apostle Peter under the top of the gable amid the four vaults of the middlemost church, covered with a polished stone. On the stone was carved an eightfold verse with a taste of musical song:

> Here lies a venerable abbot of outstanding merit,
>   Adalard, our ancient, worthy of honor;
> Royal progeny, by right a citizen of paradise;
>   A man of proven charity, manners, and faith.
> While you, O traveler, whoever you are, recall him
>   under the mound,
>   Perceive who you are and what you will be, for
>   death seizes all things.
> Released from this flesh after the octave of the Lord,
>   On the following day he exultantly sought the stars.

Chapter 88. In that place around the venerable man are buried four others who had been invested by the Lord with the same servitude of office. It did not happen by chance. As in Christ there was one soldiery in the same place to carry aloft its cross after Jesus, so should there be one burial place signally arranged in the likeness of the cross. Of these our ancient is the middle one. Over him the bells are struck at the hours of Divine Office. For his tongue was a cymbal of the Holy Spirit and the invitatory dedicated there to the duty of the Divine Work. The eightfold verse was inscribed because he died after the Lord's octave, suggesting that he had completed the work to which a short while ago he summoned all and

that he had happily arrived at the Lord's octave with no number of
letters diminished.

* * * * *

Here follows "The Eclogue of Two Nuns" applauding with
one plaint of praise. One of them represents a church which Adalard in Christ's stead nurtured in marriage; the other, which he
begot of her with marvelous balance according to monastic discipline. Of these the latter is called Galathea because of the brightness of her countenance; the former, Philis because of her love of
charity.

(a) *Galathea:* Mourn devoutly, O men, mourn with me the
father. Let every age more advanced implore pardon. Sprinkle the
earth with tears, scatter the field with flowers. Let everything
sweat with sobs at the burial of the father. With duty of tongue let
crying so betray hearts that even the stars far and wide may together re-echo the roaring. Let the rustic Romance and Latin
tongues together do honor. Let the Saxon equally lamenting sing
for a song, "Turn this way, all men, for a very great man has completed his song. Build the mound; add a song to the mound." Bring
the blessed body of the ancient to this celebrated little place. Eager
he was to open hot veins for us. At his funeral rites let clergy and
mixed throng relate divine poems with alternate voice. Let pastors
relate with verse how great a man he was, he the more handsome
guardian of a handsome flock. And on the other side let the multitude re-echo, "O God, bountiful Creator, grant pardon to your
servant; grant him realms of paradise, we pray and beg. Have
mercy on the ancient, have mercy on your own people. You know
how worthy he was to receive mercy." So let heart's love, sorrow,
and mourning resound. So let youths observe valor and old men
the name.

(b) *Philis:* Who is there, I ask, who does not bemoan the man
elevated beyond the stars? To be returned to ashes, to be covered
with unyielding marble? In whose orbit the fame of virtue flies
through all, the offspring of royalty is food for worms. Alas, what
we do for him, we wretches placed under death! We grieve, we
mourn, but we cannot recall him. Although repeatedly summoned

he does not return nor does he hear his lovers. Hearts are broken, bowels are torn with grief. But he hears neither tears nor threnodies of the sorrowing. Because we are tortured in heart, we are torn by commotion. Grief is present to our spirits and deaf death cares not. We save for her the dusty clod of the body, but that shining one, restored to the stars, rejoices in choir. So, men of valor, youths, and maids, mourn with devout heart, bring forth salty fountains. For sad birth has given what we all suffer, and from of old is this nature one of earlier ones. One also may be compassion of mind for all. Let sobs of sadness and tears together beat the air. Far and wide let one sob flow into the mouths of the monks.

(c) *Galathea:* I pray you, elder Corbie, bury the ancient in a mound. Then I, the lesser, so soon widowed of such a patron, will utter with alternate voice a groan for a song. How long ago as a happy mother bringing forth a happy one, by one, even of your own, name you speak, "O beautiful one, you will now be to me another self forever, you whom that blessed one exultantly founded thrice by his own hand, attributing many oracles to salvation-bringing words." For where evil power, the demon, thus raged, and the cult of his shrine had polluted the whole soil, he changed the altars of cattle and dedicated the fold to Christ. When the grove was entirely uprooted, he established holy monasteries full of monks.

(d) *Philis:* O much too fortunate one! I am compelled to enter upon such sorrows, however much the noble things are gathered with divine favor. Amiens knew you before you merited to be in charge of the flock of Corbie, O most holy pastor; the Saxon sod knew you as father. You may therefore report to God the doubled talents entrusted to you. O unfaithful death, you know not how to spare him or us with your poisons. But you also care for no rewards. You know not how to love men; you know not how to protect patrons. For all you remain the one lot of an irrevocable hour, you, death, who immediately snatched away the blessed one whom with querulous voice we all equally mourn and bemoan, sob for, weep over, love. But you, wretched one, know not how to be merciful and to have mercy on wretched ones.[232] Behold, O grief, alas, though hated, you draw all men with you. Whatever you have already conquered, you still swallow up all things.

(e) *Galathea:* (Then said the venerable but smallest of our sisters:) O how mild and sweet in word was the master! Why have you so suddenly left us while we are still tender? May you always through the ages remain happy. But I, fierce virgin bloody with many battles, am drenched with a rainy fountain of tears. With deep groaning I beat my guilty breasts. I wash my stained face with salty tears, although I am black with stains and dusky with venoms. With color of roses bespattered on a snowy countenance, may I become golden, may I glitter, may I be fragrant, may I be drenched. Too fortunate I lament for you in time as long as the last mournful part of life remains.

(f) *Philis:* (Then also she says, the mother adorned with his name:) You will never conquer one with tears and sobs. Not to sing light songs, not to unfold vows, but when you mix honeycombs, I will adorn you with flowers. You gather pale violets, I gather lilies. I will scatter over the mound sweetest herbs, since this one was worthy of these gifts. He provided us with many delights and painted you with the rosy blood of Christ which the bard Isaiah had foretold long ago. So they bring to you holy forests of proven comeliness. There exult myrtles, firs, and pines, the vine and glistening grape. Even the olive grows richly. Like Paradise and the garden of delights, you are nurtured with living waters from the peak of heaven. The sterile region which you were, a descent to Avernus, you now lie open as a gate of heaven or door of life. The earlier treachery of death cannot rival so swift a course such as you now boast or on which you can plume yourself. Already you touch the highest stars of heaven with your head, and with your splendor you gleam far and wide in the world more quickly than any earlier nourisher of monks. Could she be more fertile under the square pole? So, my sister, I demand that you make lamentation in place of song because the father had scarcely completed eighty years.[233] Not yet perhaps would your breast trickle with milk. But lo, suddenly the urn of the fountain has perished or it is broken, the counsel of the fatherland, full of Christ's wisdom.

(g) *Galathea:* Ah! mother supported by God (replied the daughter), why do you wish to relate and renew such great sorrows? Or to recall the day, than which none was more savage or even can be in the future? At once it deprived us, as our patron perished, of all the beauty of life, cutting away the vows of virtues. Alas, how wretched we are who live without him! Into what depths are we plunged by malignant lot! So situated, we were unable to go to heaven with him with whom I have reckoned it better to die than to live.

(h) *Philis:* So, people of Christ, whom the wave has washed, bring forth the "rivery" waters deep in the heart. Let us dutifully bemoan my virginal husband, foresighted, sober, chaste, filled with charity, gentle, humble, as well as just and kind, of proven nobility, than whom no one was wiser. In his eloquence Christ's wisdom gleamed. A leaping fountain of life was obvious, the doctrine of salvation; shining in manners, full of the teaching of virtue; meek, peaceable, clement, and very modest. Those were, you know, the rewards of his right; those espousals of my dowry exhale in manly fashion. Blessed love for him grows in me so much, as in early springtime the world enriches itself with flowers. But henceforth grief grows up more hour after hour, because insatiable ardor burns too much in him and because before now there has been no medicine for my sorrow, unless I am allowed to grieve for the holy name.

(i) *Galathea:* (Most fortunate Galathea replies:) Begin now to lay aside such anxious complaints. Perhaps the muses marvel at such a great funeral. Songs and melody have left you benumbed. All the rocks groan with your threnodies. Would that that return of love may come again by which we are compelled to great waves of tears for him. May we at length be renewed by a taste of his sweetness. In the meanwhile, hand in hand let us go to the citadel, to the chambers of the realm to which the same one is still summoning us. Let us graze with him in the heavenly meadows forever, where the elder happy Menalcas has merited to enter, who as long as possible drew our loves with him and still draws sighs from our heart after him.

(j) *Philis:* The laws of prayer ought to join us with him. Hitherto, however, the middle way for us is the sad sepulcher. But if we constantly seek, knock, ask, there is no doubt but that after ashes we will come to the city wherein piety, goodness, peace, light, riches reign. The fruits of happiness, rest, and joys shine. Every good gleams double; sweet concord caresses. Glory, laud, and honor [234] trickle from one fountain. Eternal life exults, meadows of virtues flower. Angelic flocks are happy, heavenly rewards grow green, and they are finally established with eternal gifts. Where God is always present, riches are disclosed. Amid the bands of Apostles and patriarchs, how sweet the odor breathes, sweeter than all herbs! Mossy fields lie open with the choir of martyrs glistening. The fields of the prophets are redolent with a taste of sweetness. Gleaming columns are golden-yellow with the flower of virgins. All the joys there together rejoice, and all singing with one voice re-echo honey-flowing voices, so each one sings such songs.

(k) *Galathea:* Cease, O my mother (says Galathea). Perhaps we may indeed sing better what we contemplate, when paradise will be green for us also as it rejoices. Still, therefore, cut the flowers of the field and the lilies, until the joys of alleluia [235] laugh out. Scatter the way with violets, the fields with flowers of virtue. Paint the street with roses; spread lilies in the squares.

* * * * *

The Life of Wala

OR

An Epitaph for Arsenius

by PASCHASIUS RADBERTUS

BOOK I

INTRODUCTION

(*Interlocutors:* Paschasius, Adeodatus, Severus, Chremes, and Allabigus. Arsenius is, of course, a pseudonym for Wala, and Antonius for Adalard.)

(1) *Paschasius:* I often wonder quietly to myself, brother Severus, what new has happened [1] to our Adeodatus. For although the limit of grief has been reached, he bids me, according to Maro's adage and, I suppose, at your urging, to renew unutterable sorrows.[2] He proposes that in the manner of Zeuxis [3] I depict as a memorial for the ages a representation of the character of our Arsenius. He does not think it enough that I, unworthy artist, am afraid to appear even more unworthy by giving through the medium of letters an image of a man so great, so renowned for his virtuous ornaments. Yet it is a satisfaction that, although I may be perplexed by many things, I am enlightened by the merits of his virtues, even if "I cannot find any suitable beginning for these matters. I shall therefore undertake to relate in part those things which I have observed with these eyes, in part those things that I have heard with these ears" [4] and perceived more fully with my mind.

(2) *Severus:* It is amazing that, capable as you are, you marvel if you are ashamed to produce a likeness, beautiful in uprightness

83

of character, of him whose imitator you ought to be and whose fatherly features (as they say) you ought to reproduce. Although I too am bound by the same vows of discipleship, there is nothing more cowardly or dastardly which you grieve not to feel nor dare to bewail, even with the anxieties with which you are weighed down.

(3) *Paschasius:* I shall strive, I shall do, I shall attempt what you urge, Severus, since no one should mourn who does not know what he is suffering. There is no one in the midst of torments who would not dare to groan. I will therefore release the soul hence from the body rather than love it. And I will omit to commend it by prayers to whom it would be useful.

(4) *Adeodatus:* Of one who has abandoned the body, it is best to reveal what was his excellence in spirit, that what seemed to have perished with him may again flourish in us. Virtues are always green and blooming for reward. They do not die in anyone unless they are slain through vice. Yet they can be slain or annulled forever. It is naturally faith's assurance and hope's consolation to take for granted of anyone whom you have known well that he has gone to God; it is charity's obligation to follow him with prayers and to esteem him. Otherwise are we to be reckoned as "down, carried away by the wind"? [5] Heaven forbid! But since such men have led the way, it behooves us to believe that they are happily present with Him who says, "No one who believes in me shall die forever." [6] They are not to be lamented as dead, but to be entrusted with prayers as advocates.

(5) *Paschasius:* Let us lay these things aside, my brother and sons. The result will be to render us worthy of those gifts of the Holy Spirit who thus adorned him with the fresh flowers of virtue. I fear, however, that while I strive to please you, I will offend many. You are not unaware, are you, Severus, that the years of our unhappy life made him another Jeremiah? As I recall, even you yourself have often heard Arsenius say with tears streaming down his face, "Woe to me, my mother, why did you give birth to me, a man of contention, a man of discord in the whole earth?" [7] Yet you bid me pour out lamentation over the grave which time has brought, besprinkle a funeral oration with tears after the manner of

the ancients. Now you wish the devastation of fire to be kindled from ashes after quarrelsome disagreements have been lulled to sleep. Do you not see, Severus, that even now all things in the whole earth are on fire with flames of desire and that deceiving jealousy is laying everything waste?

(6) *Severus:* I see clearly, for, according to the Apocalypse, before our eyes "a great burning mountain is hurled into the sea" of this malign world while our errors thrive, and "a great flaming star from heaven, like a little torch," runs to and fro and reduces the minds of people to ashes.[8] Arsenius chose rather to extinguish its flames, bringing the peace of Christ in reply to them. But under compulsion of sins the bitterness of absinthe overcame the sweetness [9] of such a great man. From that time onward, therefore, he could not prevail against the wanton inclinations of people.

(7) *Paschasius:* By Hercules, you are not at all in doubt about his sense of right. But, refreshed by your words, I will relate what I saw with my own eyes before these things came to pass. I saw from afar as it were a mountain of wood set on fire, piled high almost to the clouds. In front of it someone tall of stature was toiling, stirring with a stick everything already burned out to see if it would blaze up once again. Of that conflagration I could not discern the end. These things, I believe, foreshadowed later events.

(8) *Severus:* As I see it, our Adeodatus has sought to utter lament, but you want to provoke laughter. For unless you had gone to sleep, you would have approved what I said, which you yourself perceive with no hesitation at all and with no fanciful dreams. But I want you now to bestir and apply yourself to what we ask.

(9) *Adeodatus:* Severus, you often employ the sharpness of Crisippus [10] and refute even choice jests with the keen edge of your speech. I beg you not to act more severely (to pun on your foreboding name),[11] but rather to deliberate with us to fashion in gentle style the likeness of our father.

(10) *Severus:* I agree with your advice. A picture of this man's character, however, will not be fully fashioned from the face of one person, for by his actions he displayed the worth of many illustrious men. It seemed to me, for example, that when he wore the mantle as Prior Arsenius, he was truly playing the role of Father

Benedict. As we have already hinted, he occasionally performed the office of Jeremiah, pursuing bitterly with inflexible expression although he was gentle in spirit and mildest of men.[12]

(11) *Paschasius:* In any case you indicate amply that you have etched him in your memory as long as it survives, etched him with pen of reverence which, according to the Apostle, is useful for all things.[13] Even so, if I should wish to pursue those matters, scarcely any but a rare person would believe.

(12) *Adeodatus:* "Who ever required sworn compurgators of a historian? Yet, if it should be necessary,"[14] there are a great many honest men who will set their right hands in oath to your statements. It is therefore quite unworthy to evade a friend of truth and to be timidly silent about truth to those who seek.

(13) *Paschasius:* Have you not read that an ineffective matter which fails of performance requires endeavor?[15] As often therefore as truth has been trampled upon, you have known more fully the things beaten out of those seats. So if I should prove that no one in our time has more adequately borne the manner of Father Benedict, even if that sun which gazes on everything should bear witness, he is a rare one who listens, although truth may remain safe.

(14) *Adeodatus:* I do not believe that matter fails of performance if it brings a disposition of love and piety. Even if heedless ones become envious, it is not absurd to release for a little while the disposition of love. It feasts well on tears;[16] it is bedaubed with tears.[17] It is released by gazing at him whom you love. As he flowers again, he is rendered immovable. It is therefore not absurd for the grave of so great a father to be bedecked with the flowers of lamentation.

(15) *Paschasius:* But you say, you piously urge us, to pursue God's holy and pleasing victim to the court of heaven with tears, not because we have possessed him but because we have lost him and because we, burdened with faults, can no longer accompany him. If the ancient maxim is true that misery alone lacks envy,[18] then we should pursue him willingly with prayers. In our tearful wretchedness, however, I have come to know that much envy of certain ones will not be lacking. They will swear with outstretched

arms, especially if they give heed from whence the story [19] is woven.

(16) *Severus:* That is what I mentioned earlier. It seems to me that you are suffering from drowsiness. Did you not say that you would portray a representation of character and as it were weave a narrative of what was done? But now you bring us a *story*.[20]

(17) *Adeodatus:* It is surprising, Severus, how you always make use of sharp words. It seems to me that he said "story" not to you but to those to whom everything grounded in truth is a "story" and a game. But in your conscience you recognize his *account* [21] and therefore to you is set forth not a "story" but the truth.

(18) *Paschasius:* You are acting properly, Adeodatus, if you favor with your vows the one whom you weary with prayers. But what will strangers do when we are complained of by a witness? Have you not read about a topic of the pagans recently brought forward, how a certain person saw Drusilla going to heaven? [22] Perhaps the same one will relate that he saw Arsenius on the way to heaven. If, therefore, you do not trust us—willingly or unwillingly—ask him. Perhaps he will declare that he observed what was done in heaven, since we do not believe in divine matters. But if you ask him, he will relate it to one person only, for I believe that he will not speak a single word in the presence of many. From the time when he swore in the senate that he saw her ascend to heaven, no one believed him so good a messenger. Whatever he saw, he made certain that he would thereafter tell no one in expressed words, even if he saw a man killed in the public square.

(19) *Adeodatus:* I feel that you are pretending more timidity than is profitable. Do you imagine that you could relate anything that would please everybody equally and that everybody would believe? What, for instance, is clearer, happier, or (best of all) truer for a messenger than the fact that Christ, victor from hell, sought heaven in the flesh, prepared the way, opened the gates, forgave sins, granted grace, and made all this possible through faith to those who wish to go where He is? Yet some do not believe, many gainsay it by their deeds, and few come to faith. Where else do so many miracles shine, so many representatives of patriarchs as-

semble, and proclamations of prophets point out as by one finger what has happened? The elements understand; the angels worship and proclaim. All the apostles are witnesses to these firmly promised events and utterances, Christ's martyrs are witnesses, innumerable confessors and virgins are witnesses, and by the merits of their faith miracles are accomplished. Yet when so many utterances and witnesses from so good a messenger are despised, you have no reason to complain. Many will not believe the words of their salvation, and there are those who feel good enough about their unbelief.

(20) *Paschasius:* Solomon's statement is true that "iron is whetted by iron." [23] You, my brother, often whet the friends you love to advance by loving. So wherever you lead, I follow devoutly. But take care that the cause of salvation may cease to be investigated where profit is lacking.

CHAPTER 1

1:1. *Adeodatus:* Since he was very well known by face and nation to almost everyone, will you unfold, I pray, the character from which the inner, untainted man was prepared? Or, as Severus has suggested, tell us to whom he should be compared.

1:2. *Paschasius:* The truth is that from boyhood Prior Arsenius extended his fame by soldiery and high office. He was a first cousin of the greatest of the august ones and dearer to him than all others. He was "in speech truthful" (as is said of one whose ashes recently brought among us have glistened with many miracles [24]), "upright in judgment, farsighted in counsel, and most faithful in trust." [25] In meetings of the senate he was by his talent more capable than all the others. If he were questioned about any kind of transaction, he replied immediately whatever could be said or devised, and his words flowed as if from a fountain of wisdom. Already his virtue was the loftiest, his authority vastly extended,[26] both recommended by goodness and nobility of character and nation. His wisdom became bright when it excelled in human affairs, as it advanced in divine matters. He possessed a modest fluency in both languages,[27] by which the wisdom of many was greatly enhanced, and eloquence of speech to persuade what he wanted. As long, therefore, as he shone with good of this kind, he was beloved by everyone.

1:3. *Adeodatus:* If he was that kind of man, why did he so often lament that he was begotten as "a man of strife and discord," [28] although you say that he was beloved by everyone?

1:4. *Paschasius:* I grant that zeal for religion grew in him and that his virtue became richer from grace. He had not yet become aware of flaws in the commonwealth which he rejoiced to see increase. More eager he was, therefore, to cultivate intimate association with nobles and holy friendship with people than like Jeremiah to bewail the sins and flaws which indeed had not yet begun to flourish.[29] You know, of course, Adeodatus, that a good man takes counsel not for himself but for the country and its citizens. You have also learned about Scipio and other men of that age who endured hatred and peril of death for the greatest and most abundant good of country and for the virtues.

CHAPTER 2

2:1. *Adeodatus:* Alas, how the greater number seeks the lowest things! Would that I had not come to know about such things among the religious men of our period! How did he come to monastic discipline?

2:2. *Paschasius:* Truly the glory of the world is never without envy nor prosperity without peril of some adversity, but an upright man employs both for salvation. While Arsenius was being buffeted by the artifices of certain men and when he observed the shamelessness of extravagant men occupying unwonted seats, he discovered for himself that welcome time which he had in his mind devoted to God. This was particularly true as he observed how ingenious men held the places of skillful ones and how the lowest had with Marsic hands [30] overthrown the ones best known and most friendly to the people. When he discerned that such ones acted with powerful force against the wise and that in estimation of the masses they were superior and worthiest, he predicted that many misfortunes and many shipwrecks would befall the people.

2:3. It was then that, despite many attempts to dissuade him, he laid aside without regret the world and its allurements insofar as he had clung to them, although without loving them. Inflamed with divine love, he abandoned everything and sought a place of monastic discipline [31] so as to be governed not by his own law but by Christ's and by the Holy Spirit. He had read that "those who are governed by God's Spirit are God's sons." [32] He therefore earnestly held up not himself to himself, but Christ in all things. As for where he was professed, ask Severus. For up to this point I have listened to you carefully; I have tried to endure lightly what I am suffering.

2:4. But now that I have mentioned him whom I once looked upon, whom I once held great, I have found fresh, new griefs which I thought had gone away. I want to be silent for a while until my eyes find the fountain of tears [33] and drain themselves. For my comforter, "converting my soul," [34] has departed far from me; far from me because Arsenius has departed to God, worn by much vexation for the people and for Christ's religion. None of us is unaware of how many great stings he was tortured with when he was preparing to die. There were persons acting toward him as similar ones said in a passage from Jeremiah, "Come, let us smite him with the tongue and let us heed none of his words." [35] Depressed by their extreme loathing, he sought now and then a place where he could tarry in the help of the Most High and in the protection of the God of heaven,[36] a place where no enemy could enter violently. But when he took counsel with himself, he left us desolate and full of grief during that hour. "My bowels have therefore been disturbed enough, my liver has been poured out upon the earth" [37] at the absence of so great a father, and now, by reason of tears, I cannot contemplate a likeness of his character. But I shall weep continuously until my eyes waste; only thus may I be consoled in my wretchedness, I who have suddenly lost such a comforter of mind.[38]

2:5. *Severus:* Please rest from your lamentations for a little while so that your vitals may not again be freshly disturbed by tears. We cannot erase what we have known. But before your eyes darken with mist, let the likeness of his character be depicted in his more graceful colors. Then recollection of his shining countenance will open up the hot fountain of tears.[39] While he looks down from heaven in joy, we shall pour out laments; indeed rejoicing, yet sorrowful; sad, yet happy; dejected, yet transported. For if what we have lost is a matter of sorrow, it should be a matter of joy that we have sent on ahead to heaven's palace such a great intercessor.

2:6. You recall Jeremiah, do you not, whose image our beloved one bore? Although cast by his people into a foul pit,[40] he was at length elevated to the stars because he prayed much. If Jeremiah ceaselessly poured out prayers to God for those for whom while he lived he was forbidden to undertake "prayer and praise," [41] what do you think Arsenius does for his suddenly desolate sons who were so dear to him? We read that it was said of God's prophet Jeremiah, "He is a lover of the brothers; he is the one who prays much for the people and for the entire holy city of Jerusalem." [42] If therefore he, although forbidden, undertakes praise and prayer for the city and people over whom he formerly wept while he was living, for whom he composed Lamentations and undertook mournings, what will Arsenius do for his own whom he loved? He will, even as that one, be an intercessor not only for us but also for the ones he endured as enemies. The invectives of both of them against the people, however harsh, were not products of hatred, but of love.

2:7. The people are not yet willing to believe that, but we who knew him doubt not that one who endured such pain for truth is in any way deprived of the promises of Christ. If faith could be bought at a price, we would pay them to cease pursuing with hatred him whom charity nursed, justice advanced, and piety adorned. I warn them to be quiet, to stop cursing lest they betray their own evil deeds, for they should emulate what they call his craftiness and faithlessness rather than their own distorted faith.

2:8. *Paschasius:* You are too acrimonious, brother Severus. I wish that you would heed the warning of Terence, "Nothing to excess." [43] For all whose conscience is not secure "are in some manner suspicious. They take everything as an affront and believe that they are always blamed" [44] for everything they do.

CHAPTER 3

3:1. *Adeodatus:* Will you describe what is true faith toward one's neighbor and what is the kind of faith that should be maintained when promised to one's lords? Each of us could then gaze more clearly at his own conscience and judge it. For the impression is abroad that Arsenius did not keep faith with the emperor.

3:2. *Paschasius:* I am happy that you urge it to be made manifest how many corrupt and pervert true faith, unaware of what they have promised. According to the Apostle, the faith of Christians "is brought to fruition through love." [45] So take away love and faith is destroyed, for love encompasses all oaths of fealty. Love for Christ and one's neighbor permits no sin, at least not willingly. It is therefore obvious that anyone who cherishes injustice or agrees to it is wicked, hating both his own soul and him with whom he indulgently agrees to evil. It follows plainly that fealty must not extend to what one might wish, namely, to rise up against God's commandments at the behest of an earthly lord. Otherwise, by evil consent the faithless one will lose that faith which is brought to fruition through love for one's neighbor.[46]

3:3. One must weigh what relates to love and through faith fulfil with more consistency and caution what belongs to a neighbor's safety. If the reverse were true, then Herod and his accomplices to whom he was bound by oath would have been guilty of no crime,[47] that is, if fealty required to be fulfilled whatever he wills or indeed whatever you may promise. First, therefore, you should avoid recklessly promising anything in fealty; then if you have vowed, shun any advance toward worse things. For, as the Apostle says, we owe nothing except to love one another.[48] Let everyone fulfil what he owes and owe what he fulfils, namely, faith that is achieved through love.[49] There are times, however, when faith is not faith because it is not of love toward God and one's neighbor, but is of earthly, animal remonstrance and of diabolical obligation. Consequently, no one keeps faith if God is despised and a neighbor's salvation to future life is neglected.

3:4. *Adeodatus:* Alas, how miserable the years of our age in which the will of everyone leads the way. What each one savors and can do is now lawful. He can with degenerate desire bring to completion what is in conflict with this purpose. Formerly it was necessary, first, to discern what one should will; then, to will what one discerned; and finally, to accomplish whatever good one could. Now, however, minds [50] give birth to monsters. What ought to follow comes first and the head which ought to come first follows at random. Indecisive and playful authority swells on all sides. So comes to pass that statement by the comic writer, "I will, I won't; I won't, I will." [51] And everyone is possessed by a vastly unhappy, childish giddiness.

3:5. *Paschasius:* Hence quite properly one of the leaders among the senators—two years ago I urged him to correct himself—overcome by reason and scriptural argument, has said, "Have you not heard? In that age, place, and time into which we were born, those matters that you are relating, even though divine, perhaps had an opportunity for affecting life, had indeed the force of commands. But now, in this age in which we live, you know that nothing useful and reasonable is effective." After that remark we parted, he sweating after his own will and I resting from my effort.

3:6. *Adeodatus:* My dear Paschasius, such matters appear to me not so much blindness as an astonishing madness of mind. For to realize where one is or what he is doing, to recall indeed where he was or what kind of person goes staggering, yet be unable to turn back (or go forward) to what he once was, and indeed to act so unfeelingly as to go after his own will lest he return to himself —that is madness.

3:7. *Severus:* Who can be more imperceptive than one who does not perceive himself,[52] who cannot hear what he himself says? I suppose you think those who are diminishing so obviously cannot even hear "raging silences." [53] You are consequently not at all frightened to speak freely.

3:8. *Paschasius:* We speak of faith, what it should be toward neighbors and what kind should be preserved. I have therefore thought also that there should be no silence at all. As you know, our Arsenius held this faith truly, he displayed it, he kept it; the faith which is operative in love [54] is supported in all respects by truth, is strengthened by justice. There is another faith which deceives wickedly by adulation, which extols every vice. In every action and word, in every fact and agreement, Arsenius examined thoroughly to see if friendly truth were present. He investigated minutely each particular case of facts and actions lest falsity create a flaw in it. Thereafter, that all the various parts of faith might with one accord sing forth the harmony of justice, he assigned all things for himself in the presence of all eyes. Moreover he daily offered himself to the Lord in prayers, that charity might inwardly accomplish everything.

CHAPTER 4

4:1. *Adeodatus:* I marvel how with varied and innumerable involvements he had time so earnestly for God wherever he was, especially since we distracted him so often even when we wanted time for God. But when we seek now, we can scarcely find.

4:2. *Paschasius:* I admit, beloved Adeodatus, that wherever he was he was always with God. For he did not, as it is said, surrender himself to things, but entrusted himself to them. Amid crowds of men, treating his own thoughts, he was always doing something in his mind healthful to himself. In order for faithless ones to recover faith, I bear witness that I never saw anyone who was present everywhere and who moved anxiously far and wide, so that seldom or never did he withdraw himself although he was busy with numberless weighty matters. Even at banquets, either when he had guests or when he was the guest of the great ones, I could never understand how he ate so abstemiously over long periods of time. His refreshment at lunch would have been deemed abstinence and frugality of diet by many who could scarcely achieve such fasting even during the days of Lent.

4:3. Alas, how unhappy now that I am deprived of his presence! Now I do not blush to do before many what I once feared to do before him, for I knew that he would not spare any expression that was immoderate. I wish that you would ask Severus about such matters, for he underwent with me such discipline as often as possible.

4:4. *Severus:* At any rate I give heed to what you assert that it may sometime or another be manifest, perhaps because I stretched out my hand greedily to your mouth. We often had what he introduced among us and still today we are flogged by conscience instead of his severe invective. Yet of what you are speaking, the fathers, brothers, and fellow students are witnesses who understand that after the manner of a farmer weeding he quickly used word and sentiment of reproach at the beginning of sin as a garden hoe so that Christ's harvest might sprout richer. Unlike certain ones he acted unhesitatingly at transgressions before they grew. At any early stage he cut down the source of sin with the sword of the Word. How indeed could he listlessly spare his own, since at no place and time did he yield to the more lofty ones, but admonished them? He made Solomon's opinion his own, "The words of the wise are like goads and nails fixed on high." [55]

4:5. With the spear of the Word he pierced the rank growth of vices and on high he strengthened more securely the beginning of virtues. Absorbed in such great and alternating courses of events, he was exceedingly happy and blessed as a harsh critic of himself who devoted himself in high retreat to studies, to God, and to charity. This then was his business and the reason for his business; this was his leisure and labor; this was his fasting and vigil; this was the constant care and anxiety of his mind; namely, that he might never cease what he had once undertaken in the soldiery of Christ. It is therefore abundantly clear that what he was to himself he was to God and his neighbors. He was no more severe with another than with himself nor did he judge another more than himself.

CHAPTER 5

5:1. *Paschasius:* I am pondering, my brother, and recalling what you are referring to, but it is not yet the place to speak of it. Reluctantly therefore I pass over what you are setting forth. Nevertheless I admit that I occasionally questioned him why he was so severe with himself and why he moved along so sorrowfully even when he was alone. To that he replied, "You should understand that I am with myself and I perceive what is within me. So I rejoice with no great joy as yet, but in hope alone." Let them therefore ponder, our men who are trying to disparage him and charge him with the faults of others, charge him who took such a view of himself. Do they suppose, contrary to the Apostle, that he will be adjudged by the Lord as an alien from wisdom beyond just men? [56] No, he sings with rejoicing to Christ to whom he clung in life while still in the flesh, "You have freed me from the snare of hunters and from the harsh word." [57]

5:2. But while he himself is now set free from such great evils, he has left us wretched. I do not want them to know if we slip into tears very secretly in solitude. We have repressed them lest we seem to weep for him whom the wicked have freely hated. Now, however, we shall at last abate our mourning for those who "are at peace," [58] for weeping and tears are mitigations of desire and desire is the happy memory of the lost. Even if harsh death is frightening, the recollection of a dear name is pleasing. For that reason a certain one says, "The death of friends may hold a kind of pleasure and their memory may be sweet, as apples which seem sweetly bitter." [59] When, therefore, an interval has elapsed, the pure joy of hope returns to us. We love those whom we once had as if we ourselves also were about to go hence suddenly, and so we have lost in order to have. Glorious and blessed is sweet hope.

5:3. So, father Arsenius, we rejoice over you; we solace ourselves; for we take for granted that you have achieved that blessed hope, and we trust that we will there be aided by your merits. Although we grieve from this moment to that hour, yet somehow we rejoice, for a good result is happier for you than the end that remains for us, unless your earlier departure will intervene for us. Perhaps it was expedient that you go away so that the comfort of Christ [60] may come; that we, abandoning all things, may in mind be quickly with you; that with untiring prayers there may be the faculty of eagerly seizing indulgence and our mind may receive the confidence of achieving. So, my father, not wretched, but blessed are they whom your spiritual presence does not fail, for whom the shepherd's care is not diminished, but rather grace is increased.

5:4. What then is death but a sleep, as we can demonstrate from many places in Scripture.[61] But if in the quiet of night, still clinging to bodily bonds and bound in the prison of the members,

souls can perceive higher things distinguished by their likenesses,
how much more do they, divested of every stain of corruption, see
(as a certain saint says)⁶² with a sense now pure and ethereal?
Hence the more readily have we relied upon you as our father for
what in this life we have been looking forward to in abundance.
We believe that his sweet absence is everywhere readily present to
us, for then all things cannot be as his bitter presence is absent now.
He is believed to be in Him to whom all things lie open, to whom
all things are present at once. Great therefore is the power and unutterable is the virtue, so that neither death nor time can snatch
away those whom God's majesty has blessed.

5:5. You, my father, who are living better for yourself, are
now believed rather to live for us. Tears are already becoming
sweet and weeping more joyous, for although death is a matter of
enmity, your love for us is life. Death drained has been swallowed
up in life.⁶³ You are, therefore, O father, not only alive, but
blessedly alive. Be present for us, we pray, before Him in whom
you live better, in whom all things live. We are moved in Him and
we live in Him.⁶⁴ By the promises of hope in Him the burning
mind is truly refreshed and the assuaged mood is somewhat alle-
viated. I pray, therefore, that the likeness of your mind may habit-
ually fly hither and pour out sweet visions of a true dream (if it is
proper to say this), that you may be fully present, albeit deprived
of bodily appearances. Your daily intimacy arouses a yoked memory, the mood evokes the likeness; but when they are removed
they renew sorrow.

5:6. Sometimes, my father, you are present, embraced by mind
and spirit. We embrace you often, we converse, we understand. I
am unfortunate who, so long absent, drained the last warnings of
your words. As our Chremes ⁶⁵ has related to me, you say, "Act
my sons, so as to do well whatever good you know and you will
not be found less than yourself." Those, my father, were your last
words to me; those were the mandates of your esteem. You were
attending carefully, not that I might know what was perfect, but
that by knowing I might make progress. Unaware that what one
may not escape would soon come to pass, supposing that it might
be delayed a while longer, I replied more truthfully than jokingly
that to know, to will, and to do do not belong equally to a man at

all times. For many things that we know to be good we are unwilling to do when sins press upon us. Moreover, if an opportunity to be willing should present itself, we then no longer have ability to act.

5:7. It is God alone whose knowledge is not greater than His will nor His will stronger than His ability. But whatever He knows He both wills and accomplishes; [66] in His wisdom, therefore, He does all things. For men, on the other hand, none of these is possible without Christ's grace. So, I beseech you, refresh us with your prayers, aid us with your vows, for then the teacher's warning will be made perfect if he aids with abundance of prayers the one whom he warned. This is indeed the office of our praise: here below you have been without offense toward anyone, because you would not proclaim God's will to your own people until you enveloped them in your prayers and merits. The result was that God permitted them to will and to accomplish what is pleasing whom He permitted through you to know what was appropriate.

CHAPTER 6

6:1. *Adeodatus:* I would like to express my profound desire for you to relate the beginnings of such a great man from his youth onward, for we believe that his merits grew more and more perfect with time. True virtues do not advance without innocence, yet innocence is founded on the efficacy of virtues. As merit increases by practice of good work, lasting solidity is established. As simplicity may reply to prudence with another analogy of the perfect man and prudence may renew simplicity, so what is in flower may show forth fruit and the flowers may promise fruit of good hope. It is possible that a blossom may sometime fall without fruit, but fruit does not put forth without flower. Unfold therefore, I pray, the flowers first so that a richer fruit may abound. For even if fruit is useful, the fairer bloom of a young life gives a sweet odor. The grace of Christ was present in this one, for although he flowered earlier the virtue of future flowering was even richer.

6:2. *Paschasius:* You are asking, Adeodatus, you are perhaps asking about some things before I was born. I have, of course, learned many things worthy to record from the accounts of reliable men, since he shone forth from the womb as a well-known person. From boyhood he was devoted to liberal studies amid the neophytes of the palace, demonstrating strong nobility of manners and honesty of feeling. The emperor, although favoring his effective talent and although being his first cousin (son of his paternal uncle), decided by an inspiration of some kind that he should be humbled and forced back among the weaker ones. The action was not by chance, but by a dispensation of divine judgment, so that his tender age might be proven like gold in a furnace of trial and so that while still a youth he might learn not only to endure adversity with courage but also prosperity with calmness. It is written, as a furnace proves gold, so trial proves just men.[67]

6:3. The witness of his justice was, therefore, already shining so that more extensive grace might be evinced. Later he shone forth as very mild where for so long a time he was severely beaten in the forge of humility. Entrusted under a free guardianship to some of the magnates, he was honorable and compliant. Hence his great fame was daily increasing and public recognition of his life and praise was building up. Who, then, would not admit that he was already proven in a divine novitiate? Although no neighbor accused him of crimes, although he was innocent and just, he was kept in subjection as though he were a criminal and as though he were not related by blood to the emperor. Some tell that once when he was on the road, despondent, goading the oxen pulling a wagon, he encountered a certain rustic who was girded with baldric and weapons. Him he addressed thus, "Man, don't you want to lay aside the arms you are wearing as a poor man and take up these with which I am girded?"

6:4. At this the gullible wayfarer harmlessly divested himself of the arms and carried back the unexpected gifts with the wagon.[68] Thereupon our Arsenius said, "Lowly things suit me better, since I am not occupied with soldiery of the present age, but with affairs of common life." What more, my brothers, did he say than what David once said, "I am become yet more vile and I will be humble in my eyes"?[69] Anyone who appears before God as unworthy in his own eyes becomes more acceptable to God. But if great and adequate to himself, he is certainly deemed very little before

God.[70] What more? When his humiliation had been accomplished, divine power shortly thereafter exalted him with great honors and he became to all more pleasing and much more estimable.

6:5. He was restored to court; he was elevated by favor. Daily advancing and growing, he was constituted by the emperor steward of the whole household. Far and wide he was revered as second to Caesar, as though another Joseph was wielding the scepter of the kingdom.[71] He was on everyone's lips and pre-eminent in everything whatsoever, especially as a supervisor of justice. His skill administered the civil law for good without sub-terfuge, and his presence frightened criminals no less than it re-lieved dutiful ones. A senator of senators he was, if I may speak thus, even then more effectual in all private matters because he wished nothing other than ability to understand everything more wisely. Everywhere he was cautious, everywhere ready; faithful, too, and everywhere active.

6:6. In his presence no one dared to express about himself any-thing but the truth. Before him the right of citizens was never for sale, but acting freely in all respects, he seemed willing to hear peti-tioners, He was therefore ever entrusted more particularly with those matters which properly should have been done by the em-peror. Consequently, already exercising leadership, he led the army against enemies in a brilliant manner in place of Caesar.[72] Subdued by his kindnesses, the wild barbarian peoples loved him very much, as you have learned. And when at length he became a monk, faith-ful followers continued to flock to him from everywhere.

CHAPTER 7

7:1. *Severus:* We have often discussed why he loved those same peoples so much that he applied himself to them quickly and waited upon them wholeheartedly and untiringly, while the leaders of our order were bypassed. Understanding, however, makes it eas-ily clear that he did so from love of duty to arouse by his example and to incite to honorable manners those who had just recently come to faith in Christ.

7:2. *Paschasius:* True, my Severus. Among them he was for

that reason more welcome than all others and more esteemed than everyone else, a fact which I have myself often tested. Perhaps you recall, when we were there with our Antonius in the business concerning the new monastery,[73] what sort of person and how great a person I have shown him to be considered there. If I may say so, although he was actually a monk, he was venerated as if he had come down from heaven rather than from the court. When we approached certain ones who did not recognize him in the new habit, who had in hostile manner laid waste monastic fields, and who had plundered adjoining lands, our Antonius wanted in the spirit of kindness to reprove them with mildness, so he was not heard to say anything. Then he presented Arsenius to them and bade him to urge them to curb themselves. When the latter had expressed himself, they began to scrutinize more carefully if it were indeed he whom we acknowledged. Although convinced by many evidences, they could hardly believe that so distinguished and powerful a man had come to such profound lowliness and appearance of defeat. One of them asked him, "Are you indeed the one whom our world praises as so renowned?"

7:3. "I am," he replied.

7:4. The other thereupon declared, "I confess that although you do not exercise so much as the tips of your finger, you are said to be an even greater person than you were." At this we all smiled and departed.

7:5. *Adeodatus:* I wish that you would be serious. I do not see what good the things on which worldly pride relies may serve. Even if they had been pleasant, our death will completely abolish them. Are you unaware that he who loves the world loses things without price?[74] What is it to seek again the pomp of the world but to deny Christ's faith?

7:6. *Paschasius:* I feel the same way, but upright men, although they may appear to act in the ways of the world, maintain a wakeful spirit. They do not permit themselves to be summoned to all outward shows, although everything outside may resound loudly, although everything outside may be supported by great upheavals. Which do you account the more strongly, to wear purple as if it were goats' hair and use vessels of gold and silver as if they were earthen pots; that is, not to be moved by such things? Or, on the other hand, to employ cheap objects as if they were costly; that is, not to be influenced by poverty?

7:7. *Adeodatus:* I would call each one a man of surpassing virtue. But scarcely or rarely is such a one found whom high degree does not cast down, whom lowliness does not move, whom eminence of riches and honor does not excite, whom poverty does not influence, and whom occupation in different affairs does not weaken.

7:8. *Paschasius:* Yes, Adeodatus, yes, but true virtue lies in both—which a good, devoted mind displays—where neither greed nor avarice kindles the spirit, but generous manners and upright lives freely commend. Virtues are not remote, vices do not pursue; one passionate disposition does not plague the other; those things that are external do not devastate. Otherwise what good are the harshness and silence of a region for a hermit, if wicked desires rage within and vices pervert the spirit? Gentle and true peace is that which reason creates everywhere and which serenity of religion graces. Although certain ones withdraw from the world, we have found that they are still vexed by its tempests, for they are shown mentally not to have sufficiently left it. Some, however, whom the beginnings of virtue have nourished in military affairs, have afterward come to Christ's soldiery tougher and sharper than if they had been without that experience.

7:9. *Adeodatus:* Yet in these persons there ought to be an experience in the virtues for which they may be esteemed extraordinary. Even pagans seemed deserving and upright among their own people at least, and some are reputed in estimation of the masses to have been carried up to dwell among the gods.[75]

7:10. *Paschasius:* It seems to me that you falter over everything we bring forward, that you are imbued with a vulgar color. You think that no one else can regain an accomplishment of mind, especially since changing gossip poisons changing minds with spatterings of things. It may be, therefore, that you also are so corrupted by the ill reports of many that you cannot again recover another faith about this one whom the multitude mangles and whom the ignorance of the masses gnaws.

7:11. *Adeodatus:* Do you not recall the statement of Cato that many persons say many things and therefore confidence is rare? [76]

I have the highest confidence, however, about this one to whom I clung to the very last, whom I came to know late. I loved him who was distinguished above all by virtues. But confidence should not be easily bestowed in all matters. For that reason even apostles are said to have believed slowly lest their faith seem perhaps rash.[77] So it is fitting that we, too, do nothing hastily, nothing unadvisedly. It is not fitting to be so imbued with perception of the masses or of anyone that we are unable to regain the better things; nor, may I say, be softened like wax so that we receive the imprints of all the seals on the sculpture. The image of anyone must therefore be demonstrated and confidence must also be demonstrated, so that when once you shall have proved it clearly you will not again judge concerning it.

7:12. *Paschasius:* You speak truly, but I want you to ponder how upright men have lived amid highest honors of the world, how able men have presently come from soldiering to the grace of Christ. I therefore say nothing about David whom royal dignity did not entice with rich supplies, nor did concern with affairs drive him back from the gift of grace. I say nothing, moreover, about all the others who, when at the peak of greatness they were adorned with the flower of virtue, are said to have "pleased God" [78] and to have shone with many sacraments of mysteries. I shall now come to our own people whom Christ's church has taken from warfare of the world and made glorious prelates. I speak of Ambrose, who by and by arrived at the chair of episcopate from the office of prefect; [79] and Hilary, whom all Gaul celebrates as a distinguished teacher.[80] Often the world has advanced men of this kind, or rather the grace of Christ has advanced them from the world. Consequently no one can doubt that this one also, marked with the jewels of virtue, was set by God's providence amid the fillets of senatorial dignity or that by God's mercy he was prepared by fire so that when he had changed from so great a height to monastic lowliness he might become "a vessel of honor." [81]

CHAPTER 8

8:1 *Severus:* For a long time I await this, namely, why you wish to present doubtful things about one whom we have known better than ourselves (if I may so confess), of whom we have been aware, who was without doubt a devotee of justice and truth, in whom we have more readily trusted than in ourselves. Perhaps, like certain philosophers, we hold all things doubtful and we philosophize that nothing can be held certain. Otherwise ask our Chremes [82] or Allabigus (whose blast of the trumpet will perhaps furnish confidence for the deaf),[83] how that up to this point he has lived more brightly than others in integrity of manners and morals.

8:2. *Chremes:* [84] No one was ignorant of this, for he was well known to virtually everyone; but spite denies what conscience demonstrated to many. It is abundantly clear, although it may offend, that he was acknowledged even by the envious as more preeminent than all the nobles of our time. Even though it may not be pleasing to them, he was nevertheless acclaimed as good by all. In the world he was a distributor of alms and an even more generous dispenser of tithes. You might indeed judge that he was not distributing his own possessions for this purpose but things that had been entrusted to him. After the yearly tithe, he ceaselessly paid out to Christ's poor a daily tithe both of every return and provision of food and of various outlays of gifts. He deemed this a part of his heritage, this the price of gain, this the merchandise of his compassion. But, look, our Allabigus, reviling, becomes angry. He is rubbing his bare tonsure with his hand, and he thinks ill of all those matters which you present.

8:3. *Allabigus:* [85] Why do you jestingly cultivate games? Even if I seem bald to you, why do you despise Elisha? [86] Do you not know, Chremes, that many winds have weathered me? Perhaps I have diminished my hair in swearing by this head. In any case, since they do not believe, I have this new word of Terence, "I may pursue them who wish to be first of all, but are not; when they laugh, I laugh and marvel at their talents; whatever they say, I applaud; even if they deny, I applaud; whatever anyone of them denies, I deny; they say, I say. I have ordered myself to fawn on everything, for that profit is now exceedingly rich." [87] Nevertheless I may at all events summon a small faith, I who am very well aware of him. I will pretend nothing false, since I find no one dearer to my heart. In his own time Arsenius was pleasing to all, even though the unnatural last period of this world hated him unwisely and spitefully, indeed pursued him with lies.

8:4. But do not, I beg, think me so spiritless or ungrateful, inhuman or mad, that the morals of so great a man, his stable manner of life, love, or shame of forgetfulness do not move me. On the contrary, they warn me to keep faith with him—with whom I have endured much, from whom I learned much, from whom I have come to appreciate whatever is best of virtue in the world, for love of whom I first abandoned the world for God. If any of you has opposed me with some kind of horn, let him hear the trumpet of truth. Even though envious ones become too dull to comprehend that Arsenius was Christ's true athlete; even though unskilled in speech, I cannot enumerate more; I am nonetheless unashamed to lament, as often as I recall those matters to mind, that so I may be fully refreshed with the grief of our distress. For if I think there should be rejoicing that we have had such a man, there should also be weeping among us, who have always lived with him, that at the last we were absent. Even if we had been with him, we might perchance have shared his spirit the more. Have you not read what Elijah said to Elisha who was begging a double portion of the former's spirit, "If you see when I am taken up, what you desire will come to pass"? [88] So, brothers, had we been with him when he went hence to the skies, the pledge of his spirit might have flowed back strongly upon us. But now how wretched are we who were not permitted to know the hour of departure of him whom we thought still living!

8:5. *Paschasius:* Listen, the beardless youth who seemed so unsophisticated has suddenly become a philosopher of lamentation. No doubt he has been inspired by the spirit of him whom we mourn. For if he had not been touched by him, how would he have anticipated such things before the pen came by which there will be an opportunity to lament with flowing heart? He is not one who agrees to falsehood as he pretends, but, so I think, one who proclaims the truth. Let someone think little of what he may hear, especially since there is none of my friends today to whom I dare expose all my secrets. For unwittingly one may betray our secrets to enemies. Sometimes dignity prevents one; folly of the deed itself chagrins another. May I not seem faithless and shameless. It is therefore ours to understand whenever and wherever it may be needful to agree and comply or perhaps to be silent about Arsenius.

8:6. Since we cannot consider in advance or foreknow the death of so great a man, we must now think over beforehand what, to whom, and when we may speak. Our spirit was sufficiently terrified at first to think such things about him, such things at which we grieved as have at length happened. Not, of course, that we might be unaware of the condition, but a certain one, relying on our prayers, had concealed our awareness of universal frailty so that we might not think about him in any way but favorable. Thus once when I was sent by the emperor on business about which you know, before I returned to Cologne I found that he for whom we now shed tears had endured exile instead of the reward wherein we monks are refreshed. There is a reading in the middle of the prophet Isaiah [89] which says, "Let Egyptians rush against Egyptians and let Egypt be shattered in its vitals." [90] Then indeed I growled; then, as though drenched with a rain of tears and broken with grief, I fainted. Everyone marveled; some conjectured correctly what had happened, while others presumed that I was perhaps aware of the supposed guilt of that one. Not one of them is here with me today, although yesterday they seemed to be my best comforters. I confess, however, that in the same hour everything that later happened came to my mind. One should therefore doubt not but that the divine Spirit everywhere completes everything, even those things which He does not possess.

8:7. *Severus:* I will tell of those matters that are in my mind; you decide. As long as Arsenius was alone, as long as there was no other hope, as long as his power flourished, many, many people were well inclined to him and they gave him approbation. But after the situation was changed, they too were changed concerning what they strove to gain. But not for that reason shall I say that such things happened by chance, as both reading and tears made known, namely, that our affairs like Egypt were shattered in their vitals. Perhaps even now the innermost vitals wail like a lyre against future abominations.

CHAPTER 9

9:1. *Adeodatus:* While varying situations are happening, the pen is confused, orderly speech is difficult to maintain, and a rich supply of wisdom is not drawn from the fountain of the heart. I want you therefore to open for us a burning fountain [91] and make known what kind of person and how great a person he was who came into the monastic community. Virtues are beautiful even under the concealment of a military mantle, and they do grow amid the very allurements of the world. Yet they become more beautiful in the school of virtues where, with vices cut away, the field is redolent with sweet odors of other fellow soldiers, where only the holy affairs of God are meditated by all.

9:2. *Paschasius:* If you ask, Adeodatus, what kind of person came, I assert such a one as your Vergilius Maro describes, "whole, polished, and rounded." [92] This verse, although given high praise in your Vergil, is indeed read much earlier in Horace.[93] Although he was speaking of the wise man, he says that he is strong and is "in himself whole, polished, and rounded." It is obvious that in a great many places your ingenious and able Vergil derived praise from the sentiments of others and from many fragments of the philosophers, and as a beggar has prepared foolish entertainment at least for boys. But this one of ours is even more praiseworthy, being illumined by the grace of Christ. He has shone forth from this age; he has come, as they say, strong in God and "polished and rounded." For nothing is rounder in every respect than a point, as if the virtues agree with reason and with God.

9:3. Does not virtue seem to you a certain equanimity of life everywhere consonant with reason? But if one thing in life differs from another, it is (unless I am deceived) offensive, as that famous man says, as if one part of a circle is unlike the other parts by a greater or lesser distance. Consequently it is virtue and true reason which make a perfect life; that is, a life perfect in every respect, if it accords with truth and if it attains the virtues. He who lives so well and honorably that he seems to live by the virtues commanded by God is assuredly deemed proper and upright in life. But of that one such beliefs are scarcely held since everywhere he is destroyed by hatred and envy. I therefore consider him too stintingly praised where truth is stifled by clamors and justice is killed by envy.

9:4. *Severus:* If you had lived at the time of the persecutors, you would either have declared that you knew nothing about Christ or you would have at any rate kept silence. But now put fear aside: here you will again swear nothing to the one demanding. Otherwise say that, if I harm what I love, I will harm endlessly. There is surely enough love for me, because I once for all drank from it. I could not receive anything else. If therefore what is seen does not advance, let us ourselves come to the weapons of virtues. For if I cease not worthily to praise God for men of such kind and such greatness, I will be more blessed, although I myself am less than his counsel and his manners.

9:5. *Paschasius:* We strive for great things, brother Adeodatus, but virtue is nothing if not difficult. Let us relate a tale exceedingly well known to all the world. As you say, it is a mean virtue to maintain silence in such matters. On the other hand, it is a severe defect to speak of what should be kept silent, although it would be useful to many to conceal what should be presented and to present what should be concealed. Our Arsenius now came, as you have learned, to monastic life already almost perfect, even though he was in time believed to have grown greater and better. For there is no one who can fail in this life to make progress in virtues. He came, I repeat, as your aforesaid poet once said, "The good and wise man, such a one as skillful Apollo has scarcely discovered among all the thousands of men, as very judge of himself, was proving himself entirely to the fingertips." [94] I confess that I have never seen anyone examine himself as carefully as this man, who pried into his innermost deeds not only daily but continually as not even the cleverest judge penetrates those of another man.

9:6. *Adeodatus:* If he came already "polished and rounded," how, I ask, was he in time greater and better than himself? Can anything be rounder than round? If that is possible, it stands to reason that he was not rounded so that the circle of his virtues might be fashioned by the immediate point, that is, by the work of the Godhead.

9:7. *Paschasius:* As far as pertains to geometrical learning, what you say would be true; but not if to the virtues, for with Christ measuring inwardly on every side they are ever being rounded most evenly into a sphere. Here a beginning is being inaugurated according to pattern; there, where the city of virtue is, it is brought to perfection. Therefore, in comparison with God, as no one is good, so no one is perfect; and as no one is perfect, so no one is "polished and rounded." Yet a man is called good or perfect; and if perfect, by all means polished, because he is fashioned in Christ in whose circuit indeed we read that there is a certain rainbow [95] and from whom every perfection of virtue is marked. No one, however, proceeds to them who is not found daily greater and better than himself. Hence also the prophet says, "Blessed is the man whose help is from you; he has set in order the risings in his heart." [96] What it is to "set in order the risings," he continues concerning each one, saying, "And they shall go from virtue to virtue." [97] Thus, as the form of all virtues, let the peculiar love of each soul accomplish the size and kind. It is therefore fitting for the soul to increase in virtues but to decrease in vices and in movement toward nonbeing. But as our illustrious one strove daily from virtue to virtue, so from being to greater being; and as to greater and better, so although already polished in virtues he was carefully molded by the hand of Christ that he might be more prepared and rounder.

9:8. Such as and great as he already was when he laid aside the warfare of the world, the present abbot and brothers are witnesses. Attentive and anxious they examined him with many proofs and skillful disciplines while as novice he was knocking at the gate of monastic training. They are witnesses indeed that he was tried as gold in the furnace amid all rough and harsh harassments to such an extent that he was held to be no longer a tyro but already a knight of Christ. The Spirit of God was in him. He was, so it is said, crushed by no stings of annoyance. Yet he strove daily to be more excellent than himself. How true is that statement of the Apostle that "all things work together in them for good; they are called saints according to purpose." [98] To him also what is usually introduced for evil was immediately an advantage. He sang praise to the Lord with the prophet, "Because of the words of your lips I have guarded the rough ways." [99] I confess that what seems rough for many was easy for him, for he was indeed a monk.

CHAPTER 10

10:1. *Adeodatus:* What praise is it for you to proclaim him a monk? Are not we and many, many others also deemed to bear the name of monk?

10:2. *Paschasius:* We are truly deemed so, but in name only; in reality we are found false. Well said a certain father gazing at himself, "Woe is me who bear the false name of monk!" [100] If you look closely, they are found rare. But our illustrious elder was one who alone out of thousands was pointed out by finger. Do you not recall the eyes of those coming to us? They were all quickly gazing upon him, and they were entranced at the light. Seeking him out, they wanted to talk with him alone. Even when he was farthest from a beginning, he was before others venerated by all. No one wanted to be found blameworthy in any respect before him, even in levity. His gravity and probity of manners illuminated everyone. Each one, therefore, in his presence lowered his face with modest mind. You would more freely allow something blameworthy in presence of the sun than in his presence. But now without him how wretched we live; how enticed by many allurements! We are all indeed the worse with a license which often loosens restraints of gravity when it falls into anyone's mind. But ask Severus if you want to learn about him.

10:3. *Severus:* Brothers, brothers, what shall I say or where shall I find supply of speech, when nothing about him has remained in me except ability to weep and mourn? It was better for me when I was bearing the yoke of my youth with him. I was then, like a solitary, silent in his presence. It was better than now when permission to speak has been granted. I think it safer to allow those things which I then feared to admit. I submit to a practice which is now that of all men: I see and judge better the deeds of others than my own. Hence the shameful things that I often commit, especially since I often act with those who know neither law nor the good or reasonable. Better, worse, useful, hurtful—they neither care nor see. Nothing is acceptable except what pleases them. They knowingly defend only what they want, even if it does not permit them to be as they wish. Moreover we give the palm, we boastfully exalt him who has such great force and power and ability to deceive. He can build up false things for true and adjudge the wicked as the best.

10:4. It is not now the time to publish anything praiseworthy about Arsenius. But since all know, though they hate and envy, there is no need to praise with eloquence when he is proclaimed by each one as a man more religious and perfect than any other of our time. In all respects he was a student of monastic discipline, serving a long, long time under the *Rule* and the abbot. He was, I repeat, a student. To all he held himself subject and humble. He rejoiced to be behind rather than in front.[101] He was careful to be as profitable under the yoke of a master as afterward when he was prelate. At length, therefore, he was found a perfect father and master, because as disciple and son he was approved as more perfect than others. Such kind you will find very rare, for each one enjoys to be out front rather than to be behind or to be profitable. Otherwise there would be no great paucity of perfect prelates nor great difficulty of making progress. Although they have authority, most of them strive to be profitable only to a few, but injurious to many.

10:5. This one was praised by the mouth of many while he was still under the discipline of obedience. For example, while he was still a novice, the channel of a river became swollen. An order was given in usual manner for the brothers to go out and cut back swollen grasses to prevent further inundation. Soon he began to encourage the others to go in clothed with tunics only so as to make better headway. With this encouragement many went along with him. As they were enduring the bitter cold, the abbot of the monastery, when he was informed, ordered them dragged out and restrained from further such daring. If one may so speak, an excess of blame often results from warmth of good love. For charity compels when the mind takes less counsel, so that the Apostle Paul may say, "Charity never falls away." [102] We read that such happened to Peter, that he expressed himself with his mouth without taking counsel.[103] If I may so suggest, such excess is a sign of ignorance, not of love. Its flame, therefore, is more easily purified.

10:6. Have you not seen him when he was in charge of our hospitality? What a wonderful person, how great, humble, de-

voted! Have you ever seen any of our notables longing for such
vile tasks, enduring such harsh matters, and assiduously handling
such repulsive, stinking things? I am not referring to dirty shoes of
guests, but to sores of the poor and their stinking clothes. He always washed them as though he were carrying spices. All such
matters he endured tirelessly, never growing weary.

10:7. *Paschasius:* O good Lord Jesus, how tireless you made
him in all the duties of love, how vigorous, effective, devoted! He
did so much during his crowded ministry for care of the poor,
guests, infirm; anxious for them before and above all things else
during the day. At night, however, after very little sleep, he, like
Mary unwearied at the feet of the Lord Jesus,[104] lay prostrate on
the ground before the holy altar before and after the vigil of the
brothers.

10:8. You know, O Lord Christ, how he bedewed the soil with
a rain of tears, begging you, longing for you, seeking you, knocking for you to open the door of your pity; for you to open what
you had hitherto closed to him; and for you to admit where you
had mercifully opened to him. With doors opened, so we believe,
he then knocked with faith to penetrate, but now he embraces with
love of charity to enjoy. With the prophet he could have said,
"My eyes have failed at your speech saying, 'When will you comfort me?'"[105] I have observed his eyes almost exhausted with
weeping. You, too, I suppose, have often seen him wasting with
anguished vigils; you have seen him wet with tears; you have seen
him bursting with sobs; you have seen him weak and thin from
frugality, skin clinging to his bones, face wasting with sweat of
laborious life.

10:9. He lived both kinds of life in his time, the practical during
the day, the theoretical during the night. On one hand, besprinkled
with flowers, he knew with Mary what was the one thing necessary, although he was constantly with Martha.[106] Consistently he
strengthened one life with the other. Panting with sighs in this
duty of love and driving to this end, he labored enough in the daytime to cause the field to flow with his sweat; but in the night, with
his tears. In the morning you might observe him bathed as it were
with purple dew and drenched with a rain of tears. If, however,
you wish to know the truth more fully, ask Severus, who was al-

ways more zealous and able than I to keep vigil. He should know better about all these matters.

10:10. *Severus:* Even if you say that about me not quite truthfully, it is true that I observed much about him (such as it is) that ought to be published. You recall, do you not, how in severely cold weather he sang Psalms to the Lord? There were nights in which he scarcely once left the holy altar to go to bed. If you asked whether he wished to overcome the night by singing, asking, seeking, knocking, or by groans and tears, he would reply with Cato's statement, "If I would or not; if I could or not." [107] He helped me watch because of the text, "Blessed are they who watch at my doors, for if they shall seek me in the morning, they will find me." [108] He would never have maintained such great duty of vigils, except for the blessedness of perfect labor. There was no one who could not see the moist floors on the site where he waged war for the Lord during the night. O how great was that time! Then you would have seen all the others around night after night at cockcrow; you would have seen them everywhere murmuring with deep groans. Now the longer we slumber, the less we are alive, for while we are slaves of sleep we are dead although we live.

CHAPTER 11

11:1. *Paschasius:* You are telling only about the vigils. You are not recalling how great was the kind of man he lived; or you are not daring to unfold what you censure in me.

11:2. *Severus:* I dare by all means, but one should not speak rashly about anyone.

11:3. *Paschasius:* Take care, brother, lest you fall into a characteristic of the comic writers.[109] One cannot distinguish, they say, a free man, "a compliant one," one who "can deal rightly with truth," one who can know anyone or be known by anyone where one "does not live uprightly." Perhaps you do not wish to show how "great you deem him nor has that one dared" to believe you in respect of "what is just" to the abbot. If these matters were so, you could never be silent about him, even if you wished.

11:4. *Severus:* I wish in every way to show what is virtuous about him whom I trusted more than myself. He never hid from me anything about myself. He made himself transparent in order to fashion in me a resemblance to himself. He never relaxed time for himself nor looked back; he committed himself wholly to God and set himself toward those things which are not seen.[110] If with his own hands he heated the wintry dwelling of the brothers, it is clear with what great virtue he anxiously withstood and with what pungency of smoke he was warmed, although thoroughly blackened with pitch. So much indeed was he burned by fire and heat of the furnace that you might see him no longer clothed with flesh but as a certain apparition existing with the breath of soot.

11:5. *Paschasius:* I recall and remember well. Although the Lord proved him as gold in the furnace,[111] He received him at length as a whole burnt offering. He purged himself freely by labors, seeking to endure for God in all respects the evils of the world rather than those things that are sweet. He wasted himself with fasts and forebore even meager food. He cared for all and he was burdened with holy solicitude for the brothers. Infirm guests and brothers he served with zealous obedience. When many avoided his indulgence out of a mood of reverence, he often exclaimed, "You there! Why do you want to make my duty vain and take away the obedience entrusted to me?" At his voice each one soon offered himself pliant in his hands. Fame therefore daily bore him increasingly to ears everywhere and commended him as praiseworthy. What more? Shortly after Antonius died,[112] this distinguished father was presented in his place.[113]

11:6. In the interest of his election, I by direction of the brothers soon secured at the palace of the emperor what many were at that time desiring. In order to conceal himself, he had earlier gone to visit and improve our brothers at that second Corbie which is of the mother's name; which is also a mother itself, but a different one; another, yet the same. Recalled from there, our election quickly seized him. At that time an effort was made by some of our nobles (I clearly perceived the emperor in the background) to persuade me that we could not endure him nor copy the footprints of his life because of his asceticism and his firmness in correction. To that I replied with a laugh, "You there! Don't you know who we are? Do you want to choose the tail instead of the head,[114] as certain are unnaturally accustomed to do? As great as he is, how much more excellent do you think any one of the saints was? Since we can't move back and forth, is it becoming to prefer him who moves behind to him who goes in front?"

11:7. I am sure that he later smilingly reported this conversation to the emperor. In any case, after this discussion, I obtained completely everything that I wished as I wished. So at the emperor's insistence, he, who a short time ago had shunned high office, yielded unwillingly to our prayers.

11:8. *Adeodatus:* I am sure that those who snarl at such a person will think that you should speak more clearly about him, not so enigmatically.

11:9. *Paschasius:* We are not speaking about matters unseen or unknown. Although the title is represented vaguely, the marks of his deeds are revealing. As in the case of painting, those who know how to paint well can often depict the countenance so that it speaks without letters and voice. I have not yet spoken; I am still guarding certain hidden matters. But there will be a day, I believe, when it will be permissible for me to declare openly the facts of the case and to unfold more plainly the most important truths about him. In the meanwhile, however, as even you suggest, "lest anything" be done "to excess," [115] it is advisable to speak more prudently and to lament more copiously, that is, for us who live without him, with whom I reckon it would be better to die. His death has been transmuted into life before the time preferred by us, perhaps lest spite should alter his heart and mind. But it was not thus.

11:10. *Adeodatus:* I truly believe that the word is trustworthy, "He who believes in me, even if he dies, shall live." [116] That one believed not in a perfunctory manner but totally and lovingly. For the faith "which works through love" [117] is the sole faith by which one lives. Because he so lived and because he believed in Him who gives life to the dead, he will not die forever.

11:11. *Paschasius:* For you, too, faith supplies abundantly because you believe this. How much more should one believe that even now he who is fragrant with odor of such great works of virtue already enjoys fruits that never waste away? From the day of his profession he bore in his own body the dying of Christ.[118]

Later, when he was chosen as abbot, he advanced everywhere to the field first as if His standard-bearer in the battle array against most savage foes. For as the warfare changed, the soldier also changed. He who had once borne arms against the Abitrices,[119] an unyielding people, was at length proclaimed even more gloriously to have borne the banner of virtue against the monsters of vice. He who once despised the honors of the world for religion now wears the palm for reward.

CHAPTER 12

12:1. *Adeodatus:* We have learned all those events. I wish you would now tell us how he was converted under Antonius. I wish this in particular for the sake of our brothers dwelling in Saxony —he was of that people [120]—so that they may know fully what great founders of the faith they had.

12:2. *Paschasius:* If I should undertake to relate that, I would not know where to begin, where to turn, or where to proceed. Their life and deeds were so inseparable that you would not find what one of them did without the other, even after I had made them known. Some particular work might be unequal to one or the other by reason of strength, time, or office; yet there was a common longing and one will. You might see them as it were drawing the plow good-naturedly under one yoke in the Lord's tillage and bearing each other's burdens.[121] If they occasionally happened to be apart by some distance or time, you might see one of them searching for the other with sighing and longing, as one ox looks for the other. Neither considered himself entirely present if the other was absent. In fact each of them was mentally where the other one was rather than with himself. Just as an ox, separated from the one with which it is accustomed to draw the plow, indicates a dutiful disposition for the other by constant lowing, so they sighed deeply and longingly for each other. So solicitous were they that they wondered what each other was doing until they came back together.

12:3. Although one of them was older and the other no more

than a youth, their desire was equal. Although one was sturdier in body, the other was more exalted in burning charity. In them was one attention, one purpose, one will. Antonius was indeed sharper in perception, but our old man was broader in understanding and charity. The former was more glowing for justice; the latter, more timely in foresight, more profound in prudence. The former replied quickly and more sharply to each matter, but the latter pondered a longer time, yet promptly, what would be profitable and what would eventuate adversely. Although they were brothers in the flesh and the fullest of brothers in faith and will, yet in manners they seemed different in this respect, namely, the latter manifested himself as an extraordinary father to all, but the former as a student of monastic discipline and a most dear son in all humility.

12:4. *Severus:* No one doubts that they were unique in holiness and religion and most zealous in goodness, although of royal stock. It is no marvel that they who offered themselves as examples to others supported each other with mutual virtues. Wearied with age, our Antonius seemed more slack in labors and cares, but he was nonetheless broader in charity. The other, always more solicitous, supported him zealously with his own holy devotion and humbly fulfilled the cares of government along with his own duties. You might see him as a son attending to everything, displaying respect as a younger one, service as a servant, faithfulness as a very dear brother, and always tender love as a father. As an elder, moreover, he displayed powerful counsel with humility. He had such great patience in all matters that he was moved by no hurtful vexations.

12:5. *Paschasius:* By reason of one necessity you appear to enumerate for us at once the duties of many necessities, so that in one and the same person we grieve to have lost not one person but many. Such great grief requires remembrance since we lost in him what we lost earlier in Antonius. Their brotherly charity and pleasant life not only toward us but toward the entire realm was so conspicuous and resplendent that you might see as it were the two luminaries of heaven shining everywhere. Arsenius was less, I admit, and Antonius was greater, because the latter was a father and the former a son. The latter was older, while the former was keener and nimbler in manners as also younger in age. In neither was there any flattery, but in both model devotion and no disparagement.

12:6. You might not find anything to add to the similarity of their purpose, since one spirit and one faith was in them both, as well as one harmony of peace and a true religion of holiness in all things. Between them you might detect nothing other than charity and devotion which vicissitudes could not change, nor would you recognize any other will toward each other. They had such beautiful quality of manners that if one excelled in any virtue there was a single concord of honor toward each other and a single balance of virtue. What each had you would judge common to both. One might be called a half of the other, as indeed Arsenius was deemed the complement of Antonius. So it was, beloved, that as with one mind, so with one devotion they sowed seeds of a new plantation in Saxony. With the Lord's favor they built from the ground up monasteries of both sexes.[122]

CHAPTER 13

13:1. *Adeodatus:* I wonder if you want to make them equal since it was not Arsenius but Antonius who, when he was the shepherd of this place, built when there was an opportunity to build something. Arsenius was simply one of many, although more pleasing in grace than his brother, deeper in counsel, quicker in will, stronger in help, more thoroughly moved by religion. And so, however much they loved each other, and however much each wished his labor to be the other's recompense, nevertheless to Antonius rightly belongs the reward of work by whose labors what accomplishments were made were set apart. For never did one of them will what was just and holy without the other doing it. By right, therefore, he to whom the power of accomplishment belonged is set apart, although the laborious toil was common.

13:2. *Paschasius:* The more externally one looks in human judgment, the more frequently fame evokes praise among the masses. But the divine Arbiter discerns inwardly the grace which He has given to each one and thereafter the labor which each one expends. But since there was only one will among them and each depended on the will of the other, it was obvious to all that, when words proceeded from the mouth, it was first divinely inspired in Arsenius. It was particularly obvious when an opportunity arose, namely, when certain of his fellow countrymen came to us in conversion and gave us their own lands where a monastery might be erected. Arsenius glowed with love toward God and holy religion, toward his tribal kinsmen and his fatherland. Consequently he strove more consistently and more often to persuade the illustrious abbot of the same name as the older man [123] to expend labor for this work and to furnish the cost. By that time Arsenius was already the one on whom the care of our monastic household as well as attention to hospitality rested. When these matters had been discussed, the abbot made his own the prayer and will of our Arsenius. And in such manner the virtuous work was undertaken and happily rendered until the old Antonius was returned from exile and restored to favor.

13:3. When the latter returned, the will of Arsenius soon became that of the old man. You might think that the son had given birth to a distinguished father by this grace. Abounding encouragement on the part of each made one the intention of both and one the mark of desire for those to whom God had given a common will or its opposite. They had always been undivided when neither wished to live without the other, when both had one disposition of mind, one desire, and one care for holy religion. The prudence of their sons, especially those whom their faith has equally begotten and their charity has equally dedicated to God in this grace, may therefore inquire whether a greater reward ought to go to anyone but him who with persistent exhortation made others seek this first after God and then compelled them to perform. He supported them by his own strongest help rather than by their own shoulders. He strengthened them more solicitously by his own counsel. With every ability, every art, every zeal, he also did this in matters before Caesar, before dignitaries of the entire realm, and before all whom he could. He did so that the laborious work which had been undertaken at his urging might be brought to completion.

CHAPTER 14

14:1. *Severus:* What you have said was not concealed from us.
With these eyes we have clearly perceived and seen all the things
that he did. Many indeed cried out that he pillaged the goods of
our monastery to enrich those places at any expense. But it is part
of his praise that without offending good people he enriched those
places from the goods of all, made them opulent with ample supplies, yet did not diminish ours very much. He governed the household of his brother and soon displayed in himself the office of
abbot—which was destined to come to pass. Inwardly he maintained the solace and form of holy religion; outwardly, however,
he exhibited the shield and rampart of defense and the glory of
complete honor. He soon bore with the father, as I have said, care
of the monastery, as if he were a judge in planning and an arranger
of matters, having care of everything.

14:2. He was, moreover, an anxious overseer of souls lest in
some way our old man displease God; so he labored to please all.
He was a guardian against grief and a staff for the old age [124] of
the saintly elder man. He was also a stimulus of all our virtues. The
holy old man took great joy in him and in turn wished him the joy
of flourishing grace, all the while illuminating him with holy and
virtuous admonitions. You might observe them here and there
mutually refreshing and advancing each other in all things. Perhaps
Paschasius knows all these things better, these things that they did
as they did them. He should, for he was their special companion
and indeed a third one with them in every matter.

CHAPTER 15

15:1. *Paschasius:* I surely agree with what you are adding, especially how they jointly built monasteries of both sexes among the
aforesaid people. How great was their devotion and burning
charity! How strong was their humility and virtuous exaltation!
They sought to demonstrate in themselves the form of holy religion and an example of perfection, so that in days to come their

disciples following in monastic discipline might have what they ought to emulate. For the Lord, "the teacher of truth," [125] says, "Every disciple will be perfect if he is as his master." [126] These men have, therefore, truly become imitators of Christ, that placed on a sure foundation the future flock may be built up in the Lord. Thus the roof was not erected without squareness of virtues and firmness of faith, nor were the foundations laid without a roof of highest perfection. Since, therefore, they offered themselves to be emulated, they should be followed before all others and their admonitions and example should be kept. So what was laid on a firm foundation will not totter at the roof. So what was in the best way planted as seed will not sprout badly.

15:2. Let our lamentation, then, for our lost fathers be common, for our gain was common since we lived with them under such discipline. The mind cannot be unaffected in repeating their activities and in enumerating their virtues. Yet in that very perturbation and grief of mind we are refreshed, and the mood of that time is renewed, especially for those of us who saw them. As for me, who was with them when their activities began, it is "with bowed head" [127] that I look upon their absence as always present. I recall when they went on a journey, when they were here, when they were disposing of particular matters, when they were in counsel, when they were chatting with each other. With my eyes I drank in their grace; with my ears I listened [128] to the discussions they propounded and caught up [129] the words they spoke. But if it is a joy of mind now to look back [130] upon those events, how great, dearly beloved, do you think was the grace then, how great the happiness, how blessed the times, when I saw them meditating on such distinguished plans? I cannot even repeat how much I silently marveled at their virtues, how often I congratulated myself that the Lord had given such patrons, in whose fellowship I, though unworthy, was indeed a third. Not by merit or by grace or by honor of any dignity, but only by their condescension, was I present with them, and even then only as observer and listener.

15:3. Clinging to them modestly enough, I did not despair the efficacy of any simplicity and innocence. When I observed their foresight, I greatly marveled at the dove-like simplicity [131] in them; and if I should look back at their simplicity, there was almost no spirit in me to marvel at their foresight. They always united simplicity with their marvelous virtues, and what they said in words wisely agreed with their example. What both could scarcely do at once, one of them completed alone. If occasionally one did something without the other, it was as though you were observing both, so habitual was their practice of doing things at the same time. Occasionally one might display a flank uncovered, but even so he presaged in manners and duty the disposition of the other. Thus you marveled at the singleness of mind in them, one holy and unbreakable grace, not indeed of body but of vigorous mind, one purpose, one unassuming modesty of contemplation. Although at work they stretched the lines by hand and measured by reed and arranged both places whereby separate places might be made, it seemed that they were measuring the structure according to Ezekiel, inclining toward the south [132] that they might locate both the foundation and the roof in heaven. When they raised their steps equally, they lifted up their countenance and eyes thither that you might approve their committing to God in those heavens whatever they set in order on earth and then to their locating the bases of the foundation which the roofs of others scarcely reach.

15:4. *Adeodatus:* After the manner of the Apostle Thomas, I now see.[133] They set the foundations of places and the structure of houses which would never grow old. They built workshops and erected roofs which would never fall down. I do not believe that they would have attempted those things in so distant a region if it had not seemed to them that they might establish on earth a heavenly dwelling place among those where the new light of Christ had recently shown through the Holy Spirit. Thus that nation might be able to say in spirit with John, "We have seen the new Jerusalem happily descending from the heavens to our places, adorned in each sex with its own jewels." [134] From these very same places, therefore, it is proclaimed that among the same people are these divine camps with their twinborn nurslings dedicated to the Lord.

CHAPTER 16

16:1. *Severus:* All your assertions are true, but I would still like to know what our Arsenius did more than any of us who were fellow workers with the saintly old man, especially when he had no

more time or capacity than his other fellow workers. We must beware not to attribute to him something more than is fitting, for
truth restrains itself. Perhaps such great will was divinely inspired
in him, so that afterward he had a common will with his brothers: a
common ability or inability to do something common and to obey
in individual matters.

16:2. *Paschasius:* First, he had, as you declare, this grace in the
work, namely, prerogative of merits. Before all others he conceived
these matters in his mind. Then, as they became clear, he worked
more because he willed more than others. In particular, his prior
will begot the wills of others in this business. He incited, he nourished with prudent counsel, with prayers, with persistent persuasion. Antonius indeed had power, pre-eminent wisdom for accom-
plishing, and great virtue in completing. Yet in Arsenius was seen a
finer grace, however common. Whatever the former did or desired, the whole by God's grace took its rise from, as it was nourished by, the latter. And not only what the former wished and did,
but also whatever others evinced by their suffrages, as, for example, the very delightful, rich, and fertile place where the monastery
was dedicated and all such things with which the place is surrounded. No one is, therefore, unaware of our brother whose heritage it would have been,[135] which he yielded in life to no other
person, not even to the king. But by divine conviction he was constrained by Arsenius, whom he could not gainsay, for from early
life he was most beloved and most intimate. Impelled, therefore, by
Arsenius' prayers and advice, he freely gave to God whatever he
dearly possessed on earth. Such grace is for that reason rightly attributed to Arsenius, who was able to obtain a place designated of
old by the Lord as suitable for this work. No other mortal, I suppose, could have done that.

16:3. Among the aforementioned people, he was beloved and
famous in an immeasurable degree. There was an interesting
demonstration when Antonius came to a certain assembly not far
from that place. A multitude had gathered to see them. After we
had been honorably received, everyone began to direct attention to
our Arsenius and to surround him lovingly and admiringly. Their
joy and desire might have impelled them to kidnap him from us.
None of them looked back at Antonius, although he was the one
who had power and although we all supported him on both sides

and to the limit of our strength venerated him as master. Even so, no one looked closely at us or inquired who he was. The latter, humbly grateful that they ignored us and humbly rejoicing at the reception of his brother, thereupon turned to me and smilingly said, "Brother, we can withdraw, for no one here cares for us or gives heed to anyone else." So after the two had been formally received and all else had been forgotten, we gladly returned alone to the appointed place.

16:4. I have introduced this incident that noble sons may know what kind of founders they had. In all respects they thought humbly of themselves and they were moved by no favors of the world, as is usual of others. The latter was not confounded by shame nor was the former made arrogant by honor. The popular reception and fame of the younger were joy and gladness to the elder one. Arsenius was pleasing to all and beloved of all, but even more he was worthy of love and acceptance. No one could be more outstanding in humility unless he had wanted to match their deeds. Although each was of pre-eminent worldly rank, they vied in turn that either of them might be found humbler. Hence it was that Antonius, albeit abbot and master, devoted such great respect upon the son and younger brother as one might wish to measure out to an equal. On the other hand, how great was the diligence which the younger displayed that he might not be anticipated by anyone in compliance, in regard for due honor, in care and solicitude, in every service, in speech and dress, and even in pace.

16:5. Let someone dare to ask why no one can emulate him! As one example among many, I will now indicate the profound abjection he demonstrated. He was very abstemious even with the cheapest food, and he stated that he sought to be content with the clothes of his fatherland. He declared that it was not worthy for a monk, who ought to be content with cheaper things according to the custom of the province in which he lived, to clothe himself with more elegant clothes or have more sumptuous foods than fellow provincials among whom he lived. He therefore ordered prepared for himself shoes after the mode of the land (they call them *ruhilingi*). And he would have worn them if he had not been discreetly forbidden by the abbot.

16:6. I wonder, however, why Arsenius, who (if I may lawfully say this) can be deemed prophetic, wanted to be so discreet.

On one occasion during a journey he allowed no provision to be made at night for shelter against rain, as travelers are wont to do, nor did he permit us to erect a tent for him day or night. Drenched we lay down upon the ground to rest, and according to a statement which someone makes, "the grass gave us wholesome slumbers." [136] For himself and me the blessed father provided the singularly adequate deep furrows of the field, very full as is usual in that land, where he ordered me to spread our bed. Both sides supported us with beautiful bedposts as we traveled. The saddle of a horse placed in the middle furnished one Alp at the head for me and another for him. Nothing else did we have except what we had above and below in the daytime. This was the only mattress for a bed, a sufficiently honorable vanity!

16:7. *Severus:* This does not seem as prophetic to me as it does to you. When Jacob was going with great difficulty to purchase a wife, he is said to have had on the journey nothing other than a stone at his head [137] and to have carried with him no luxury other than a staff.[138] Arsenius was going to espouse a virgin to one man, Christ the Lord, and to exhibit a chaste wife. Why is it, therefore, surprising that he was supported by no dignities, equipped with no provision? He ought to have foreshown in himself and in us the whole story, namely, to what extent he wanted to preserve the bride whom he was leading to Christ. Hence he should always pursue most holy poverty rather than delights of the world and embrace the hard and harsh difficulties by which Christ is fully approached. Our holy father should himself be an example to be imitated not only in this respect but also in everything with which Christ's religion is entrusted. But you perhaps call attention to such matters because it is a rare person who exhibits himself in that manner. Most people pursue all the pomps of the world. Arsenius showed far greater examples of virtue for his sons than those merely on the occasion of the journey which you have related.

CHAPTER 17

17:1. *Paschasius:* What if by reviewing their functions, by recounting their virtues, I shall devote my soul? The recollection itself, I believe, will renew our griefs, but the memory is a delight of mind and an incitement to virtue. To recall is a sweet grace. A holy remembrance is pleasanter and happier than any enjoyment of absent pleasures. This is particularly true at the present moment when there is no happiness without sadness, no sweetness without bitterness, no honor without soiling, no mental enjoyment without sorrow. For wherever there is distress, there are anguish and sighing.[139] Daily, no, hourly are evils everywhere heard of and nothing but confusion is reported. Because they were men of virtue, those two could not leave us completely despondent, although evils were already increasing. They comforted us with their own words, equipped us with their examples, strengthened us with their advice, and nourished us with their holy teachings. Today, therefore, they still remain with us and they will ever remain with us, if we are true imitators of them and lovers of their virtues.

17:2. If we truly love them, we have already undertaken not to remain here complacently, but we have become pilgrims at least in desire and our portion is better. For never are we whole in ourselves, if we loved them truly. But we are whole only in them because they are the head in which our greater part existed. And because each of them lives in Christ, it is fitting for us to undertake the pilgrimage thither where there is a totality of everything and the portion of each. Hence the remembrance of them is more pleasant than all riches and dearer now than all good things. In it is all our enjoyment. Before they left us, they sought to transplant all their possessions so that they might lift us upward whom as infants they had nourished in Christ. How fitting it is that even there they are still with the sons whom they begot to flourish as lilies in heavenly places and as cedars of Lebanon in highest firmament!

CHAPTER 18

18:1. *Severus:* Rome was built in one manner by two brothers; new Rome was built in another manner from our name. The former was erected carnally in the earth; the latter, to be spiritually enlarged in heaven. The former was built to subdue nations under its dominion; the latter, to extricate its own from the world. The former was constructed to grow in wealth and in abundance of riches; the latter, to have its foundation in heaven, rich with blessed poverty. The former, founded in blood, increased in wealth by bloody wars; the latter, loving spiritually the poverty of the present life, grew rich in heavenly matters.[140]

18:2. *Paschasius:* It seems to me that you, who used to correct others severely,[141] are creating mischief in your fashion. Perhaps you are looking upon them whom the two brothers with single mind established to grow and increase in riches in heaven. Already you think they are violating their precepts and mandates, their adequately cautious warnings. You think they are growing in worldly affairs, abounding in delights, enriching themselves with honors and ostentations of the age. Otherwise it would be superfluous for me to mention the two structures except that the earthly one was built in blood, but this one, dedicated by them to the Lord, was erected according to the passage in Ezekiel, inclining toward the south,[142] with the same measure upon the same foundations, with the same breadth and length, with the same number of gates and windows, and with no need for any increase. For this purpose these two notables placed it toward the north of the city as foundation for the nations along with its towers and ramparts. They expressly warned three things: not to rejoice in being enriched, not to seek for the wealth of the world to set their hearts on it, but to flee completely delights and pleasures as if they were poison. They feared that, if they became pleased with honors (even for the sake of religion) and proud ambition, they might become foolish and thus perish into nothingness.

18:3. We have observed in the Gauls that many churches once well established have fallen away from religion. These men, therefore, taught by such examples, forewarned their sons, not to abound in human vanities by which they might be enslaved to the world, but to be poor in spirit, humble and meek, gentle and merciful, ever hungering for uprightness.[143] Thus everyone would wish them well because of their purity of heart; would think well of them, not envying because of possessions and felicity; and would not seek to oppress them by slavery to the age. By God's favor everyone still proclaims good concerning them, still deems well of them. They are in truth still remarkable and famous for their virtue and probity of life. For upon such sons the odor of our two abbots is still fragrant, their virtues flourish, praise is raised on high, religion is magnified, and surpassing nobility is proclaimed. Their benediction still flowers in their sons; the highest worth of life is entrusted; the richest fruit of merit increases; and luminous grace sprouts and grows high.

CHAPTER 19

19:1. *Severus:* Whatever their virtues everywhere highly extolled, it would be praiseworthy, brothers, if the properties solemnly confided to our monastery and all other matters assembled for us had been transferred by law to this monastery. They should have sought for the brothers to live on their own property. He is a rare person who does not wish to enrich the place over which he presides, that he may be able to rule more broadly with pride of power even though under the cloak of religion. But these, on the contrary, not only declined to seek as much property as possible, but also disposed of things assembled here and returned them freely to the use of the brothers so they could not belong to us.

19:2. *Paschasius:* What they taught by words, they did that they might confirm by examples. They warned us as well as themselves not to receive unnecessary things and not to go about to procure full means as though for the sake of God's religion.[144] We should set a limit to the possessions of the church lest, as the prophet warns, they themselves should stretch forth a finger to join field to field to the boundary without restriction of desire.[145] You may consider this free act unjust, but it was in fact more fruitful and honorable. It was more just and useful for them to serve the Lord freely in usages of the monastery than by right to heredity to rule us unseasonably and superfluously. An inheritance is shown to serve the Lord of His church when it is expended with charity for the use of His servant in religion. The gift of grace is greatly enriched when from one root of perfect love two convents of monastic discipline are doubled.

CHAPTER 20

20:1. *Adeodatus:* It would be enough that you are thus far revealing both equally, one with his virtue of labor, the other with his intensity of mind. But since we have decided in this treatise to pursue with lamentation Arsenius who labored far more fully in these matters, he alone should be graced with our tears. If he had not departed hence so quickly, he who demonstrated in all matters contempt for the world, he might perhaps have made citizens of heaven those brothers of whom we speak. He might have made them even despise themselves for the faith as he had first despised himself. He might have by the grace of charity brought back together the hearts of all so that none would strain himself beyond the standard and measure of monastic discipline toward those disciplines that are outside.

20:2. He clearly indicated this in the prelate whom he advanced to his place until he should return,[146] that is, when, driven out again so quickly, he fled to Italy. We have learned for certain that he presided there only a short while before he learned to think humbly of himself. He learned not to be inflated because of lineage, not to embrace delights, not to sport with trifles and vanities of the age, not to run after affairs of the world. You might have seen rising here and there buildings of a heavenly fatherland according to standards of the city which I mentioned earlier, that city which always inclines toward the south,[147] which is measured by heavenly measures, which is not spread through the world by human means. You might have seen today in that place towers and fortresses of the faith humbly stretching toward the skies. You might have seen all kinds of virtues rising upward and the place being expanded with possessions, but not for pride and arrogance. Today his odor permeates that place; his virtues grow green; teaching of morals thrives; nobility of life remains; gravity is admired; charity is praised; and honor of discipline in all things is proclaimed.

20:3. Thus from the daughter's fruitfulness, the glorious mother's fame is announced everywhere and the offspring's richness, spread here and there, increases through everyone. These, therefore, brothers, are the celebrations of our Arsenius; these are the distinctions of his labor and the badges of his virtues. While ages remain, the religion of the churches will be his. His praises and the fame of his good life never fail from the mouth of men. Not unjustly in this true, for fruit will abound in double seed, which the praise of the sower increases again at the harvest and through the years the harvest is multiplied more and more.

20:4. So is confirmed that statement of the true God, "Whoever will abandon everything that he possesses for my name's sake will receive a hundredfold and will gain eternal life." [148] This one abandoned many things, but he achieved greater things in the world when by loving the church he made his own the goods of the church. He abandoned innumerable things when he clearly trampled upon himself and upon all the lusts of the present life. He abandoned all things when he lay himself so low that we saw him daily wearied with labors, suffering from numberless vigils, his body ceaselessly pained by fasts and abstinence. You might see, with the prophet David, his skin clinging to his bones and the strength of his flesh perenially wasting away with too much fasting.[149] So at last, clothed with Christ's poverty, he, who for religion's sake despised the accustomed honors of the world, was rightfully prominent, fortunate, and blessed. But Severus, who did much more with him, is witness how vigorous he was toward the virtue of works that the brothers might go forward by example.

CHAPTER 21

21:1. *Severus:* "With this law I bind my faith" [150] that I will be silent about many things I know of him and I will fix memory best. When the time shall come and the torches of hostility have burned low, I may set forth fully and openly to those who wish to hear. If anyone now relates anything about him publicly either false or vain or feigned, it is more pleasing. For that reason, as Allabigus admits, "I first truly found this way." There is, you know, "a class of men who wish themselves to be first in every respect," although they are not. "Them I emulate; with them I compare my-

self, so that spontaneously they may laugh at me and I at them." [151]
Because such persons think that they are disparaged when they
hear others praised, there now exists no opportunity of speaking
about good men.

21:2. *Paschasius:* Good Jesus! "In what respect does one man
surpass another?" [152] When one has lost touch with reality, let
him by no means dare speak what he knows. Perhaps "all known
friends" and fellow soldiers "have deserted" [153] him so that none
may dare speak of him.

21:3. *Adeodatus:* What I hear, Paschasius, is frightening, that
to secure the approval of evil ones good persons dare not emulate. I
pray for you to gain strength. Do so that you may dare. If it can be
done, recall Severus so that he will not fear too much and so that
he may not be deceived by vain hope and thus "waste the good" [154]
accounts that he has learned.

21:4. *Severus:* Shall I fail to praise him whom I long for day
and night, whom I think about, whom I admire, and to see whose
appearance is to be refreshed? When I recall him, I am more
sharply inflamed with love. When I praise him, I become a partaker
of truth. Shall I refrain from praising this one among the upright?
Even among those by whose grudges he is bespattered, he is proven
incontestably praiseworthy. For he wears the palm of praise even if
like holy Jeremiah he is challenged by those who speak falsely in
the heart.[155] Not only the entire congregation over which he presided, but also the familiar knowledge of many more monks, is witness that as prelate he was without exception the lord of delinquent
ones and abbot of us all.

21:5. Abbot indeed he was, because as father of all, he displayed himself with pious disposition, showing toward each one a
heart of charity filled with the dew of Christ. Lord indeed he was,
because unlike those who hold pastoral care lightly, he indulged no
one to be wantonly slothful. As observer of all he excelled each in
manner of life, yet so that he might draw lagging ones with his encouragement and so that he might with Christ lift up the bad-
smelling ones and carry them on the shoulders of his virtues. He
left no one lukewarm whom he did not heat with poultices, no one
whom he did not spice with the salt of wisdom, no one whom he
did not cure of chicanery, if condition of the disease permitted and

the grace of Christ cooperated. Diligently he accomplished the functions of a physician to cure the wounds of sin. He furnished an example of life to persuade virtues and also demonstrated faithfulness of warning "in season out of season." [156]

21:6. In all matters he maintained one charity and one discipline, neglecting nothing, counting nothing of small worth which might tend toward salvation of the souls committed to him. I wish now that Paschasius would pursue other details, although he always followed him more in agreement of counsel than in example of works. Of course he says that I am now the flatterer, but he was everywhere with him, an irremovable companion.

21:7. *Paschasius:* "I have never known a man craftier" [157] than you. Although you have not so professed, are you not in some manner shunning the very things that you wished to be undertaken in this deliberation? Yet I will not keep silence about that which everyone knows. I have never seen anyone like him in government. He glowed with greatest zeal of virtue; everywhere tirelessly he flourished with holy anxiety; whether absent or present he tended the flock entrusted to him; he thought of nothing so much as how he would render account for each one before Christ's tribunal. He therefore very often admonished everyone in general and in particular about the choice of free will and the power of one's body so that none of ours who had professed monastic discipline should pursue his own will. "Otherwise," he was accustomed to say, "how shall I render account for each one unless he relinquishes to me the power of his body and the function of his will? If he should keep his own power of will, he should know that he must render an account, not only for his words, thoughts, or deeds, but also for the fact that contrary to monastic law which he professed he retained his own power or will. Certainly I shall be free," he said, "insofar as power not due to me remains unyielded, and one's choice of his own will becomes his own responsibility. Yet whatever I can, I will weigh out for charity so that I shall be free of power and of will lest I be deceived by ostensible power or misled by will of eager pursuit."

21:8. Good Jesus, how ceaselessly beset he was by great care for the sheep and anxiety for souls! Now he generally instructed all, now especially warned each, marking out this one by threats, that one by appealing teaching. As the prophet says, "I will bridle you with my praise," [158] he dealt with one as if recalling him with flattery and praise. Another he repressed with reproaches. But all he ever stimulated with his own examples. His words were, as I have said, "like nails fastened on high." [159] When he addressed everyone in chapter, it seemed to each as if he spoke especially to him. He left nothing untouched, nothing undiscussed, from all the texture of the *Rule.* If he found anything everyone was neglectful in practicing, he set before them many persuasive words and commended them not to ignore a divine precept no matter how small it might seem. If anyone departed from all the words of the *Holy Rule* and would not in any respect make amends, he censured that one openly, the other one secretly, and seasoned them with the salt of doctrine. For he deemed nothing to be of little value.

21:9. Since he considered the salvation of souls "before and above everything else," [160] he judged even the least matters to be supreme and indeed pre-eminent. Every one of his sermons was therefore seasoned with salt. He cured wounds lest the flock perish with deadly impulses or he implanted virtue in minds to guard the health of souls. The sheep entrusted to him might thus always lie down in green grasses near the fountains of waters [161] and thereby grow richer and fatter. He also incited certain ones with bodily benefits that they might maintain the law of the *Rule* and so fulfil Christ's commands.

21:10. *Severus:* A certain one says that there never was anyone with reason well balanced against life, to whom wealth, age, custom may bring nothing new, and may warn that you do not know what you thought you knew,[162] and that what you might consider primary for yourself in actual experience you will reject because it turns out now as something too grievous for us. For in a very short period of time we have lost the harsh life we formerly lived with him. We therefore already judge the fact itself with ease; and according to Solomon's Proverbs, nothing is better for a man than to abound in delights and to enjoy his own labors for himself.[163] It is now quite easy to know when someone lives his life in leisure and banquets: he is indulgent to himself and happy in excess of passion, daring to offend no one accused for the sake of truth, accustomed to speak against no one, to smile upon all, to contradict no one, to live for himself, to spend for himself.

21:11. Behold, all bless him, love him, and glorify him. But they are accustomed to point out how rustic we are, how savage, how gloomy, how grim, how niggardly, how slanderous of others. Although we strive [164] to please such people, all we do is grind away life, age, in seeking to do so. In the meanwhile we receive from them animosity as fruit of our labor, and they take possession of our goods. Others love and cherish them while they shun us and wish for such ones to flourish. They trust their own plans to them; they commend their own vows among them. They wait for our death and promise that they will be free, if we cease to blame those matters and burden them with no duties. If, therefore, we praise Arsenius, they think that they are themselves reproved.[165]

CHAPTER 22

22:1. *Paschasius:* "Come, come, let us now try," if possible, "to say something courteously and do something kindly." Let us seek "to be loved" again by our own and to commend to later ones matters that are worthy of praise. Let us also attempt "to soften things by giving, yielding," [166] persuading, caressing them to love the good although they may not be able or willing to emulate it and also not to despise the truth we set forth. Do you not recollect what our Arsenius would do when one of ours became enraged with envy at the preferment of another? How he would stare at himself covered with the cheapest winter wool, then at the one preferred?

22:2. *Severus:* I recollect clearly and remember well enough, since he soon found an antidote out of his own lowliness. Although rage was already vanishing, three days later the father clothed himself in a fine cowl of best weaving and came to meet the brother. He fell upon his neck and kissed him. Then he laid aside his own cowl and clothed the brother with it, dressing himself with the other's cowl. Thereupon the brother, adorned with flatteries, returned to himself quickly and sensibly. Thenceforward the father boasted of his own, and he was delighted with the other's, because he had found a remedy for a wound, bringing increased merit for himself and sanity to the brother. Many days he wore that garment as a challenge to our pride, for we were sometimes excited with a costly habit when it would have befitted us to be abject. Thus he emulated that greatest father and householder who ran to meet his returning son and caused him to be clothed with the first vesture, so that charity might incite him to love whom luxury had driven into exile.[167] Therein have we observed three elements: remedial action for a brother, enrichment of the father, and an example of religion for us all. But we are not persons of that kind; we should be deeply grieved. For while we are delighted by greater elegancies, we are disdained by secular people who know what we ought to be.

CHAPTER 23

23:1. *Adeodatus:* He was of such great charity and such great holiness that I wonder why some people insist that he was austere or harsh. They are cutting the tip of the hem from the edge of the cloak, for in the other virtues of his life they praise him to the skies.

23:2. *Paschasius:* Please do not marvel at what you recall from the Gospel. The lazy servant calls the master harsh not because he is harsh. The lazy servant works to defame the master because he himself is useless and his faults oppress him. Such ones who call him harsh should return to a good conscience. For they but increase severer scourgings for themselves and amass vindication for him. Even if the master is said to gather where he has not scattered, he has exacted with usury where he has not sown.[168] Why do you suppose that he was austere when he was pious and mild, unless lazy, slothful ones deem that very virtue severe? Those who do not wish to follow prove themselves indolent. They call him harsh who lightly (if at all) restrained vices and incited to virtues by any means other than by his own example. If he seemed harsh, the torments of the deceiver will be harsher, for Arsenius blamed nothing but vices and cultivated virtues, lest he should bring back empty handed the talent confided to him.[169] But if Jeremiah had been in charge of such persons, he would no doubt have been blamed as harsher, since the Lord made his countenance harsher than their countenance.[170]

23:3. Indulgence always judges men of virtue as harsh and rude. Arsenius, however, was kind and pious, who always indulged others far more than himself. Yet he either restrained vices or cut them off completely at the beginning. If, therefore, he was harsh, it was toward those who were neither turned away from their efforts by punishment nor stirred by rewards; it was toward those whose hearts had become so insensible that they felt neither his nor Christ's admonitions. With them fear rather than love had succeeded. For it is written, "The beginning of wisdom is fear of the Lord." [171] To make us Christ's sons by adoption, Arsenius acted now with threats, now with blows, now with benefits, now with flattering persuasions. He cared for each with zeal and shrewdness that none might be misled by craft of the devil and perish. Did you not observe what he did about a brother who was longing to depart, a brother who was destitute of reason, who was unwilling to suffer, who was allowing his faults to drive away what he had yielded?

CHAPTER 24

24:1. *Severus:* We have observed quite clearly. Indeed together with him we constrained that brother not to leave here to be rebarbarized. We even stationed soldiers at the gate to deter him. Compelled therefore by fear, that one returned within and, drenched with tears, fell prostrate at Arsenius's feet.

24:2. *Paschasius:* I am happy that you recall. And I am joyful beyond measure that the one of whom we are speaking is, I think, making progress toward the virtues, maintaining above all the moderation of the more perfect life. Good Jesus, how great was the joy at that time! It was as if you saw a prodigal son returning and a father exulting.[172] The latter was weeping for joy and the son was weeping since he had already been tamed. Even I bellowed when I saw them weeping, and at the same time I mingled many tears with theirs, giving thanks to God as if we had received him from the dead. Such then was the austerity of the abbot! Such the bowels of his coldness! Such his will! Such his disposition! But now how wretched are we to whom freedom to sin is granted! If no one then sinned with impunity, yet recurring falls rose up,[173] how much more now when we are flattered for our evils.

CHAPTER 25

25:1. *Adeodatus:* As I see it, Arsenius was of perfect charity, who loved his own in the same manner in which Christ loved.[174] What is found in divine disciplines he accomplished in deeds. But they say that he was not sufficiently conformed and that he was less loved in return and less visited by many.

25:2. *Paschasius:* I often mentioned those words to him, although I knew that he had done everything for almost everyone. He replied not with excuses, as certain ones are accustomed to do, but with deepest humility that he did not have such breadth of heart (as great as the sand of the sea) to do everything. "To whom do you want me to be conformed? To the sluggish or depraved? To the boastful and facetious? Surely not! Have you not read the Apostle, 'Do not be conformed to this world, but be reformed in newness of your disposition'?"[175] With such examples he lifted himself upward toward the virtues by attempting the peak, so that lightness of mind might not destroy what the gravity of charity offered inwardly to the Lord.

25:3. My brother and sons, I marvel why devotees of wantonness and pleasure want the more perfect ones to be conformed to them, when they ought rather to pass over to the pattern of virtue. They will not become sons of adoption in any manner other than by being foreknown and predestined to become like the image of God's Son. Arsenius was foreknown and predestined to this pattern. Consequently he did not adapt himself to childish sports. Occasionally, while standing on a high rock, he might with pleasantries urge boys "swimming far apart"[176] to come to shore at close quarters. Although what he said provoked a little laughter, yet it was with gravity, so that rich virtue might not be annulled, but also that nursing infancy, deprived of its rattles, might strive for more perfect things if wheedled by fatherly hearts. None believed the smiling countenance before him if he did not receive him with gravity. As Job said, "Even though he laughed at them, they did not believe him." [177]

25:4. Although he relaxed gravity of speech, "the light of his countenance did not fall to earth." [178] He acted subtly in order to incite to zeal for virtue those in conversation with him. When they listened to him, they waited for his opinion and they were silent, paying attention to his counsel.[179] Although he was far inferior to Job in virtues, yet the listening ear blessed him and the discerning eye bore witness that he set free the poor man crying aloud and the orphan who had no helper. The blessing of one about to die came upon him, since from childhood he was clothed with uprightness as with a garment.[180] He also carefully investigated a case he did not know.[181] Let us ask Chremes what he did in decisions or in disposition of properties and in exercise of justice when he was preceptor of the august Caesar beyond the Pennine Alps.[182]

CHAPTER 26

26:1. *Chremes:* I hesitate to praise a man lest I be thought to be agreeable simply by assenting rather than by presenting what I have about him. Yet I would not remain entirely silent about him: how great a seeker for truth, how prompt in sentiment, how vigorous against the highest judges of wickedness, how effective in character against those who are corrupted by bribes. I will relate one event out of many,[183] by which I have learned nothing more unfairly at this time.

26:2. A certain noble widow entrusted her possessions and herself to a justiciar as her defender. By instrument of surrender she also assigned him almost half of her possessions so that the rest would remain safe for her. Soon he craftily laid hold on absolutely all the deed for himself and produced witnesses. When the woman wanted to return to her properties and make use of her possessions, there were guards to prevent her from entering her own lands, claiming that she had assigned everything to her defender. There is a joke that he defends everything who leaves nothing for the owner.[184]

26:3. The unhappy widow, bereft of her properties, approached the emperor. By imperial documents he commended her to a certain bishop and other judges of the land. They were enjoined to make careful investigation of her case and reach a true judgment. "Each of them, however, had turned aside after his own greed," so that "the plight" of widows "did not interest" them.[185] They indeed contrived a lie for themselves and made common cause with the aforesaid witnesses. As a result people had no insight into such matters and everyone, even Christ's priests, practiced guile.

26:4. When the case was brought to a conclusion, the widow was driven from her properties. The defender received from the elders of the people assurance that there would be no further dispute about the lands. But the widow, although plagued by many ills and grievous distress and exhausted by her long journey through harsh heights of the Alps, went on foot to the Gauls. Immediately she began to besiege the king with her wailing. The king, deeply moved by her grave plaints and woes, entrusted her to our Arsenius. The latter was then dispatched by the father as a trustworthy kinsman to be with his imperial son for the sake of stabilizing and governing the realm. Sending her ahead, he ordered her to return to her properties until he came back to that country, at which time she could present herself before him with her witnesses.

26:5. When news of this action had been broadcast, all Italy trembled. The justiciar turned to crafty and fraudulent arguments and began to contrive plots for the woman's death. For he saw one coming whom he did not deem corruptible by bribes. In the past he had been successful in softening the minds of all and inveigling them into his own greedy clutches, because almost everyone "pursues rewards and loves gifts." [186] But since nothing in Arsenius could move toward impiety, the justiciar turned to frauds and deeds of iniquity. When he was enjoined to restore at least some of the properties that he had unjustly and guilefully stolen, he knew that he was trapped. Surreptitiously he sent three of his men along a certain road to kill her secretly.

26:6. With three in the plot, however, it did not seem safe enough for complete silence. He thereupon added crime to crime so that if perchance they were questioned they might not lay bare the villainy. As they were placed long distances apart from each other, he ordered one of them to murder the other two so that there would be no one on the face of the earth to disclose the innocent blood shed by guile. The wretch deemed of no importance what the divine Judge might think, provided he could evade human judgment. But our Arsenius, inflamed with zeal for God, employed many arguments that what was obvious should not lay hidden in secret. But he by whom the deed was done could not be held either by judgment or by witnesses.

26:7. In the meanwhile, one of them was discovered concealed in a certain underground cavern. A difficult conjecture emerged from this development. The man in whose cave he was found was held responsible, but when the other incriminated the one by whose instigation he had arranged the matter, neither of them could be convinced by the other. What sorrow, then, or what grief, do you think, was in the mind of Arsenius? O Lord Jesus, You who once heard the blood of Abel the just crying from the ground,[187] You have seen what devout prayers, how many tears, he would pour out before You, that You might indeed declare by which one it was shed. But all Italy and its senators, corrupted by bribes, disputed and acted against him, lest he find the responsible person, one who was very well known to all as a ravisher and murderer. Even You, "O God, who search the hearts and reins," [188] although You know all things, even You treated your athlete with much jealousy; You did not reveal to him but to their accomplices what was clear to most people.

26:8. With one accord everyone strove to prevent discovery of the culprit, for in your presence, O God, the many were as responsible for the deed as the one who committed it. With what evil reports the wicked ones mangled Your soldier! With what calumnies they gnawed at him! As though he alone was unbelieving; as though he alone, contrary to law, was a subverter of innocents! Those who did not fear to violate justice were the ones who set forth the law. All the while guileless blood was crying from the ground.[189] Even those guilty ones who were slain and already received among the dead were making public that they had shed it unjustly. What more? Now with laws, now with witnesses, now with many persuasive arguments, all the nobles of the palace were acting so that he might dismiss the culprit as an innocent man.

26:9. In the meanwhile they were wearying him with entreaties. But no artifice made a fool of him, no scandal broke him. Unconquered, Arsenius did whatever he could so that in some manner truth might at length be known. Ultimately, perceiving his constancy, they decided that unless he came to a judgment about it, they would do nothing further in this dispute although the law was manifestly on their side. The people applauded as though Christ's soldier would not wish to come to a judgment. He heard about these matters and resorted to his usual weapons. He appointed a fast for himself and for us who were with him, lest, as often happened, some deceit of the enemy might prevail in the judgment. Accordingly we spent a whole night in vigil and prayer that the Lord would soon reveal the one responsible for so enormous a crime.

26:10. In the morning, trusting in God's faithfulness, we went in procession as to a spectacle to the place where the entire populace was already assembled. There was much taunting from the magistrates, so that many bishops were misled. Certainly a case of such magnitude did not involve them. Then Christ's true athlete began to urge them to prepare the judgment immediately.[190] Standing in the midst he prayed to God with outstretched arms and with tears that no folly of judgment might stain upright ones. As soon as these prayers left his mouth, they penetrated heaven.[191] Since bribery had overthrown the tribunal of human judgment, tears stand near the throne of Christ's grace together with innocent blood crying out from the ground.[192]

26:11. Soon the inner judge, as if again chiding the conscience of old Cain, compelled the justiciar to confess the secret so wickedly covered up; soon he fell at the feet of Arsenius trembling and groaning. Inwardly the divine Judge was chastising his wretched conscience. Smitten with new fear, he began also to implicate others whose aid he had enlisted to dare his deeds. And so that nothing indeed might remain of all that he could have had, except that he was alive, he related everything to those who were standing around him. In their blindness they had certainly perverted justice in afflicting Arsenius with their hatred and in wearying him with their plots. But now, convicted by divine judgment, they all departed in confusion. The wretch was mercifully sentenced only to penance.

26:12. *Paschasius:* O far too unhappy time, when someone wishes anything well and no one is disposed to comply; when each one gives attention to his own will, not to God's. "Everyone loves a bribe, pursues a reward." [193] The zeal is equal in all; persistence is the same. With one and the same game they seem to look forward to malice, even if one of their own kind is ridiculed. Little faith can they produce. By their efforts they judge our Arsenius as if he could be nothing other than what they are. There is no truth among them, for it has disappeared from the public squares.[194] Equity cannot enter them. So the widow's blood did not come near them, but because she was innocent she was exposed to prey.

CHAPTER 27

27:1. *Severus:* Why is Chremes so excited about these transactions? When Arsenius lived among us he was able, almost intuitively, daily to expose to public view the secrets of just judgment from the hidden receptacles of the heart. Scarcely anyone would dare conceal hidden faults from him. Yet when shocking crimes have been examined and acknowledged, he presented for the ill ones Christ's lightest medicine.

27:2. *Chremes:* What you recall is true. But here in our community all of us, together with him, were striving eagerly toward salvation. Outside, however, no one, or only a rare one, was to be found who would not corrupt truth and justice but would also keep at arm's length anyone refusing to condone wicked crimes. For example, a certain one fraudulently removed the testaments of another's inheritance and produced witnesses. He then hid the documents in the sheath of a sword and thus craftily repaid his own pleader. The latter, not knowing what he would receive, sought to return a page of his inheritance, accidentally bypassing the very place where the documents were. The other man thereupon produced witnesses that he had returned all the instruments of his right. But since an oath is the end of every controversy and since false witnesses had sworn, the poor man did not get what he was eagerly seeking. He then appealed with many complaints to our Arsenius. The latter smiled and ordered the culprit to approach and declare if he was aware of the course of such a great crime. "O much too unhappy one," he cried, "how is it that you have produced so great a trick of cunning in such a manner?" The latter, aware that he was caught, fell at his feet and disclosed what he had hidden.

27:3. *Adeodatus:* The wisdom of Solomon was in him, I believe, making him shrewd in the investigation of secret transactions.

CHAPTER 28

28:1. *Paschasius:* What Parmenus says has often happened: some man without foresight may on occasions act more unaware of good than one who knows beforehand.[195] But this man of ours, from the day of his profession, never did anything imprudently, although by his closely woven conjectures he laid hold of hidden matters, as we have often seen in the delinquencies of certain brothers. For those who sin always lurk in the shadows and undertake to shun, lest what is open to divine observation may be open to those with power of censure. Because it was a long time since we had been in Italy, we were strangers to them in respect of the Pennine Alps, where we saw "golden Saturnian realms" [196] and malignant arts, and where the world reigns and Ausonian sod is prostituted. At length, however, we returned to the Gauls. Almost everything had been corrected and Eugenius had been ordained most holy pontiff of the Apostolic See.[197] He is said to have labored much in administration so that through him matters might be corrected, matters which had for so long been distorted.

CHAPTER 29

29:1. *Adeodatus:* It appears to me, Paschasius, that you are perhaps blaming with bitterness no less obscurely than craftily or ingeniously him whom you had decided to praise. It would seem that you had noted trifling gifts offered to the brothers which he carried away, the kind of treasures or ornaments by which the world reigns, such things as none of us has ever seen all at once.

29:2. *Paschasius:* Never would I have believed that you were so suspicious or capricious that you would turn to accusing me of what has been spoken in sincerity. About such matters you are perhaps motivated after the manner of certain men, one of whom you particularly note. There is no one who doubts that all those blessings (that is, gifts) were of pure love or that the allegiance of the magnates was of due veneration (for he was deputy of the realm and teacher of the emperor), if one can judge rightly about a neighbor's conscience. Certainly assured in his conscience before us all, he said, "Everything that you observe you can accept without hazard, without utterance of desires or loss of anyone's properties. Thanks to God and to you I have received what was offered me for the sake of an acceptance and for the honor of the emperor, as well as for your use. No one has either acquired or lost anything unjustly. There has been no grief in respect of what was either given or received. No, since I have no desire to receive from many, they have prayed that these things be given to you for alms."

29:3. Since these gifts were received in this manner, it should be clear that what I said was a prediction of their employment for use of the country and welfare of the realm, and not as you have supposed. I knew that this one, so liberal in all matters and such a despiser of the world, had abandoned himself according to the voice of the Lord.[198] In the case of one who abandoned himself so perfectly that it was clear for all to know, what could he secure for himself even lawfully, much less wickedly or greedily? No, as I have said and is quite clear, he accepted those gifts for two obvious reasons: first, that those who are accustomed to give presents might not be offended or vexed; secondly, that if he returned empty handed, we would not accuse him of spurning what was sent to us for our expenses.

29:4. *Adeodatus:* It is good that I reproached you for finding fault with him, for now we have heard about the gifts which he brought. All may now understand how liberal he was, how alien to our age, how dead to the world. He did not ignobly require thanks from us for all those presents nor from outsiders for certain other benefits. He was aware in himself that in all things he ever sought to please God.

29:5. *Paschasius:* So it is, my brother, as you declare. Certain ones of us did not at that time understand that those gifts were not offered to him as bribes, but to be transmitted through him to us from our magnates or indeed by the supreme pontiff of the Apostolic See who made so many grants. One day, for instance, one of our brothers happened to be lauding him for such deeds. Another brother is said to have replied, "Why do you speak so much in praise of that one? Weren't those presents which he brought back directed to us?" We all laughed at those questions.

29:6. The former thereupon exclaimed, "It would be more fitting, I suppose, that such great gifts be sent to you."

29:7. "O wretched human ambition," I replied, "so stupid, envious, and ungrateful! If he had labored for some other one of us, nothing at all would have been said."

29:8. It is certain that our Arsenius was at that time more beloved and famous than anyone else in this realm. He was amused that, though unwillingly, he was compelled to accept such gifts so that love and delight might not be offended. Let others do what they will; let them sell justice for bribes; let them rage with fraud and guiles; let everything stand as venal for everyone. Even so, no such outstanding gifts are multiplied to them as were freely offered to that one for love and reverence alone. When these remarks had been uttered, let us bring the book to an end, since we finally turn again our pen to the Gauls. Those matters which should be pursued inexorably with groaning are so fearful and so monstrous that scarcely anyone can mentally comprehend, so dreadful and disturbing they are.

29:9. Since the pen has touched upon these matters, I do not know if letters can be formed because of tears (although the writer has a heart of stone); I fear they will be washed away by weeping. How much less can a chronology of the account be established! In the meanwhile let us console ourselves with joy in awareness that we have known and had with us such a great man about whom we do not fear to rejoice in God. Foresight should be taken that we may not be shattered by calumnies. For now in this present time the majority, even the honorable ones, rail out against good men, so that no one can go away untouched.

The Life of Wala

BOOK II

INTRODUCTION

(*Interlocutors:* Paschasius, Adeodatus, and Theophrastus. Pseudonyms employed are Arsenius for Wala, Antonius for Adalard, Justinian for Emperor Louis, Justina for Empress Judith, Honorius for Lothair, Gratian for Louis of Bavaria, Melanius for Pepin of Aquitaine, Naso—and once, Amisarius—for Bernard of Barcelona, and Pashhur—Latin, *Phasur*—for a person as yet unidentified.)

(1) *Adeodatus:* After numberless cares of duty within, after immeasurable cares of tasks without, after various occurrences of affairs and business and expending of life, after long weariness of diverse travels hither and thither with throngs on all sides, after indefatigable pressures of all kinds, quiet and freedom of mind have finally returned for you, Paschasius, by the disposition of divine judgment and with no others left to complete the work. It is now fitting for what we formerly omitted to be recorded, that we may bring to fruition the pattern of the father's epitaph which we long ago undertook to commit to writing. Otherwise it would have been more honorable not to have begun than having begun not to finish.[1]

(2) *Paschasius:* I admit the cogency of your remark, my brother. But after the dumb silences of life, after the neglected study of letters, I fear to seek again what oblivion has stolen away or levity of manner loathes to hear now. Above all, even if there should be occasion for speaking such matters, I no longer have

facility for writing, although once I might have had it. Yet I will attempt what you urge so that what we once undertook may not pass unfinished to dishonor. That would only cause our enemies joy and serve as an example for indolent ones. I will begin, although unsatisfied are the lamentations which remain for deeds done. In the meantime, however, Severus is happy,[2] having entered upon "the way of all the earth," [3] and Chremes has departed amid our crises.[4] It is therefore necessary for us after the manner of the holy fathers to choose another from those who along with us were with him. Truth will thus be better commended if presented by three witnesses,[5] and our lament will not be found different in number. Since it was yours, brother, to renew what we began, it should be yours to choose our associate.

(3) *Adeodatus:* I am less suitable for judging and discerning, but since I am devoted to your commands, I will not refuse what you urge. We do not indeed need a philosopher for our lament, but one by whose remembrance or by whose disposition we may be aroused to tears. So, if it seems well to you, let us choose Theophrastus although he is beardless.

(4) *Theophrastus:* I would not have thought that you might wish to interweave jokes in this game or to follow childish trivialities.

(5) *Paschasius:* Do not marvel, brother, if Adeodatus has chosen you, a beardless one, for this purpose, since he would not bypass me, the decrepit one, long since forgetful in such studies. Upright and knowledgeable lovers only ought to commend themselves to those listening for lamentations and truth. We two, therefore, although harassed for a long time, can in many matters unfold our grief to sons and friends.

CHAPTER 1

1:1. *Adeodatus:* Before we come to the lament, however, please point out to us the beginning of such a great crisis. For there is no one of sound mind who believes that these things happened among a people without offense to God.

1:2. *Paschasius:* What you say is true, by Hercules, but it is not yet permitted to disclose all to everyone, particularly to those to whom truth is an object of hatred and to those to whom crimes are pleasing. Yet even if good pleases them less, truth must not always be hidden. This one of whom we are speaking uttered the word of truth freely even to those who found fault with him. Before these evils of the empire appeared and different calamities and scourges began to spread abroad moment by moment, day by day, among the people by the just judgment of God, before all this happened, the emperor together with his senators and the magnates of the land demanded to know why it was that the offended divine Majesty had so long ago foretold so many dire occurrences among the people at this time. For as Scripture testifies, "hardship alone gave discernment to hearing." [6]

1:3. It was thereupon ordered that each person inquire more carefully about this until the next assembly.[7] Each should inquire wherein God was offended and how He could be placated. After the order had been made known, our Arsenius before our eyes soon gave stability to the wretched world, to divine laws, and to the decrees of the Fathers. Therein he noted in what ways Christ's churches would be seduced and with what carnal works all the people would be corrupted. To this end he published a small booklet to aid his memory. In it he effectively depicted in letters all the vices of this realm. So guardedly did he do so that no adversary could deny all those matters. Returning then to the retinue, he expounded one by one before the emperor, all the prelates of churches, and the senators the various duties of each order. He showed how evils were growing up and how all things are corrupted and disfigured.[8]

1:4. *Theophrastus:* Since we are challenged by his great examples, I am astonished that none of ours dares to relate to posterity the full truth about him, although he may dare to expose the people's sins accumulated over so long a period of time, disasters, pestilences, famines, changes of weather, and even terrors of visions. The earlier false invention of dust [9] certainly outstripped these evils. Under it there was much harassment and evidence of mendacity that it might be allowed a prudent man to understand that all the earth was assailed by the hands of the enemy. Hence it is manifest that sins of the realm, which have not yet been completed, are daily growing worse.

1:5. So it remains that in many ways we learn a fact only for it to be destroyed. We should therefore fear lest what has happened to many nations also befall us. But I would not say without reason that the miracles of saints long since asleep in Christ have recently been gleaming. Never before in the history of the world have such great deeds been accomplished at one time by relics of the saints.[10] Everywhere the saints brought into this realm from hither and yon have aroused each other in symphony of song as at cockcrow.[11] So that what our faithlessness has, according to the Apostle, compelled may be understood, he himself is witness, since signs are most truly vouchsafed not to believers, but to unbelievers.[12] After the darkness of our blindness, let us, finally awake, rise up to the true light which is Christ.[13]

1:6. *Adeodatus:* Perhaps if that one were first summoned to utter lament, he might, as if a traitor, not able to restrain his spirit from speaking, disclose us. Even, therefore, if what he teaches is true, he does not wait to speak in his own place.

1:7. *Theophrastus:* Everything that I have set forth is not more properly deferred to another place, since the evils which have increased throughout the land are to be struck at the first opportunity. This empire has grown by favorable success to the present, as if to a perfect age of plenitude. Yet vices, which have usually been committed in prosperity throughout the land, have multiplied and become inveterate. By God's just judgment they are disclosed no less by scourges than by new miracles. Unless I am mistaken, they should, for that reason, be specified and bemoaned here and now. They may become, if not for us, at least for posterity, an example of correction.

CHAPTER 2

2:1. *Paschasius:* We cannot deny that. On the other hand we ought not bypass what our Arsenius formerly set forth before all the highest nobles. For by these and other matters he was driven, as if another Jeremiah, by divine authority showing to everyone wherein each had offended God. In his charity he constantly admonished that they destroy, scatter, and uproot the evils which they perpetrated and that thenceforward they should build up the good that they bypassed and then implant it in others.

2:2. "In the meanwhile," he said, "do you know in what orders Christ's church consists? The discipline and condition of the commonwealth should be sought according to each one's function. It is fitting that divine matters be pondered inwardly and human affairs outwardly. For the entire church is regulated by these two orders. May the emperor and king be surrendered to his proper duty; may he not do other than what is suitable, proper, and right; may he not ignore such matters, because for these the Lord directs him in jurisdiction. May the bishop and ministers of churches perform what is more particularly of God. May the king establish such helmsmen in the realm as the Lord commands. Let them inquire carefully into the law. May the king remain secure in those and for those whom he recognizes as upright and fit to rule the holy people of God. Let them be persons who do not act according to their own pleasures to indulge the people, but who hate greed and love God and justice. It is their duty always to dispose what is right and just, and to correct what is corrupt. Otherwise, O king, unless you observe that has been commended, a severer punishment lies ready for you and, if God is shunned, one death comes upon all through you. Care must be taken that you neglect nothing, for in you alone, according to Solomon, is the stability of the entire realm.[14] In divine matters, however, do not force yourself more than is appropriate."

2:3. *Adeodatus:* Not without warrant, I think, have you called him another Jeremiah, because of the constancy of his faith and the grimness of his countenance as he daringly inveighed against the emperor for his excessive sloth, nor did he bypass also the worst practices of kings, the affairs of his office, when he was preoccupied with vanities.

2:4. *Paschasius:* There are harsher matters, brother, which were then brought forward. I will say a few words about them. For example, he said to Caesar, "I wish, most devout and august emperor, that you would tell us why it is that you so often abandon your proper duties and transfer your interest to divine matters? Or why is it that you sometime grant the honors of churches (or rather, I think, their burdens) [15] which you lavish? But if properties have been legitimately dedicated to God by the law of alms, they belong to His churches; they are legally given to His poor and to those especially serving Him. If, however, you think that by divine authority you give benedictions and the Holy Spirit, which God's chosen ones worthily receive only from the Lord and His holy consecrated prelates, you should know that what you presume is not your function. But if by authority of the holy fathers what you are doing is more well considered according to God and what you are lavishing more fruitful, the manner should be regulated in consultation with God's clergy, people, and holy pontiffs. Otherwise either you choose for yourself and arrogate to yourself [16] divine matters or the multitudes (or someone) will confuse such great favor for another. In that respect nothing but divine matters and the testaments of our salvation should be considered.

2:5. "There is identity in matters of the churches: their riches are nothing other than the price of sinners, the vows of the faithful, and the patrimony of the poor. Because it was once legitimately devoted to God, it may be freely used by His soldiery among His soldiers and the poor. Let the king therefore possess the commonwealth freely to care for the uses of his soldiery and let Christ possess the property of the churches, as another commonwealth entrusted to His faithful ministers for the use of all indigents and of those serving Him. This is the function of the king to entrust to such ones who will both faithfully distribute and wisely provide. So may everyone glorify God and rejoice in Christ no less from promise of future matters than also from comfort of present matters. But if otherwise, as the Apostle says, those who plunder another's possessions will not obtain the eternal realm.[17] How much worse are those who defraud what belongs to God and the churches if they are joined in these sacrileges?"

2:6. *Theophrastus:* If it is as he has declared and there is no providence with God about such matters, I do not know who of our princes can be saved. For to them nothing is so sweet and nothing so gratifying as booties stolen from churches, as it is written, "Hidden bread is more pleasing and stolen waters are sweeter." [18]

2:7. *Paschasius:* True, my brother, and for that reason God's wrath has been poured out upon our princes, making them wander in a roadless place and not in a road,[19] while worldlings lawlessly throw themselves to despoliation of divine things. But Christ's priests and ministers of the altar thrust themselves and divine matters from inmost affairs to outer affairs. What is worse, they now also shamelessly divert them, although they read in the Scripture that "no one fighting for God involves himself in worldly businesses." [20] Hence the worst daring and confusion are born, a consuming flame of desires, abandonment of virtues, and kindling of sin. Either Christ's ministers, allured by thought of losing their supply of possessions, are impelled toward what is not advantageous for them or worldlings, inflamed by heat of desire, despoil what is God's and as if defended by royal authority are haughty against God with rash law. When such matters were clearly set forth before the king, before Christ's prelates, and before the princes of the land, none of them has denied.

2:8. *Adeodatus:* I marvel how what is public to all and what no one gainsays can be denied. No, although they are provoked in turn, everything deteriorates hither and yon; everything is turned to the worst uses.

CHAPTER 3

3:1. *Paschasius:* Alas, that such a one daily thrives now on frenzy so that all are turned worse by such deeds and words rather than to increase of reproof. Now all, especially churchmen, have undertaken to question and to gainsay how the dignity and honor of churches could otherwise stand, as if they had never read the decrees of the holy fathers. To them our Arsenius said, "Consider what opposes divine authority that it may be corrected by authority of God Himself. For in your hands are the laws, no less the human than the divine."

3:2. Then the worldlings say, "Although everything is thus and since the commonwealth, weakened by many causes, is not sufficient to itself, we must act with ecclesiastical properties and soldiers. We must be aided by the weight of their riches. Unfold, therefore," they say, "what you are suggesting."

3:3. But he replies, "I marvel that you ask. Look! As it has been pointed out, our king takes many things from the goods of churches for his own use and that of his retainers. But there are anathemas beyond measure in the holy fathers, derived from divine authority, if the goods of churches should be abused by the force or power of any judge. You yourselves know how they condemn in those compilations often assembled from them. If anyone of the faithful should bring his vows, whether little or much, to God's altar and someone should heedlessly seize by force or theft what has been given or consecrated, I ask, do you think there is any kind of offense greater than this? At the same time, as if touched inwardly by a new oracle, they have decreed it to be sacrilege."

3:4. Continuing he then said, "Let no one deceive you, most eminent emperor, for it is exceedingly dangerous to despoil by violence properties once devoted to God in faith for use of God's poor and His servants, and contrary to divine authority to pervert them to worldly use. But if, agreeable to the statement of truth, whatever the holy pontiffs have bound are bound both on earth and in heaven,[21] the many anathemas of the holy fathers in the holy canons pertaining to such matters should be feared. For the authority of those who already reign with God flourished no less. If therefore, as you declare, the commonwealth cannot subsist without church properties, a means and an order must be sought with reverence for the religion of Christendom. Only so may you and yours receive anything from churches for defense, but nothing for plunder lest you also incur the curses and execrations of the holy fathers.

3:5. "If anything must be presented for use of the soldiery, let these holy pontiffs make this clear. If it is thus in some matters, let them not be constrained to pass over quickly to secular affairs and in a nonreligious manner serve the pomps of the world which they have renounced. For, as I have indicated earlier, according to the Apostle, 'no one fighting for God involves himself in secular businesses.'[22] If it happens otherwise, he is not a true Christian, he is someone else, because he is still serving the pomps and works of the devil." When he had spoken thus, they began to inquire what were the pomps. "It is your duty," he said, "to determine that and to produce a man of the Gospel more than those in whom the world reigns and at whom it boastfully gapes."

CHAPTER 4

4:1. *Theophrastus:* This is what I still hear today that some people misrepresent about him, namely, that he wished church properties to be divided, that only so much remain to them as would no more than suffice them, and that the remainder should serve the soldiery of the world.

4:2. *Paschasius:* That is in no wise so, as you erroneously suppose and as at the present time many (perhaps most) people feel. That one predetermined and signified nothing so rash about this matter. He urged only that whatever had to be done should be done with full consideration, so that no one would sin against God in earthly affairs. Thereafter when some of the bishops attempted what he wished, no one could ascertain anything other than what he had said to all in the presence of the emperor. At the same time that those negotiations were taking place, he also enumerated the dangers threatening monasteries. Many were then held by laymen. At present such are fewer than those governed by the proper orders, but even so almost all have been distorted by usages and practices of the world, no doubt as punishment for sins. Concerning these, the king [23] indeed began well, but in the end, as evils have increased, they have been penetrated by worldlings.

4:3. Again and again Arsenius leveled bitter denunciation against episcopates unlawfully and uncanonically granted, without semblance of an election. His criticisms were broadcast hither and yon and no one could deny them. But since ecclesiastical order had not been entirely corrupted, it was decided that synods should be held at three places [24] to inquire more carefully about this, not indeed to correct the situation (as events have proved), but simply to please the king. They had already set in motion those human activities which were later pointed out, and divine matters received even less attention.

CHAPTER 5

5:1. *Adeodatus:* I marvel at him now that he is absent, although we did not marvel when he was present with us, for now his statements are recalled. He was so humble that no one seemed humbler, no one more dead to the world. Why is it then that, out of so many supreme magistrates of churches, both prelates and senators, he was the one who spoke so deliberately and persistently in the senate before the emperor?

5:2. *Paschasius:* Do not forget, brother, that he was one whom no terror of threats, no force of circumstance, no hope of things present, no dread of things to come, no promise of possessions, no kind of endless humiliation, no authority could distract from love of Christ,[25] from affection for country and people, from devotion to the churches, from fealty to the emperor. It was for that reason that, like another Jeremiah, he could so persistently speak about such matters and indeed many, many more. In particular and perhaps most of all, he pointed his finger at the army of clerics in the palace (whom they popularly call "chaplains"),[26] because it is not a proper ecclesiastical order. They serve for no reason other than revenues of churches, advantages of the world, the sake of profit without consent of the magisterium, and ambitions of the world. They are not under monastic *Rule* nor are they enrolled canonically under a bishop. But except for these two orders there are no other recruits for service of the church.

5:3. Arsenius declared that one ought to be a canonical priest or a layman or a monk. The chaplains, however, appear to belong to no order and to be without a head. Although this group would indicate their title from another source, surely it should be acknowledged as a heresy than which at this particular time there is no worse leprosy for the churches. It violates all the rights of churches so that almost all monasteries of monks and canons and even of women are presided over and despoiled by laymen. For this reason, he, who had anticipated the future, never hesitated to speak for establishment of the realm, for safety of the people, for stability of the churches and religion, even if in so doing he might displease someone.

CHAPTER 6

6:1. *Adeodatus:* As far, then, as one can understand, such people were not consuls or providers for the country, but bandits. Their base minds the darkness of impressions had blinded, deformed humility has filled with shadows, desire has stained with filth. So true is it that they could neither understand nor contemplate, neither take heed nor hold the very name of consulship or the brightness of that honor or such greatness of empire. They should be called not consuls but merchants and salesmen of that great dignity and corrupters of churches. Not only did they not take counsel with him as he warned them, but they also resorted alternately to subterfuge, subversion, and betrayal, lest either such matters be corrected or hinder, if they could, the worse situation which was impending. As Paschasius grieved a few moments ago, such things did not occur unjustly. No, since they did not wish to receive the spirit of truth for correction, they received the spirit of error for giddiness. Hence it is that today no prince has yet been able to straighten the roads of the commonwealth toward justice.

6:2. *Paschasius:* It was indeed just, for they did not want to stand for God nor to seek first the things that are of God.[27] They did not want to correct what had been perverted. If God had withdrawn from them, counsel would have perished in the land, faith would have vanished, peace would have fled, and the flourishing of any properties would today lie helpless. The one who shows allegiance to kings is already rare. There is none who rightly counsels the country or its citizens, none who weighs out due charity to associates and friends. Judges do nothing except for a bribe. The people are not favorable to imperial duties. The authority of prelates does not flourish and even the imperial authority of kings has perished. The commonwealth is bitterly impoverished of churches because plunderers are ravaging them. Many mute persons, perhaps all, have become most eloquent now that the virtue of doing and speaking has been emptied.

6:3. Nothing more is known by the world against these parties, nor is anything more plausible for thought. Yet ability and knowledge sweat after the willing of each one. Since they did not listen at that time to the voice of Arsenius nor indeed the voice of God, all their prosperity has turned into adversity and their strength has been broken. Counsel shunned them and, as the prophet says, all wisdom was devoured.[28] Foreseeing future events, Arsenius clearly forewarned them at the same assembly, after he had explained those matters. Soon violent infirmity (which physicians call diarrhea) seized him, and by that infirmity an end came to his strength. Thereafter he fell silent until God's judgment should apprehend us and until sins which had already been completed should be revealed in deeds,[29] that is, until what we do should finally be not only sins but also the punishment of sin.

CHAPTER 7

7:1. *Theophrastus:* When such things have happened, they are already more clearly manifest than light. But what their beginning was is not to be asked. We believe it was just that their hearts should be hardened lest they hear if their faults compel them. There was divine vengeance afterward that it might justly rage more furiously against us sinners.

7:2. *Paschasius:* Alas, that day which almost brought eternal darkness and peril to this orb; which split to pieces and divided this empire formerly at peace and united; which violated, broke off close blood relationships, begot enmities everywhere, and scattered fellow citizens, destroyed faith, erased charity, defiled churches, and corrupted everything! Civil wars—more than civil wars[30]—occur daily. Hither and thither the army of the whole country almost perishes. Far and wide, provinces, the countryside, and cities are depopulated. If any are left, they flee everywhere without strength or they are hewn down with swords. On all sides are invasions by pagan enemies. All the people perish. Villas and cities without number are burned. Alas, wretched day which a more unhappy night follows!

7:3. But no more unhappy day there was than that when the accursed Naso was summoned from the Spains, that Amisarius who had abandoned everything honorable in which he had been reared.[31] Vain he plunged into the hog wallows of filth. Like a wild boar overturning the palace, he destroyed counsel, scattered abroad all the laws of reason. He drove away or trampled upon all the consuls, both divine and human. He occupied the bedchamber; and in partisan manner penetrated everything openly so that his snares might be seen. Blind so that nothing could be other than what he had found, he set aside divine matters and through both law and crime immersed himself in human matters. He shattered and defiled everything and emptied every royal dignity. He broke treaties, confounded order. He completely altered everything so that no orderly arrangement might exist. He turned day into night and then night into day. He caused sons to disavow their father and father to disavow his sons. He accomplished his tyranny so that it might encompass everyone and might leave nothing untouched.

7:4. Those who held deserved honors lost them. Those who had not yet attained them pursued them unworthily. The best of men, the most distinguished and the most worthy nobles, soon neglected authority to act, because no one thenceforward had any other more convenient way to secure and retain honors or whatever he might wish or desire than to follow what the tyrant Naso at that time preferred. In the meantime the power of a woman had shattered all the bones of virtues. Stupid, eyeless, and feelingless, he had thus plunged himself into everything. Already the giddiness of the entire empire was stirred, so that no one might acquire power, honor, and possessions without crime or without ruin of others as cost. That is indeed the fruit of faithlessness and discord. It is therefore advisable always to sow the seeds of prudence, justice, fortitude, and temperance,[32] so that you can reap the fruit of labor a hundredfold. Do not sow desires and vices from which judgment may again be measured and the vengeance of perdition may grow. O that day, O day of darkness and gloom! O accursed day [33] when such counsel was undertaken! This is the hour of God's fury, the hour of our repayment to vindication, in which the eyes of all are opened with the prophet Balaam.[34] Here we all have fallen and the rod of God's fury has been wakeful.[35] Here all the rights of law have been violated.

CHAPTER 8

8:1. *Adeodatus:* Alas, dreadful it is that such monstrous, such horrible damages have grown up in the realm, although sins added to sins through partisanships have required it. When we seek why it was that Arsenius should again have thrust himself into such sharp and such pernicious kinds of danger, perhaps he could not foresee what end they might have whom he wished to meet. We beg you to clarify.

8:2. *Paschasius:* It is true, brother, that he saw the ills which daily arose without number and without measure. But he could not foreknow the future. As much as he could, Arsenius wished to meet and resist them for loyalty to realm and king, for devotion to country and people, for the religion of churches and safety of the citizens. All these were dearer to him than his own life. But since such matters had not been checked and repressed initially, since faults were compelling, they had superior power with impunity toward the mischief of everyone. There was no one already strong and wise enough to prevent. When he recovered from his infirmity, the same one began to hear from all sides infamous and obscene, shameful and foul reports, not of ordinary kind, but of such kind as had never been heard in this our age. Because of this, his heart, so fond of religion, was soon disturbed.

8:3. The palace became a theater, formerly of honor, in which such great recurring illusions of soothsayers were welling up as were believed not to exist in the whole world. He could not restrain himself from tears of grief and love when these matters were reported to him day and night by good men, most eminent and most truthful. The more Arsenius loved Christ's church and emperor with his people and offspring, the more he was afflicted with grief. Chiefs of the palace of both orders were coming and declaring all such things to be true or rather worse than popularly reported. He thereupon decided to come and try by his reproof, persuasion, and counsel to help, so that the scourge might be averted before it disturbed and overturned everything. Thus he did what he could. He spoke with the emperor and leaders concerning what he had heard. He forewarned what he felt in those matters that were happening.

8:4. The seditious monster himself he even addressed with every expression of loyalty and friendship, since the latter's father and he had been close friends. For once upon a time Arsenius had taken as his wife the latter's sister, daughter of a most noble and high-minded man.[36] From the cradle he had, like a father, displayed a holy disposition, care, and solicitude toward him in all respects, more even than if he were his father. But when he saw that he was already blind and mad in mind and that he was already rushing headlong, he said whatever he could. But Naso would not listen, for he was already abandoned in morals and drunk with venom of desire. When Arsenius realized that he was making no progress, he returned without result to his monastery, grieving and mourning over what he had observed. After a brief lapse of time, the rulers and chiefs of the palace, banished and deposed, soon followed him, weeping and bemoaning.

8:5. By one shameless person all laws of the entire empire were violated and the best men driven away. Everywhere the strongest and most eminent men were crushed, not by the strength of that debaucher, but by guile and fraud of the worst deception. Each one reported things worse than the worst. From hither and yon all were converging upon Arsenius and were begging counsel from him as if from a fountain of wisdom. Moaning and bewailing, that one was peering upward toward God with all his mind, if perchance God might send aid in such perils. One by one he exhorted each of them first to stand fast and wait for God's judgment [37] and then to return to the palace to watch, to understand, and to persuade the better qualities of salvation. Let them strive with whatever presure they could to prevent such great disturbances. But the highest ones were driven away, outstanding ones were hurled down. Wanton ones were assembled, the vainest were honored, and scoundrels were introduced.

8:6. When such facts had been ascertained, they related to Arsenius evils of the age which have scarcely ever been heard of before, how in so glorious an empire everything had thus been suddenly and completely altered. The palace had become a brothel where adultery is queen and an adulterer reigns. Crimes are heaped up, all unmentionable kinds of soothsaying and sorcery are demanded, such as I never believed to have still remained in the world. Of all evils nothing has been omitted, and everything is gossiped about by everyone. Nonetheless the sober and wary man was moved only to tears until a plot was disclosed and indeed strengthened by the very ones who were fully aware of such perverse plans. The tyrant sought by some means secretly to slay the emperor so it would appear that he died of his own infirmity. Thereafter his sons and the best princes of the realm were to be murdered by whatever guile he could plan. These matters were reported by the most sober and truthful men and there could be no doubt about them.

8:7. Severely dejected and grieving, Arsenius kept sending suitable and approved persons of holy religion to be in the palace surreptitiously among those who were in any way in those plans. They were to remain for as long a time as needful to investigate carefully what might be the true situation. As soon as anything was said, although supposedly in secret, they were able to discover just when and how the tyrant decided what to attempt. Thereupon they reported as a matter of certainty that those who were aware of the plan had ordered such crimes. Together with the supreme consuls and certain holy bishops, as well with supreme officials of the palace, he began immediately to ask what he should by virtue of faith in Christ do to avert what was designed to overthrow the whole empire. With one voice, with weeping and wailing, all the servants of God who were present, the great and the greatest, declared insistently that he would not be faithful to God and His holy church if he could aid in such dangers but refused to do so.

8:8. With many urging and with the plan disclosed, he and the choicest and most outstanding men reached a great decision for the sake of faith in Christ, the condition of the empire, peace of the churches, love of king and realm, the safety of the sons. He was inflamed by God's zeal that the adversary's deceit might not prevail, that the dignity of the country might be preserved, that safety might continue for its citizens. Devoted to the freedom of all, Arsenius exposed his own safety for the sake of justice and fealty. If he had sought to be favorable to the parties, he would have been more pleasing to everyone and more esteemed by all. But since he was strong of mind, eminent in holiness, invested with justice, established in faith, grounded in charity, clothed with weapons of virtue, he chose rather to die than to uphold such villainy and such cruel crime which would be for ruin, destruction, and eternal damnation to all, if they should consent. He therefore undertook nothing rashly of himself, so that he could come to the aid of the most Christian princes, the prelates of the churches, and all the people, and to free all from such harsh peril of death, for one death menaced all good men.

8:9. *Adeodatus:* One thing only we ought to lament, but harsher events have happened to compel us to include them in our lamentation. They are so much more bitter and cruel than what we originally proposed to bewail. It is therefore fitting to subsume them all under one lament. Arsenius should not be grieved for so much as that the tragic events should be deplored so that God's wrath may be averted from us. Nonetheless what we thus grieve should be entrusted to tears, lest this person of ours be embroiled in the crimes of adversaries. Although there may be opportunity for pleading, we cannot reply to each what is spoken for each. Let us therefore beg the grace of piety rather than hurl censorious accusations. Let us offer the sorrow of our hearts rather than undertake the part of our noble friend for his defense. If then we shall have done anything more sharply or freely than we ought or than they themselves might wish, we beg that they may be unaware of so much inexperience and intemperance as they think should be conceded to pious sorrow or justice.

8:10. There can be no profounder sorrow than this of ours, in which so great a father now suddenly removed is lamented. He who was worthy of much love is still daily persecuted, is still torn to shreds by powerful evil infamies and hatred. In him and with him we savagely deplore at one and the same time destruction of the country, upheaval of the churches, misfortunes of the poor, overthrow of wealth, invasions of barbarians, slaughter of multitudes, wars of over-weening ones, snares of all, and (most horrible) destruction of souls. When Arsenius was spurned, when he was not heeded, all these ills happened. I beg therefore, do not falter, even though pursued by threats and provoked by defamation. Let not anyone say that such things should not be heaped up nor unfolded in lamentation. Let him know that nothing is more appropriate, especially when such ills are increasing, when truth is attacked by hatred, when justice is vanquished. So it was that Jeremiah the prophet, after chidings, persecutions, and incitements, turned to lamentation and wept bitterly over what had happened because of transgressions.

CHAPTER 9

9:1. *Paschasius:* You urge us well, brother, unless things should be so great that we are not adequate to recall nor to contemplate them. I am not speaking of what happened once upon a time, but only of what happened when that infamous and impious enemy of all religion confounded, disturbed, perverted, commingled honorable matters with indecent ones and religious matters with vain ones. There is no mind nor tongue nor voice which can relate the endeavors of that mad man who was protected "by the dregs of all crimes." [38] He thought to seize everything in advance with diabolical sorceries, to overcome not by counsel but by omens, to grasp in advance by divinations. He so held the most sacred emperor by his misleading delusions that those whom the latter or his great imperial father had cherished he drove away from intimacy, from conference, from secret counsel, from faithful trust, from honors, and from every fellowship of earlier life. When this scourge and author of crime had been secured by royal power, he shone in preference because he was the punishment for past crimes and the increment of evil.

9:2. It finally came to pass in the realm that no one could do anything other than what he permitted or commanded. So, as if by a token of God's fury, all were oppressed lest anyone should dare resist or go contrary. For the power and will of the pious emperor was, even if innocently, with that foul man. This situation was accomplished for a memory of everlasting shamefulness. Since such a condition was already in progress, they began to devise plans whereby the king and queen might take the road under command of that savage beast. The emperor indeed was going like an innocent lamb to sacrifice,[39] the great and merciful emperor was going to his death. Misled he was by that of which Solomon had warned him to beware, by the snares of the same seducer.[40] The latter was serving for the sake of nothing but to grow powerful enough to steal the right of empire and for the fraud of the enemy to overwhelm everyone. There is no one who may believe, or who may reconsider what has been done and how much has been accomplished. There is no one who may understand why or how such things came to pass or who may distinguish the authors of evil from good men. Everyone, the unknowing, the wicked, and the worst, tend to blame Arsenius as an inciter to evil.

9:3. While all these ills were being accomplished, while the emperor was moving forward like an innocent lamb to the sacrifice,[41] while he was moving away from his place, and while he was pressing unwittingly toward death, the Lord's hand was placed upon all the people. For all, at the same time and as if divinely impelled, came together for the sake of fealty to the king and realm, of safety for people and country, of stability for the empire, of succession of the sons. All had heard and each had discovered in his own way that one destruction was being prepared for all. As if divinely summoned together, each reported the evils of which he had heard. Some indeed reported what evils they had seen and observed or at which they had been present. When these sentiments had exploded on all sides, it became abundantly clear that one ruin and one annihilation was imminent for the emperor and his sons and all his chiefs. Even Melanius, son of the most pious Caesar, had come with his men. This king indeed was in danger even though he was there with all his men. For a journey had been undertaken against him, his father being unaware that he would be the first to perish after the father.

9:4. While they all, drenched with grief, were faltering about what should be done, Melanius has escaped from restraints long imposed upon him by the same oaths which Gratian had just completed with his father. With his own voice he related what was said and done or what he knew would happen, for since he had dwelt for a very long time among them, he saw that nothing but death awaited him. When he had fled to them, he related every-thing that he had learned while under detention. No doubt had remained in anyone about adultery and about sorceries and divina-tions, but from him it was learned how many from every part of the world had been assembled in the palace and what kinds, such as no one believed to be still practiced. It was as if Antichrist had appeared with his sorceries. Lastly he spoke concerning the pro-posed murder of his father and overthrow of the empire. He told how it had been projected in advance by omens, forebodings, plots, and stratagems, as well as with every malign craft. Thereupon all the nobles and the two sons who were present, Melanius and Gratian, decided that they ought to die rather than agree to such proceedings. They decided that only one was infamous to them, shameful, and the author of every malice, destined for violence, ruin, and everlasting reproach to all.

9:5. Although grieving and lamenting with divine fear, Ar-senius acquiesced in this plan and explanation, because he could at that time find no other opportunity to evade it. But he did not want the emperor to be deprived of empire nor, as far as the result of the affair would allow, to be treated dishonorably in any respect by anyone. He wanted simply for the enemy and his accomplices to be driven away and for adultery, which was already common fame, to be no longer concealed to the confusion of everyone. He sought that soothsayers there assembled, diviners, seers, and mutes, as well as dream-interpreters and those who consult entrails, and indeed all those skilled in malign crafts be expelled from the sacred place. So many and so great were the forebodings of the unmen-tionable art as to drag a vast number of people into error. All the figments of devilish art seemed to have again sprung up in the world, so that when everything about the emperor was done by fraud and guile, it was possible for no one to be deeply aware of what was happening daily. Evidence that he was deluded by malicious crafts lies in the fact that he refused to heed the most faithful consuls and the most holy prelates and that he believed evil things about him whose counsel he had always employed in the past. He refused to receive anyone into his confidence except those whom Justina approved.

9:6. As long as this condition prevailed, he was unable to listen to any other or love any other or agree with any other than those whom she commended to his confidence. But even more ominously as they say, he could not will anything other than what she willed. There was, for instance, a certain bishop at that meeting with all the prelates of Christ and senate of the whole empire. They were denouncing the emperor with insistent confidence for such things. The aforesaid bishop, however, observed, "I know about the kind and the enormity of the matters mentioned, and I know that you, being badly misled by these arts, still approve. Yet when you have been divested of those regalia with which you have been clothed, you will receive yourself again and you will be, as you were before, the best of emperors."

9:7. *Adeodatus:* In our age, so far as I am aware, an occurrence like this has never been known before, that a people would act thus for prince against prince. It was, I believe, either extreme love of our senators and prelates toward the emperor and his offspring that they, when the reasons had been made clear, raised him again to the realm so respectfully; or blind foolhardiness that they dared such things without any evidence of adultery, sorcery, and other offenses, except in the opinion of the masses. Consequently it does not seem to me that the entire ecclesiastical establishment and the whole ruling class should for such reasons rise in revolt or should be incited to rebellion against Caesar, unless perhaps something lay hidden in the background which may be more serious. Since you were at that assembly and on the same business, we ask you to reveal a little more clearly so that our Arsenius may appear blameless.

CHAPTER 10

10:1. *Paschasius:* I was present, as you say, at that assembly when all the princes, gathered together peaceably, as we then supposed, wrangled about those matters against Caesar. I do not deny, but I cannot retain absolutely everything that was said or what replies were given. This is not surprising, because you too do not remember what I enumerated a few moments ago. Unless you were either unmindful or a false informer, you would never have supposed the few grievous things that I have reported. For nothing can be more infamous than for the nobles of the realm and the sons (already created kings) to have permitted what I have described. When the king thanked the people for what happened in that assembly, he spoke as follows, although he might have concealed something in his heart,[42] "You have this day done such as no people is ever known to have done in the past, because I have committed such things as no king before me has done. So thanks be to almighty God," he said, "who has brought such imminent evil to a peaceful conclusion. I do now solemnly avow that never again will I do anything further without your counsel. For I decree and will that the empire continue as formerly ordained and constituted by me with your consent. To this woman, however, whom you have judged, I grant life, since according to the general laws, as you require, the judgment against her was mine. Nonetheless she must henceforth live under the sacred veil and do penance." [43]

10:2. When all this had been peacefully disposed in the same assembly, the glorious emperor was lifted upon the throne and elevated with praises. All the people were rendered more loyal in fealty to him than ever before, if that is possible. Such was the "disloyalty" of Arsenius. Those to whom it was not foreknown imagine falsely that he had anticipated the tyrant by his own wise counsel that he might not accomplish what he was attempting, namely, to destroy the emperor and annihilate all his progeny and to take his wife whom he had shamelessly polluted. If it had worked, he would have with her spread throughout the empire and would have either slain all the seigneurs of the land or subjugated them with wicked oppression. Otherwise he would have transported himself to Spain with her. For that cause therefore Arsenius gave himself to peril and freed everyone else from the evil of so great a crime. He did nothing against Caesar, although ignorant slanderers may think differently. On the contrary he acted for Caesar and for the empire, for the fatherland and for all the nobles, for the faith and for zeal for God, for the religion of Christendom and for the safety of the citizens.

10:3. A little later, it is true, all the rights of law, divine and human, were annulled in that fact. But too much fraud lay hidden as if under a system of loyalty and the royal will. Hence it is, by

Hercules, that even today many wander about and say that good is evil and the evil which all were then disparaging is good. From this evil grew innumerable more evils, and they grow daily more savage. Then, however, everyone magnified Arsenius as liberator of all and extolled him everywhere with praises. Especially was this true when the august Emperor Honorius was summoned from Italy.[44] Justinian had once, with the will and consent of all, made him an associate in the empire and his successor to the whole monarchy. Him too the aforesaid Naso was trying to annihilate and overthrow along with the father and the other brother-kings. At his arrival, of course, a great many persons were exposed and what was being said was laid bare.

10:4. In connection with this plan the brother of that scourge [45] confessed at this assembly that he was implicated. By public judgment he was thereupon convicted and blinded, but his life was mercifully spared. Nothing that was done was from the heart of Justinian nor from his mind, but he was goaded on and fawned upon by the rivals of true fealty and justice. He was importuned by feminine instigation that he could not rule again unless he vindicated himself of the deposition that was imposed on him out of loyalty and that he must take back his wife although she had been removed from him and forced to take the veil. The deep wound in his heart was camouflaged, and accomplices were once again multiplied to split the empire. Honorius, long a partner with his father and recognized by all as emperor, was removed from power, was expelled from partnership. Oaths which had been made to him were dissolved by authority of his father. Good men and renowned ones, who not long since had striven in the interest of loyalty, had put the tyrant to flight, had banished adultery and shamefulness from the palace, who had saved the country and people, had set free the emperor and his sons (as we have related earlier), had determinedly made themselves in loyalty (after they had restored him to the throne of empire and his sons to partnership), had acted in the interest of loyalty, were themselves subdued, so that in them nothing was left but loyalty and truth.

10:5. But evils lay in ambush; time and opportunity were designated. Everyone who had earlier pledged fealty to him was scattered. The senate was exiled, as were all the magnates. Those of the palace, formerly the dearest and first, were condemned. Among them even our Arsenius was arrested and banished, but by the pleading of pontiffs and order of the emperor, as if with great honor. He was lifted up and thrust into a certain high and confined cavern a long distance away,[46] to which there was no access except for angels acting on divine judgment. Not long afterward I arrived there, by direction of the emperor, on ecclesiastical and monastic business. For his consolation I climbed up to visit him, although not without peril. We spent a happy yet sorrowful day together amid profuse and briny tears of joy and grief: happy, from seeing each other again and from a pure conscience that in him lay no fault of responsibility; sorrowful, because as a reward of great virtue he was enduring exile, hatred, prison, and dire misfortune.

10:6. Amid words sweet and bitter I sought to persuade him, first, to acknowledge that he had been excessive [47] in some respects and, next, to agree to the emperor's wishes. In such an event I could act, together with certain friends, to secure his return to favor. Caesar was indeed longing for his return if only he would agree with him. But to this proposal he replied, "I am surprised that you have any doubt about my conscience. I am aware that I have no more to do with these matters for which I am blamed than you have. It would have been more suitable for you to try to persuade me in behalf of justice than for me to be lukewarm for a while or to agree with and acknowledge what is contrary to truth or honor."

10:7. Thereupon I said, "I do not doubt for a moment nor do I wish anything from you but a word of admission of excess [48] and an expression of approval. In these two matters I believe that friendly persons and I can secure not only pardon for any offenses but also fuller favor, that is, proper and greater honors, and especially whatever from him and by him might be pleasing to you."

10:8. Smiling with a little grimace, Arsenius replied, "Perhaps you think that he and all those who befriend him are in your power? Are you not alarmed at God's judgments? What if I should abandon the uprightness of true faith and purity of heart and should bring against myself a false confession and denial of responsibility? It could happen in the stern judgment of God that such a statement as you propose might be turned against me. If for the sake of anyone or for honors, fear, or favor, I should abandon truth and speak falsely against myself, it is possible that by the action of God's just judgment I could receive sentence of death, being condemned by my own mouth. You ask me to shun lighter perils and to seek honors or favor. But I must beware lest I incur more cruel dangers. You ask me to flee temporal injuries to secure honors. But I might by the disposition of ineffable judgment secure damnation and eternal death. So, brother, once having entered upon the way of truth, let us take our stand. Let us have hope, because this admits us to the everlasting life which is Christ."

10:9. Confounded by these utterances, I fell silent. It was obvious that he had no remorse toward the emperor and his sons, toward fatherland and churches, toward nobles and magnates, toward religion and the safety of the people, except in matters relating to God. He sought not his own advantage but Christ's.[49] He errs therefore who thought that Arsenius was imperiled with exile or death because he knowingly or wilfully neglected something in those affairs; or that he injured the fatherland, violated the majesty of empire, dishonored the emperor and his sons, broke faith, disrupted peace. Not by good and prudent men was he accused of disdaining ecclesiastical laws or hating the king's glory or the fullness of the empire, but in esteeming the former too highly he neglected the latter.

10:10. In all these matters he was not properly cited as guilty of malevolence, but guilty of virtue, for blessed are the ones who suffer persecution for the sake of justice.[50] He is rightly called a new man of virtues who quenched the pernicious insanity and fury of fraud and guile. He freed Caesar from death, the sons from destruction, the realm and empire from the tyrant's invasion. From the palace of the holy empire he expelled all abominations, put adultery to flight, condemned soothsayers, restored honor. He returned father to sons, sons to father. He refused to allow the monarchy to go to pieces. He forbade violation of vows made to the imperial son. He truly wished to preserve all good things, but to cast down evil things and tread them under foot, so that everyone might live a safe and tranquil life according to God.[51]

10:11. A choice of the son which had been solemnly made by the father and by all and an imperial consecration strengthened by authority of the Apostolic See should remain unshattered for the sake of peace and concord, for the sake of an established single government and a praiseworthy principate, for the sake of the honor and glory of the Christian religion. The latter had been trampled virtually everywhere, harassed, even captured by men faithless and hostile to the great name. By vigilant counsel he sought to keep the glorious and most Christian empire from being divided, for according to the Savior's voice, "Every kingdom divided against itself will be desolate." [52] But the sad result we all sorely grieve today and lament every single moment. He wanted the vows and fealty pledged to Honorius [53] to be preserved untouched lest all the people be blackened by false oaths. He wanted the unity and dignity of the whole empire to continue for defense of the fatherland and freedom of the churches, for the integrity and disposition of ecclesiastical properties.

10:12. But now everything has been transformed and thrown into disorder. Let every foe turn and comprehend with what outstanding virtues Arsenius is adorned, with what multiplied testimony for justice he is commended. No good and upright men mutilate or defame him, but harmful and malignant or unknowing ones, misled by rumors, pursue him with hatred. The most honorable and elegant deeds commend him everywhere. His life itself is summoned as witness. Those therefore who seek to drag his life down and diminish his praise arraign themselves. They have no sense or they would not wish to strive against virtue. They have become sycophants and they have incurred what we are now lamenting. It is vain to seek glory and honor without labor and virtue. Our Arsenius receives praise because he has with Christ's grace acquired the honors of everlasting life. He has fame and commemoration, for after disgrace, after exile, life and immortality are granted him.

10:13. *Adeodatus:* I am astonished and I cannot marvel enough at the man, exalted with great and manifest praise, lauded by every tongue. The whole church and all the people are aware that he always repressed by his counsel the evils which then flourished, which were indeed increasing. They are aware that he preserved honor for the king and empire for his sons, that he sought to anticipate such great evils lest they should thrive, such evils as now the whole church and all the people of every age and rank suffer and bewail. Why will they not know and understand? Why, especially since they are harassed by the same evils? But they do not want to perceive or think when or from whom these conditions have arisen. They do not want to perceive by whom these conditions are begotten or nourished and extended.

10:14. If his counsel had been heeded, it would today have been something far different which would please and benefit all. But he was expelled for fear that by his counsel those who assailed the evils would prevail against the snares of evildoers, against the depravities of wicked men, yes, even against the emperor himself. The latter was struggling against his own sons, against the empire, against the fatherland, against the safety of the people. So much is obvious today. And he was struggling with power, honors, ability, with whatever artifice was possible, with weapons and multitudes of soldiers. Arsenius was expelled, degraded, sentenced to banishment, and secluded in a very high cavern, so that, beyond any counsel of safety, he would not be able to reach any mortal or hinder the will of the worst. Wisdom and counsel [54] did not lead the way that good will might be led to fortunate and healthful results, but the purpose of degenerate will was successful. Cunning was done with wicked genius and power so that determined cruelty and will once undertaken might not be quickly shattered.

CHAPTER 11

11:1. *Paschasius:* You see, brother, how the devouring flame of fire comes upon us. For unless the mind should be badly deluded by certain omens, power must be set on fire, unconquered will must be preserved, and loyalty of the faithful must be made humble and devout with all reverence. He could not otherwise act so destructively against his own safety and that of all, except in part by persuasion, in part by power and ability. But since their faith was pure and undefiled, those who were good, misled by excessive reverence, did not wish harmfully to oppose at first.

They therefore incurred judgment of condemnation, and one ruin for all was almost accomplished. Again and again while he was in the aforesaid cave, he was overjoyed for himself that he had suffered harm on behalf of justice. But he grieved for perils which he foresaw as imminent. He grieved because the good and the best were being assaulted; because innocent and faithful men were being trodden down and disgraced, were being delivered to exile, prison, and hurtful fatigue.

11:2. When he was lifted up almost to the clouds, he lived as far as mortal can a life of angels. To the emperor and his followers and to the promoters of Justina (who had returned to the marriage bed), his restriction did not seem sufficiently confining, because of Honorius who lingered in those parts although he had been rejected from partnership in the empire. They were fearful that he might give, to humor the nobles, a plan of safety whereby wickedness might be shattered and cruelty, once undertaken but overcome by virtue, might cease. As quickly as possible, therefore, he was brought down from the lofty cave and transported to Herus,[55] an island in Ocean, the last of all lands. If in the manner of blessed John he may have perceived divine matters, he could neither touch with human touch nor stretch forth to anyone words of recovery.

11:3. *Theophrastus:* It appears to me that the disastrous exile imposed upon Arsenius without legality, judgment, or blame, but rather because of his faith, defense, and justice, is not punishment for sin, but proclamation of praise. It did not lessen the glory of a shining name, but rather brightened it and scattered abroad his honorable reputation. If today anyone goes where he was, he will be aware of the odor of virtue which he left there, for all his life was full of gravity, of good works, of religion. Everywhere pressure and tribulation of time generated praise for him as an everlasting memorial.

11:4. Even if it is more desirable to pass the course of life without sorrow and hurt, yet the labor of holy warfare which is endless brings more recompense in the glory of immortality and in the fruit of eternal reward than luxurious quietude does. The same person was therefore always strong and constant in best reason and holy labor, always mild and patient, ready with all devotion to receive whatever divine virtue might decree. For it was not exile to him, wherever he might be, since he was with God—indeed he deemed it fatherland.[56] In every place he was, along with the Apostle, a good odor to God.[57] For the fame and glory of a holy name he was banished hither and yon.

11:5. *Paschasius:* It is as you say. It was not he who should be called an exile, but those who forced him into banishment. In whatever place they might be, they were exiled from themselves, from sense, from counsel. By their crimes they emptied the fatherland by banishing the best citizens and men. What is the very word *exile* in itself? A disastrous and shameful punishment. When is it shameful? When it is truly a punishment for sin. It is also, as in this case, an opinion of men when it is a punishment for one unjustly condemned. At that time this one did not bear the name of exile by his own sin, but by an unjust sentence, although God acted justly. No one has such unsound mind as to say that Arsenius committed sin by his holy counsel in behalf of the faith, in behalf of Caesar's life, in behalf of the sons and the empire, in behalf of the safety of people and fatherland, in behalf of the justice and laws of the emperors, in behalf of the stability and unity of the realm, of peaceful concord, and for the smiting down of abominable vices, especially the ultimate, namely, adultery, an affront to the entire empire.

11:6. Thus far there is none so raving mad, so ignorant as to deem themselves happy or intelligent who curse him but praise what is done against conscience, against the safety of all. It is as if they would be unhappy who endured such supreme injuries in struggling for justice. In his own time Arsenius was chosen from this company to receive the "honor" of insults in return for numerous pre-eminent kindnesses. Sumptuously "honored," he was led away in exile to Herus by this new breed of people. The conscience of those who ministered such counsel is witness that an innocent and good man was thus harassed for no reason other than that he might not oppose evil effort with good counsel. They acted as all former faithless ones acted against the saints. Similarly that one endured so that having suffered together with them he might reign together with them.[58]

11:7. *Adeodatus:* O unnatural and unmentionable purpose! Who has ever heard that anyone hated those by whose counsel and foresight he was rescued to life and by whose loyalty and aid his own people and possessions were preserved? Or who has been so wise that he would cherish harmony with those who were hostile to him and his, whose filthy insults had polluted his honor with their crime? Alas, the madness of such new obscenity when all the gates of vice are open! That is, when Justina, although defiled, is received again, when what is not corrected is once again admitted and no opportunity is provided for fear that it be corrected. So snares were prepared for him and he was removed from place to place. Everywhere virtues are displeasing to vices nor are they sufficiently safe from vicious ones as long as they exist anywhere. The man of virtue, lover of chastity, defender of justice, is therefore thrust about hither and yon without censure, without indictment, without a hearing, and without crime. So I wish you would unfold what he did when deported to Herus, the last island of earth.

CHAPTER 12

12:1. *Paschasius:* In the aforesaid cave I admit that there were customary odors, but there he saw the sky and the Pennine Alps and Lake Leman. Here he saw only the sea and the sky. But here as well as there he meditated in his mind on God. He bore himself with himself always present to himself.[59] Like David he observed the marvelous fluctuations of the sea; in his mind he saw the Lord in the lofty waves.[60] He pondered the wheeling and circular motion with which the world is turned. He rejoiced that he was established on solid ground and congratulated himself very much as if set in a paradise of delights, a place of exceeding pleasantness. He rejoiced because he had gone forth from the depth of iniquity where, by the impulse of demons, floods increasingly lift to the sky the billows of those fighting each other. He rejoiced that nevertheless they do not cover the earth. He rejoiced that, as there is none who can enumerate the billows and surges, so none can comprehend the force of divine dispensation.

12:2. A certain faithful one is reputed to have heard the Lord's voice speaking to Arsenius in the sea and in the world,

"Up to this point shall you come, but here will you shatter your swelling billows." [61] If he had not been firmly established on these promises and founded on the solid rock, he would at other times not have remained immovable and unshaken amid so many hurtful eddies, so many collisions and crashes of temptation. Not long ago, alas, he was permitted with blessed John (although inferior to him) to discern divine mysteries with exultation and quickness of heart.[62] But greatly refreshed with enjoyment of eternal contemplation, he left a good example to the brothers and the fame of holy religion to later ones. Yet in no place does one rely safely on what is to be feared. Even here beyond the earth, as if outside the world, he was not permitted to remain unnoticed. Even John bound in prison became alarmed.[63] So it was that when vengeful Justina despised her veil and returned to married life, she immediately inquired where he was whom she preferred not to be alive anywhere. Not only she but the devil, envious of all good people, had long begrudged his enjoyment of the delights of virtue. For nowhere in this mortal life could he be more delighted. He was therefore removed from that charming and delightful place.

CHAPTER 13

13:1. *Adeodatus:* Tell us, I beg, why no place safer or remoter was found, since he was expelled from a place that had no access or egress for men except by a long sea vessel. That was where Antonius had earlier been placed under strict guard.[64] He too had been most beloved by all, although he was long loved adequately for his good deeds and kindnesses. This Antonius left there a deposit of many virtues; he had laid up merits with God; and he had borne with himself everywhere the odor of virtue.[65]

13:2. *Paschasius:* I have already shown what you are asking, what kind of opportunity was sought. It was such as John had in prison, namely, to be struck by the sword.[66] Yet Melanius the king was near that region. Against him they had decided to send bands of soldiers. It was foreseen that he would not be aided by counsel, for he was blinded by many acts of sin. On this occasion, albeit with honor since he was revered for his merits and feared for his counsels, Arsenius was borne away to exile through the midst of the Gauls to Germany. He was borne away for his hurt, yet most dutifully as if sweet-smelling incense. But he himself always and everywhere bore along his fatherland with him, for everywhere known, everywhere beloved, everywhere deemed innocent, he was the more dearly loved by all. He feared no force, no empire, having already undergone trials even if he had not yet satisfied the minds of his adversaries nor placated the hatred of wicked men.

13:3. For a long time, however, he had satiated the perfidy and crime of traitors, although not to the fullest extent, since he was still struggling in his mind against what they desired. And so they were influenced by fear that he would still give aid with good counsels and that fraud would perish if detected. They were not indeed foes to the one in exile, but to his virtues. And with God's help and protection he could not let go his virtues. What more? He left behind a beehive of monks honeyed with virtues; and where he was transferred in Germany, the choir of monks received him again with joy.[67] So once more he was in a measure honored there, although in disgrace, by the leading bishops and abbots.

13:4. *Theophrastus:* O our wretched times! O foolish snares of our discord, which has led our peaceful realm to such mad revelry in civil matters! But happy am I about him whose virtuous fame is everywhere scattered. I believe that there is no region, no soil of our farthest lands, no sea, no islands, no shores, no place, no house, no state, in which there are no proclamations of this man's praise. There is no place not bearing the footprints of his chaste counsel, which with unbelievable dignity, virtue, constancy, and purity of heart he provided for all. For he had integrity of mind, holy religion, care for affairs, modesty of virtues, whereby authority was most of all entrusted to him. Wherever he was led, he was revered as an eminent patron. He was venerable for merit and virtue of life even in the awareness of those by whom he was condemned to exile.

13:5. To him there was no exile at all, but an augmentation of virtues; as in the Psalm, he went from place to place scattering his seed.[88] Everywhere he held Christ's confessors as intercessors; everywhere for the sake of exhortation he found their examples preserved by God for him; everywhere the confessor himself left his own seed and a band of monks. Among the latter he lived, keeping them with him, that by their prayers he might be protected, by their consolations he might be warmed, by their solemn offices he might be caressed. He taught them by his own examples, urged them with his own pronouncements, surrounded them with his counsels. Wherever he was, he is still today most cherished and beloved. He is unceasingly proclaimed and commended even by those who have not seen him, so that his fame and proclamations ever flourish.

CHAPTER 14

14:1. *Paschasius:* Yet he was not long permitted to continue in the monastery to which he had been brought, lest there he become involved in counsel or conversation with Gratian, for everywhere he was the same. Untiringly he held, according to God, what he had once for all decided, that virtue of mind might not be shattered by any injurious troubles. What more? He was returned to his own monastery, since there was no place where he was not revered; but deprived of his honors so that he would have no opportunity for acting contrary to the will into which he had once for all sunk. For that reason we were suffused with grief no less than with joy when he returned. On one hand we were grieved that he had been deprived of office, but on the other joyful that we were deemed worthy at least to see him and to have him with us. With such profound humility and submission he lived among us; so devout and ready for all things he was, I believe that here he will not be erased from remembrance.

14:2. Not long afterward, despite his weariness from many harassments, emissaries arrived from the apostolic father,[69] from the royal sons and seigneurs. All approached Arsenius with the sacred embassy in behalf of peace and unity, of compliance and apology, begging earnestly for pardon by authority of the pope and for the safety of the empire. These men brought letters weighted with divine authority. Although he had already suffered for these things, they enjoined him with many oaths to come forth to aid the supreme bishop. But if he would not, their majesties had given command to bring him out by force, albeit with honor and respect. When we had all heard this, we were very frightened, especially since the whole monastery was filled with soldiers. At first we did not know why they wanted him, and we were consequently terrified. We asked the reason, and they then explained the situation. Even so he refused to go with them. They pressed us, saying that they would take him by force if no other way. At this we were torn aimlessly by grief and terror, for a perilous choice was threatening us as well as him, namely, to do or not to do what they asked. We were exceedingly sorrowful for the dangers he had already incurred. Since he had earlier made no effort, we were afraid that he might go out again. Then the supreme pontiff's authority was shown and read in our presence, an expression in behalf of peace, or reconciliation of father and sons, of princes and seigneurs, of the status of the churches, of reunion of the people and safety of the whole empire. On the other hand there were some of the sons' partisans begging him to assist them with counsel, begging him who had endured many trials for them not to desert them at the end of the crisis.

14:3. A divine miracle was announced, a miracle which had leveled the steep ascent of the Pennine Alps before the most holy apostolic bishop. The passage had been blocked up securely so that an army from beyond these parts might not cross hither easily. It was this passage which was, so they say, opened for them on the other side. When this and numberless other matters had been discussed, we began to urge him, for the sake of peace, to obey God's supreme pontiff, even if he should die with him. "It is a great authority which summons you," we said. "Dire need and justice require you and there is no less obedience whereby a man devoted to God agrees, along with God's other holy ones, to obey the good and holy commands of so great a pontiff."

CHAPTER 15

15:1. *Adeodatus:* Many misrepresent this point, as though it were not fitting for him to have any further care to involve himself

in such affairs. No authority of any rule prescribes the grace of the
Holy Spirit. No, the providence of Christ dispenses all things as
and how each one makes progress in his office, if indeed one considers why, how, or where he acts. According to the *Rule*, cloisters
are monasteries of the virtues and means of good works by which
everything is carefully fulfilled by regulation. For this reason one
who is not allowed to do anything without the abbot's permission
must take care that it be done without transgression, even if with
permission, to throw one's self into great uncertainties. It is perilous
to abandon one's purpose and without forethought to inject himself into what is not related or agreeable to his duty.[70]

15:2. *Paschasius:* Many people speak thus, but Arsenius belonged to the dignity or rank of those who do not give heed. For
after he was elected pastor of all and after he undertook, as we believe by God's call, the duty of rector, he was also constituted a
councilor of the whole empire along with others already chosen,
even then preferred to the rest in loyalty and counsel. He was already a leader before he was elected. He was listened to by all and
revered by each for his birth, merit of life, education (which he
had gained from the very beginning of his life under the senate and
wise men of the realm), activity of mind, and nobility of feeling.
When he was chosen prelate together with other pastors of
churches, he was also appointed a senator with the very same ones
and with several other senators of the palace and realm. Since he
had been chosen to give counsel about particular matters, it does
not seem to me that he could have bypassed anything without grief
to himself, without giving counsel about the affairs we have
enumerated. For in it one annihilation was surely imminent for all.

15:3. There is no monk greater or holier than John, who was
therefore beheaded; none more welcome than Elijah, none more religious than Elisha, or other saints and prophets who manfully resisted kings and strove until death for justice.[71] Zachariah was on
that account slain, Isaiah cut asunder, Jeremiah plunged into a
cistern.[72] But Arsenius, far inferior, was lifted up to a very high
cave. One errs who says he should not stand for justice nor strive
for faith against so many and such great ills that befell. Since it was
not lawful to resist with weapons, at least he could resist with
counsel, exhortation, and persuasion. Certainly then and thereafter

those ills came openly upon all, ills greater and more savage than those which our flowing pen can or will pursue. Whoever pretends that he knows what and how great these matters were, or how bad continuing matters are which arose from them, is either foolish or mad. No one of sound mind is there who wishes to defame this one because he sought by his wise counsel to oppose them.

15:4. *Theophrastus:* I have wondered, and there are many who still wonder, why for so great an empire, for such great dignity of realm and churches, there were not found many prelates and senators of strong and great mind to risk themselves and their safety for the state of the whole empire and for the common safety. Even now there are those of ours who wonder whether they would rather see a good strong man or even a fearful one counseling for himself instead of the commonwealth, because his counsel is either nothing or very, very small, much less for the churches or the people, since there is absolutely no one who dares or can correct what is distorted or corrupted. Although we may neglect to remember the ruin of one, we can look on one hand at those who whether with counsel or with good properties might at that time rebuild the royal dignity and the miserable, prostrate, ravished dignity of the churches and free them from domestic banditry. On the other we can look at those grieving, disgraced, disloyal ones, culprits convicted in head and reputation to prisons and exile.

15:5. We can look moreover at those who had violated everything divine and human, had harassed, disturbed, overthrown with their pillaging. We can look at them not only rejoicing and happy, strongest and richest, laden with honors, boastful, but also attempting snares and perils for the famous, the wise, the honorably zealous. So they fear nothing about themselves. There are many unworthy and execrable features in this affair which should cause many shudders. They are caused not only by robbers, greedy ones, poverty-stricken ones, criminals, and those lost in their crime but also by men formerly among the best, pre-eminent in virtue of religion, lofty in nobility of birth. Peril of death and disaster of degradation, as well as plundering and oppression, are brought forward.

15:6. Almost no one maintains soldiers by his own rightful income, but by looting and violence. Naso, most foul of all men, first taught that and to the end [73] always lived as a public plunderer. But now those who are more severely pressed by bandits are the more vehement that no one gainsay them in pillage. Although their soldiery is increased, no one of them seems to have forces except for civil disorder. It is not amazing if Arsenius did speak against such people when summoned by the supreme pontiff. Like Moses he longed to be erased from the book of life for God's people, for the emperor and his sons; [74] like Paul he prayed to be anathema for the brothers and the churches. [75]

15:7. *Adeodatus:* Nor is it amazing if, wearied by prolonged exile and meanly besmirched with dire reproaches, he at first resisted. As we have observed, he would not have taken any further steps if he had not been compellingly urged by us and if the supreme pontiff's authority had not pressed him. But at last, impelled by the brothers, summoned with oaths by the supreme pontiff, implored by the kings, sons of the emperor, begged by people and prelates with whom he had been at the beginning of this case, he decided under such compulsion to come thither, to obey the supreme bishop and to join himself with him who had assumed God's work for all the people, if perhaps with him he might be able to restore peace to the realm and remove discord from it. If he should now desert the order of such eminent authority because of perilous crisis in the present life, there would be no opportunity for withdrawal, indeed there would be a severer arrest. For it is more praiseworthy to die well or to be in danger with the good and the best than to live badly or to agree with the worst. [76]

15:8. The penalty of judgment is one thing, but increase of sin another. So, not without reason, as they say, nor against the purpose of true religion, Arsenius again put himself in a critical situation. But in laudable fashion he presented himself as most dutiful and as a mediator for both parties, if he should be equally received by them. He, who had many times entered peril for others, could not be deterred by his own perils. Let us, therefore, again pursue Paschasius, who was his constant companion. No casualty of the present life could deter him from following the one whom he loved

in Christ and whom he purposed to emulate. He would also have
sought to die with him for the faith of Christ, if the time of crisis
were imminent.

CHAPTER 16

16:1. *Paschasius:* With whatever disposition you say what you
say, I acknowledge the fact because what you say is true. Whatever road he approved which we undertook through the midst of
thick ambushes, through the midst of legions opposing us and run-
ning hither and yon, through the midst of such we proceeded
"with fear and trembling." [77] Until we came to the august kings
and to the holy pontiff himself, we traveled very dangerously, fearing that we might not be allowed to reach our destination. If our
purpose had been disclosed, an even stricter guard than had formerly apprehended him might have completely enveloped us. For
at that time Justina was with the emperor. She was again swaying
the scepter of the whole monarchy, was goading the billows and
seas, was driving the winds, and was turning the hearts of men to
what she wished. Although they had forcibly removed from her
the most infamous one (of whom we have spoken),[78] others even
more infamous were serving her.

16:2. Since we could not turn away and avoid going through
the midst of their cohorts, we proceeded through successfully with
God's protection. When we arrived, however, we were received
with superlative rejoicing by the kings, princes, and all the people.
When we were presented to the most holy pontiff, he received us
reverently enough and with great encouragement. He was deeply
troubled in mind with what he found, with what he could never
before have believed. He was terrified by the emperor (a most
lamentable situation), and by all the people, even by the bishops
who had given him their right hands on the day before we came.
They, however, had become unanimous in resisting those on the
other side, the royal sons, princes, and people. Alas, they had been
won over to depose the said apostolic bishop because he had come
without being summoned.[79]

16:3. Pashhur also was there,[80] as well as the others who agreed with Justina. When these undertakings had been disclosed, the pontiff was greatly surprised and frightened. So we gave him some propositions established by authority of the holy fathers and assembled in writing by his predecessors. No one could thus gainsay that it was his power—no, God's and the blessed Apostle Peter's, as well as his own authority—to go or to send to all peoples in behalf of faith in Christ and of the peace of the churches, in behalf of the preaching of the Gospel and the declaration of truth. In him was all the surpassing authority and living power of blessed Peter, by whom it was fitting for all to be judged, so that he himself should be judged by no one.[81] When all this had been carefully written, he received it gratefully and he was quite encouraged.

16:4. *Theophrastus:* What sort of person the emperor then was or what Justina was, who by her word swayed everything, or what the princes were, of such kind also were those who were found as prelates of Christ! As the former rose in rebellion against human affairs, so also the latter against divine affairs. For like the false prophets in a former time with their horns,[82] they swayed the people against every wind and rebelled against the head of Christ's whole church, that he might not bring peace between father and sons, between emperor and princes. They rebelled so that those who had been unjustly scattered, exiled, and disgraced might not be reconciled, so that peace might not be restored to the churches, so that the statutes of former times and the kingdoms divided among the sons might not remain unshaken and unshattered.

16:5. All that was because Justina had inflamed their efforts so that they would not give counsel to the prince from heart and mind. But by agreeing and fawning for favors, by trampling upon truth, justice, peace, and harmony against those who appeared to be striving for such virtues, they fought back with all their might. Since you were present on that occasion, we beg you to disclose to us what right the sons and the people had, since all were enemies, the father attempting to resist the sons, who were in turn resisting him and who also appeared to be in revolt against their father.

CHAPTER 17

17:1. *Paschasius:* It is known that the divisions of justice are many. There is one justice of God's kingdom, another of the earthly kingdom; one among parents and kinsmen, another among outsiders and aliens. So many laws and customs as there are peoples, so many divisions as there are usages of justice. For this reason a mode of justice must be assembled from the law of God no less than from the law of the country and also from the law of nature. It is written, "Children, obey (or defer to) your parents; so also parents, be unwilling to provoke your sons to wrath." [83] If each had been prudently observed, so much evil would not have accumulated. But in order that what I have set forth may be clear, those chapters [84] should be recalled which the father-emperor had directed to his sons as if an accusation to assert what he would demand in return.

17:2. He first admonished them to remember that they were his sons, that under God he himself begot them.

17:3. To this they replied, "Thanks be to almighty God, who has granted you to reconsider what is true about us, and not only to reconsider, but also to give command. For, O most excellent emperor, we possess in life—after God—nothing dearer than you as a most sacred father; nothing more glorious than that we are and are deemed your sons; nothing richer, nothing wealthier, nothing more munificent to us as honor, excellence, and dignity, praise of name and brightness of glory. So, most glorious one, we come as humble, devoted, yielded subjects, as is fitting. May your pity and mildness deign to reconsider us, that we may not be condemned unjustly nor sentenced without charge nor disinherited without blame. For we have not rebelled against you, as they say and charge, they who as foes endeavor to ruin us. But as suppliants we beg pardon, indulgence, and mercy."

17:4. In another chapter he says, "Remember also that you are my vassals and that you have sworn fealty to me with an oath."

17:5. To this the sons replied, "We well recall that it is as you have declared. By nature, by promises, and by every vow of true fealty we are indeed your *fideles*. As we have never neglected service in your soldiery, so we will never be deserters as long as breath is still alive in us. For your glory, honor, and prosperity are dearer to us than our life. We have, therefore, not come against you, but in every respect we have made ourselves available for you, so that we may obtain the former grace and mercy. We have not led against you those who are here with us. We have brought our troops because we dared not come without them.

17:6. "There are those lying in ambush for us, wishing to ruin us and to overwhelm your glorious empire. They are, moreover, striving to disturb your most serene, pious, and mild mind against us. You, who are by nature filled with superlative generosity and illumined by Christ's grace, they are trying to disturb and currupt against us and other loyal ones and to change you to the bitterness of an alien nature. They are the ones who formerly did nothing except seek to destroy you. It is against all this that we have come to your clemency to expose them. And when their guilt is brought to light, we want to establish to the fullest degree of glory the throne and the majesty of your empire. Restore, therefore, and pardon us who have never wilfully engaged in any mischief."

17:7. He thereupon added, "It is fitting for you to know that for a long time I have devoutly undertaken defense of the Apostolic See, but now you undutifully employ it against me. You exclude me from a duty by which I have lived so long that I cannot bypass it."

17:8. Honorius and his brothers offered this in reply, "May your highness weigh carefully and deign to recall that your superior foresight in Christ made me equally undertake the care and defense of that and of other churches. Your highness and the will of the people constituted me an associate emperor in the whole empire with all power and honor, on every document and coin, in every arrangement, saving your honor and prudence.[85] Indeed your imperial excellency sent me quietly to the same See to confirm in me what your pious honor had decided, namely, that I might be partner and consort in the hallowing no less than in power and name. So it was that before the holy altar and the holy body of blessed Peter, prince of the apostles, I received from the supreme pontiff, with your consent and will, the benediction, honor, and name of imperial office, as well as diadems for the brow and sword for defense of the church and your empire. With you there is no one who should and ought to defend more than I. Because, therefore, I heard that many were lying in ambush for him, I wish it to be manifest to all that no one will harm him whom for peace and harmony I have brought as the vicar of blessed Peter to reconcile the most serene piety of your mind."

17:9. The glorious Caesar sent word again that it was not right for them to prevent the apostolic bishop from approaching him and to bar access to him.

17:10. To this Honorius replied, "Most serene, we have in no wise hindered him from coming, but with God's help we have unlocked the ways which your order had barred or destroyed amid the fastnesses of the Alps. No mortal could freely pass over them until by God's power and our labor they had been leveled. I can say with the prophet that the crooked ways have been made straight and the harsh ones level,[86] so that he and we, both devoted, might come to you. We have constrained him to undertake this labor so that he as supreme intercessor in the place of blessed Peter might meet you whose power lives in him and whose authority excels in him. We do not hinder, as we are blamed. Rather we dutifully present him here whom we have hearkened to and whom in God's cause and ours we suppliantly and humbly beg."

17:11. Again the emperor said, "You are acting unjustly, because you restrain our sons, your brothers with you, and you are making them rebel against me."

17:12. "No! No! My lord," replied Honorius. "They have been caused to flee and have been thrust down. For a long time they have been driven away by persecution. I have merely decided to restore them to your clemency, begging suppliantly that your holy paternity would deign to recall that we are your sons and not, your Majesty, to disavow and destroy us without charge. No, let the instincts of flesh move the bowels of your pity, as well as justice no less of the law of nature than of God's law. Deign to have mercy upon us."

17:13. Then he said finally, "You have also unlawfully received our vassals and you restrain them with you."

17:14. Honorius replied, "Let your beatitude know that it is not so. Scattered, driven away, imprisoned, and exiled, they have escaped and fled to us and to that blessed bishop. Him they begged to intercede for them to your most serene clemency that they might not be unjustly condemned, for they appeared out of loyalty and justice to you so that the fraud and guile of infamous ones should not prevail. In your holy councils and senate of eminent men I have always heard, in your deeds I have always recognized, from you I have always learned, in the deeds [87] of the ancients we have read this: that strong and outstanding men ought to be honored as deserving well and as embellished with glory rather than to be driven away. They are those who have circumspectly checked the assaults and attacks of vicious men. They are those who by authority, fealty, constancy, magnanimity, and counsel have withstood the daring of those lying in ambush, of those men who by their own fickleness and mischief sullied your empire with every depravity.

17:15. "Since they uncovered the mischievous ones and put them to flight, they should be honored and glorified rather than impeached by noxious men. They have always been considered the first and foremost of the palace, since they were first nourished in your training, instructed by your counsels, elevated by your Highness, and illumined with honors. We have therefore resolved to return them to your merciful pity and present them again before your presence. We ought not for that reason to incur offense, if we restore and reconcile to your use those whom the frauds of partisans ruined."

17:16. This was the reciprocal debate, these the mutual complaints; this the father's proposition and the sons' reply. But pardons could not be received in this way. The holy and supreme pontiff, vicar of blessed Peter, was therefore summoned as an intercessor. But when he had come he was not received with worthy honor.[88] He gave a blessing after his manner and set forth the purpose for which he had come. Yet the emperor replied to him, "O holy pontiff, we have not received you, after the manner of the olden kings, with hymns and praise, with the other honors of your dignity and religion, because you have not come in the same manner as your predecessors were accustomed to come to us when summoned."

17:17. But the pontiff said, "You know that we have come properly, because we have come for that peace and harmony which the Author of our salvation left us.[89] We have come to preach this and bring this to all men who have been entrusted to me. If, therefore, O emperor, you will worthily receive both us and Christ's peace, let it rest upon you as well as upon your realm; but if not, the peace of Christ will, as you have read in the Gospel, return to us and be with us." [90]

17:18. *Theophrastus:* Alas, that it should have happened that such a very religious and devout emperor acted so foolishly and unreasonably before everyone in his presence by not giving honor to God or to blessed Peter the Apostle. An exceedingly evil obstinacy of mind, an evil hardness of heart, and that feminine persuasion which deceived our first parent,[91] this is known to have wickedly deceived him also, a fact which we lament. We bewail a man of such great authority and holiness so surrounded by deep darkness that he did not recall what Truth said, "He who receives you receives me," and, "he who hears you, hears me." [92] Woe! What kind of enchantment and blindness of mind was it that thus deluded so great a man, amid so many trials and dangers, amid so many scandals that he might never be recalled or healed by any counsels of Holy Scripture?

17:19. Daily was he seen to meditate on God's law,[93] yet with hardened heart he withdrew from the law of true love. Otherwise he would never have so stubbornly provoked his sons to wrath contrary to commandment, would never have so often and so cruelly rejected and pursued them with hostile sword. They wished nothing evil against him. They wished only that the situation remain unshattered which he and all the people had first ordained and established by oath. But he should love and care for the people and for the church entrusted to him by God and even more for the commonwealth. He should never for the sake of one woman's will or persuasion have admitted such serious evils as befell the realm, such evils as may never perhaps cease, whether by ingenuity, by human ability, by counsel, or by any power. While we are grieving profoundly, we ask you to tell us what the supreme pontiff did with him or obtained from him.

CHAPTER 18

18:1. *Paschasius:* As you have often read,[94] the legates returned whence they had come without gaining peace. So also that one returned without success, without honor, without the fruit of his great effort. Yet during the night following the day on which he withdrew, the hand of the Lord was laid upon all the people with God's just judgment. The minds of all were changed and everyone was smitten and terror-struck by the fear of God. Without persuasion or urging by anyone [95] (so far as I could ascertain), they abandoned the emperor on that night. Others from the least to the greatest approached Honorius and joined his camp. In the morning all their tents appeared pitched about him, so that each might exclaim on the part of the sons and the pontiff, "Manu," which is to say, "What is it?" [96] To all who were unaware it was miraculous. On the day before they were so strong and constant, confident in multitude, in the promises of all, in the advice of pontiffs and senators, in the authority of the father, in multiplied oaths. Yet they were so utterly changeable and vacillating that without deliberation and determination by anyone they had left Caesar alone with Justina. In the course of a night they had flown completely around, like chickens under wing, to the son against whom they had resolutely come out. When they had pitched camp, only one people appeared in the morning.

18:2. In the very early morning twilight, therefore, we came to the aforesaid pontiff to relate the miracle that had happened. Behold, one of the Romans in the midst exclaimed and began to sing, "The right hand of the Lord has shown strength," and the rest following.[97] It was thereupon adjudged by the same holy man and by all who had gathered about that a distinguished and glorious empire had fallen from the hand of the father so that Emperor Honorius might take it up and receive it, since he was the heir and since he had also been made a partner by his father and the people. If he should not accept it, all with one mind said that they would choose one who would bring them aid and defense. When this had been discussed, Honorius agreed and by some kind of decision accepted the sole government of the entire empire,[98] inducing his father to his side. When I had observed the situation, I interrupted Arsenius and said, "Such a fortuitous matter seems a great evil to me, that without serious counsel and careful arrangement so great an empire should be suddenly and completely changed. Moreover, he who was made a partner in good faith might soon formally demand for himself the entire monarchy by overthrowing his father."

18:3. He replied, "It was ours to come here to labor with good will for all and give counsel of peace for all, to calm the internal war which was impending. But now, as there is no one who listens to us, so there is no one who gives attention to what we have taught. As you have read, everyone fears, desires, rejoices, or grieves.[99] They fear what has happened, lest what was done be again formally demanded. They desire, while there is time, more speedily to reach what he had or acquire what he never had. They rejoice and exult eagerly about honors for themselves, for everyone seeks his own and very few seek what belongs to God and to utility. The remainder grieve, who fear to lose, since it was by their daring counsel that the august Caesar did such things against his sons."

CHAPTER 19

19:1. *Adeodatus:* So far as I understand, they were also birds of prey rather than consuls. They believed in nothing but strengthening their own honors. Each one sought to grasp as much as he could for himself. Since the empire had slipped from the father's hand, they ought to have been eager to discuss with the pontiff, Honorius, and his brothers why it had fallen. Then they should have at once corrected, strengthened, established a condition whereby it might thereafter remain united and unshattered. It would have been becoming for the foremost and noblest ones to watch with prudence and advice that the commonwealth and the ruinous state of the whole empire should not again perish through discord. For there is usually no other end of discord among eminent and powerful men except complete annihilation or complete

dominance of the victor. Only so come unity of the realm and restoration of peace and harmony. But that one was not reasonably
confirmed on the throne, nor has the victor obtained the mastery
with God, for his father fell by God's judgment, not by the
victor's.

19:2. Full peace was not restored as long as each sought only
his own. The kingdom was, therefore, again undone by the son's
hand, and it sank lower. Since neither of them walked before God
sincerely, it still today lies weakened and divided. There also remained a concealed hatred among the brothers and a wound deeply
implanted in their hearts and seared in the minds of the greatest
men. For them the commonwealth stretches and slips from worse
to worse. Opportunities are sought and each one bides his time.
The authority of kings, which was suitable and profitable for government, has fallen, and unanimity is shattered and rent asunder.
Judgment and right have perished. The franchises of men are multiplied, but enervated in power they make no progress. Scarcely a
man is found who will set himself forward for safety of the fatherland or offer himself to dangers for its citizens. According to the
statement of Truth, a kingdom divided is daily desolated and corrupted.[100] Where there is no pilot, the people rush headlong into
ruin.[101]

19:3. Here and there individual ones have deserted God as gov-
ernor, when with lying heart they inquired into the differences. So
it was on a certain day that the chiefs and consuls of the palace entered secretly and watchfully. They divided the whole empire
among themselves with the imperial son, giving no attention to the
prerogatives of parents, the equalities of the magnates, the innumerable number of nobles, even the formerly meritorious faithful, nor still more grievously to the dignity of churches and to
heartfelt reverence for God. Arsenius arrived when this had already been accomplished. Confounded when they learned of his
presence, they brought to him the plan of distribution, inquiring if
there was anything displeasing. Very shrewdly he replied, "The
whole matter has been well arranged, except that you have left to
God nothing that is his right, nor have you arranged anything that
might please good people." But when he had presented his position,
he began to be more and more sorrowful because no one heeded

him. He was indeed overwhelmed by the greed and blindness of men.

19:4. It came to pass, therefore, that moment by moment the royal power, already tottering, was falling into ruin rather than being bolstered. Crimes were increasing; discord was again inflamed; quarrels were aroused; plots were nourished. The imperial father was reanimated by the urging of many to consider himself obliged to seek restoration to the throne of empire. Here and there seditions were incited and differences augmented, so much so that there is no house, no city, no town, no countryside, no province where discord does not still reign. On the other hand, greater perils increased until the august father should be restored on the seat of the realm and the son expelled.

CHAPTER 20

20:1. *Paschasius:* He was not expelled as you assert nor did he act unwisely as you complain; for with the august father at his side, he maintained and preserved the kingdom and empire which had fallen. In the deprivation of power and in the sentence of the prelates who induced him to penance, he allowed nothing therein but what the entire senate and people compelled. All these matters our Arsenius moderated by God's grace lest either party should act more cruelly against the other than nature permits or more detestably for such a great crisis. But when the devouring flame of discord raged more and more, the imperial father refused voluntarily to soften and acquiesce. That he might not be guilty of parricide, the imperial son, of his own accord, did acquiesce and left his father again on the throne of empire. He sought indulgence that he might depart a free man, together with all his followers, because the wrath of God had boiled over, had poured hither and yon over all the people. According to Job, on all sides abound the tents of robbers who daringly enough provoke God with their own defiled deeds.[102] Arsenius was already making less progress with his plans. Everywhere floodgates of desire were opened and greed was inflamed.

20:2. He therefore chose a momentary lull in activities to depart from their midst. Although God had given all things into their hands, no one sought God from the heart, with whom are wisdom and fortitude, counsel and understanding.[103] It is clear that none may build up him whom the Almighty himself would destroy; none may loose him whom He would lock up.[104] And so, because He was in turn destroying those whom He had raised up and was raising up again those whom He had locked up, Arsenius preferred to depart, a free man, rather than to remain among them as a servant of sin. Already astonished that no courage or ability existed in men, he deemed rightly that it would appear as wisdom rather than foolishness, for according to the scriptural testimony he knew both the deceiver and the deceived.[105]

20:3. When he had witnessed many guiles and frauds fighting each other here and there, he caused the son to defer to the father and to withdraw with his army unharmed. He also caused the father and those of his party to remain in the empire so that all might understand that He alone was the all-powerful King who brings councilors to a foolish end and judges to dullness.[106] He also loosens the baldrics of kings and girds their reins with rope,[107] as we have seen truly happen to this one. But since neither party had wholly sought God worthily, they were changed in turn in alternate successes and the people were scourged. So all may understand that He is God who renders priests inglorious and supplants magnates.[108] Otherwise, except by their own faults, would there be such great harassment and confusion of all. The lips of truthful ones had been changed and the teaching of old men taken away.[109] Arsenius alone was not powerful against all, except only what he did that the turn of events should not deteriorate further. Many here and there were urging just such, since strife and scorn had been poured out upon princes.[110] But alas, what then stood in the way to prevent civil war from arising among them, we afterward saw done.

20:4. Nonetheless our Arsenius preferred to die rather than to agree to or to be present at any such condition. He therefore persuaded the son to withdraw with all his men; and similarly, the father to resume power over the empire so badly treated. For God, who changes the hearts of "the princes of earth and deceives them to walk vainly in pathless ways," [111] had hardened His heart. To

His judgment Arsenius entrusted everything lest something more infamous befall them. For with faults on every side, it was sad to realize what Job said, "They will coax as if in darkness and not in light. He will cause them to wander like drunk men.[112] For he alone is, whose thought no one can turn aside. But by his just judgment he will cause whatever he has wished." [113] Doubtless these things which had happened, which were daily becoming worse and increasing, were judgments.

20:5. Although it was late, he foresaw that which here and there in the present is discerned as already completed. So he chose rather to take flight than to remain with any of them. I was witness that the father wished very earnestly to retain him with him with all honor and highest office, if he would take an oath of fealty from his men. Then the imperial son sought to take him with him. But listening to neither of them, no, resisting them courageously, he departed from both. Entering Italy on winged step,[114] he betook himself to the monastery of St. Columban.[115] At the urging of the brothers, he undertook to rule it so that it would not be invaded by plunderers as all others had been. As long as he lived there, he ruled it nobly and peacefully.

CHAPTER 21

21:1. *Theophrastus.* Many reproach him for leaving the place where he was professed and elected. They claim that influenced by avarice he seized another place by some kind of pact. Perhaps it would have been more religious either to continue in his own—a short while ago you acknowledged that he could have done so peacefully—or to dwell in the new place without burden of government. In one case it would indeed have been the fulfilment of a vow; but in the other a praiseworthy accomplishment of humility.

21:2. *Paschasius.* Perhaps you have not read the life and acts of the same blessed Columban. When driven away from Luxeuil by the jealousy of a certain female,[116] he joined in constructing this place, where he presided in a laudable manner over many brothers until the end of his life. For the talent which is due, one should not hide away in the ground,[117] but should appropriate it for the brothers as we read blessed Benedict and so many others did. In no wise, therefore, does it seem less that he defended it from enemies, governed it most devotedly under the holy *Rule,* and zealously caused it to grow, than to have begun it first in the selfsame profession. Because he did not believe that he could live quietly in his own nor advance in the duty of government, I believe that no one of sound mind would reproach him, if to be of use to a great many he devoted himself under the same religion to the brothers for quiet and great usefulness, if someone could save himself and us amid so many crises. For already no faith or a rare faith is found among those who desire to be or to seem the greatest. Among them it is thought to be cowardice to despise the honors of the world for religion.

CHAPTER 22

22:1. *Adeodatus:* We know how he lived among them, and if it is a matter of reproach to despise honors, it is deemed imprudent to love Christ's poverty. We have now, Paschasius, grieved over what has been done in the past, over what has happened. We have wept over crises and varied results. We have reckoned the temptations. We have enumerated with lamentation the causes. It remains only to give attention to the end and to his death. We were not present then or at his wake, but we have scattered tears instead of flowers about his grave.[118] Long afterward let us at least commend the absent ones to the Lord with prayers. Since we do not know the day of his burial or the anniversary, let us commemorate some day while life remains in us. In our mind this day is certainly the representation of the future rest in which he lived who is deemed dead. The praise of his memory declares that better is the day of death when he entered everlasting life than the day of his birth, for when he began to live he became liable to death.[119]

22:2. *Paschasius:* You exhort us well, brother, when you thus command us to approach and review his death so that you may teach us that our man should not be mourned. As through the sin of one death passed upon all men, so also through One resurrection is fulfilled, with whom all men who die piously live blessedly.[120]

Since we do not shun the author of the race, we cannot shun the author of death. If we do not escape him, we cannot avoid what is common to all. It is unfitting that we despair of that life which is in Christ, since He is Himself the sole author of life and resurrection. Thus as through one there is death, so it must be truly believed that through one Jesus Christ there is life, not any kind of life but blessed and eternal life. The day of our father's departure, most beloved, is a day of life rather than of death, when through this death he entered everlasting life. Hence it is fitting for us to be consoled rather than to lament, since death is a necessity for all and we ought not to think harsh whatever belongs to all.

22:3. It is not to be bemoaned, first, because it is the common due of all; then, because it absolves us of all tribulations of the world; lastly, because it is a kind of sleep which frees us from labors and cares of this world and affords rest after the miseries and sorrows of present life. This annual occurrence therefore rightly gives strength to faith, grants hope of attainment, and pours back the affection of love. For whom will the grace of resurrection not comfort? Whom will hope not raise up? Whom will confidence in fulfilment not strengthen? Whom will charity not inflame and whom will so great a love not inwardly vivify, if not one born of the Holy Spirit? Even if hitherto we have wept over the varied calamities happening and the labors of misery, it remains now to direct the mind forward and fix our eyes upon that day in which one lives better, to pour back our attention after him. That day in the courts of the Lord, albeit one and one alone, is better than a thousand.[121] So let us not center upon the father with all our feelings, lest grief for his absence again steal upon us. But that we may not be exiles from him whom we love and from his great piety and grace, it is well that he dwell in our mind where great joys are proclaimed and where doubtless invited he has come and where he himself has entered with joy.

22:4. *Theophrastus:* Why do you say that he was invited? Are not all invited who have received regeneration in baptism through faith? Everyone is invited to the same immortality, and it is therefore absurd to lament this one as though dead. It is also exceedingly foolish to bewail in a special manner that which you know has been prescribed for everyone. For it is to lift the spirit above nature not to receive the common law of death, to reject partnership with nature, to ignore the measure of flesh. If this one, however, came to this invited to receive it willingly, as you say, you set forth the case of the just debtor who willingly runs to meet what he owes, ready to pay what he owes.

CHAPTER 23

23:1. *Paschasius:* Not without reason do I say that he came invited, because I have heard the following story from a certain holy bishop. On the day before the end approached, he was called and invited through a vision not just once but twice, as if he were about to complete his embassy in the presence of the eternal King and receive thanks for his labors. As a result, our Arsenius, even before he incurred the fever of death,[122] said to him that shortly he would be going hence through death. As the aforesaid bishop himself could well understand, he lived thereafter more eager in hope and more unconcerned in the fever.

23:2. He did not labor a long time. When seized by fever he became more anxious for the august emperor (for whom he was at that time acting) than for himself. He feared that what he had recently assured the father, the latter would bypass when occasion arose, for he himself was harassed by fevers. Herein it is clear that he persisted unconquered in faith and devoted in charity, strengthened in the hope of his calling.[123] Bound to Christ by this three-fold cord,[124] he returned his soul to heaven[125] with assurance. His slight body earth received on the side of the basilica where blessed Columban rests. It could not be done differently: one home should encompass both equally and one neighborhood of burial should grace those whom one religion held fast and whom almost equal trial drove from their sees and put to flight in Italy as if pilgrims.

23:3. Both queens who did that were alike in wickedness. Although separated in time, they were associates in one crime of irreligion. Alike in jealousy, intolerant of holy men who rebuked their like unmentionable wickedness and who might oppose them in any way. By guile and fraud they compelled them to abandon their own monasteries and slip away to Italy. In that place [126] there was at length for them a single mode of life (even if the reason was different), one religion, one flight from the plots of two women, one rest from labors, and one burial. The former was approved by his virtues as a holy confessor of Christ; the latter, as his servant, should be supported by merits, graced with praises, and aided with prayers. I therefore do not believe that those, who presented themselves to meet crises for faith, zeal for God, religion, equality of judgment, and application of virtues, received the end of their labor in one place without God's providence.

23:4. It cannot be doubted that the illustrious father, wearing the toga, lies in eternal rest with God's holy confessor. For he, too, was driven from his own monastery into exile, cast out of his country and his function of government. But for those who had a common trial, may a common consolation of rest forever refresh them because of the quality of their merits and may a proportionate share of justice adorn them in heaven.

23:5. It is, then, fitting because of so great a hope for us to console one another rather than to grieve. Not only has confidence in his blessedness assuaged the great mourning of distress, but time has obliterated, reason has overcome, prudence has already mitigated it. Although we have rightfully lamented, we have bemoaned the various attacks on him, and we have enumerated his multiplied trials, we have also set forth the events. It behooves us now to wish him joy, as it behooves us to be refreshed with gladness instead of grief, to be reinvigorated with happiness of good hope instead of mourning, and to be inwardly clothed with exultation instead of sadness.

23:6. We know of certainty that the famous father outlived his body. Although he was absent from us when he died, he is nevertheless present, for he lives in blessedness in Him who is everywhere. After the bonds of his senses have been loosened, his released soul looks now with free contemplation as a still embodied soul cannot do. For if in sleep the soul, even while still buried in the body, elevates itself to higher things and sometimes reports to the body visions of absent things or even celestial things, how much more when, absolved of the hardships of the world, it lives entirely in the Lord who lives everywhere and completes and rules all things everywhere?

23:7. Our father has not gone somewhere on a long pilgrimage, except to Him for whom and in whom he lived, who is everywhere in himself and who lives everywhere. For this indeed he died daily with the Apostle to live more perfectly to God.[127] As the philosophers say, the life of the wise man is a meditation on death.[128] He meditated how to approach that which is perfect. Thus, not in part nor in riddle nor in shadow, but in truth just as it is, the eternal vision might appear manifest to the one peering with unveiled face. It could not be now, because according to the Apostle, we now know only in part and we prophesy in part.[129] But when that which is in this life perfect shall come to us, that which is in part shall be abandoned, and then that will be perfect which is now in part.

23:8. No one would hasten toward the end relying on the Lord by faith except to escape the inconveniences of this life, for which David lamented to God, "Behold, you have set my days before you and my substance before you as though it were nothing; yet all is vanity, every living man." [130] So, my brothers, Arsenius, after he had realized, after he had learned, never hesitated to avoid his own will. He did not wish to be vainly disquieted in the world, nor to hope in the uncertainty of riches. But he hoped in the living God to whom he went. While he tasted death of the body, he found life, because he did not incur the first death of the soul.

23:9. Death is spoken of in a threefold manner: [131] one, when we die to sin and live to God; [132] another, when we sin to death, as it is said, "The soul which shall sin, the same shall die"; [133] third, the departure from this life, by which even Christ died, and everyone who shall taste this life shall die that he may be able to sin no more.[134] The first is called spiritual death; the second, natural; and third, penal. Although what is called natural death may appear to some to be penal, the Lord did not authorize it as a penalty, as they say who have written books about the good of death. They say it was granted as a remedy, since one thing was put to Adam as a penalty and another as a remedy. As penalty it is said, "Because you listened to the voice of your wife more than to me and you ate of what I had commanded you not to eat, accursed is the ground in your work," or otherwise, "until you shall return to the earth from which you were taken." [135] Behold the kinds of penalties when he was cursed: even in his work thorns and thistles are sprouting.

These thorns and thistles choke the word of life. They also beget cares and anxieties by which the food that is from heaven is killed and removed, by which food every man lives who lives to God; [136] and death whereby the soul may live is penally hindered. That death is granted by the holy Lord as a remedy, as if the end of evils.

23:10. It was not said to Adam, "Because you listened to the voice of your wife, you will return to the earth." If He had thus spoken, the sentence would be penal, just as that statement, "Accursed is the earth in your work," et cetera. You have, therefore, a death of the soul, namely, sin. You also have a penalty which is rightly called true death. And you have a death which is the end and remedy of our punishments; by it the course of this life is cut short in an hour. This death by which Abraham died and by which also our father died, indeed by which we all die, is not only an evil but also a good. Blessed Ambrose produced an extraordinary book, *The Good of Death*.[137] If we have thus at the departure of so great a father lamented the manifold sorrows of things and his many labors, let us rejoice with him that for him to live was Christ and to die gain.[138] Let us moreover die together with him that with him we may live in Christ. Let us learn with daily practice to die to the world, that we may be withdrawn from the flesh and live by meditation as in heaven. Let us in the meanwhile undertake the image of death, lest the penalty of death assail us.

23:11. Through the good of death we can thus attain eternal life in which neither death nor grief will be any more. Let us moreover die the death of the just that we may live with them. Let us also die the death of our great father, since we believe that he already lives in blessedness, that with him we too may be able to live, as he always prayed and taught. Let us exhibit in ourselves the vows of the father. For he vowed and offered us, especially our brothers, to God as if a victim, a new oblation for sacrifice, whom he dedicated to the Lord. He dedicated to the Lord not only those whom he selected and instructed but also those who will be in the same place for the same instruction. He lived not only for himself and God but also for us all. In example and teaching he taught us to live for God. To us therefore his life was profitable, to whom with the Apostle to die was gain.[139]

23:12. Let us therefore, as suppliants, pray earnestly to Christ, who offers the vows of the saints to God the Father, that He himself may confer his gifts in us for the increase of His merits. His gifts were in larger measure for an accumulation of his reward offered for him to God the Father, that our oblation and his for us together may be accepted in Christ for an everlasting sacrifice. As in the oath of their holy confession there was one profession, so may there be one partnership of eternal reward in joy.

CHAPTER 24

24:1. *Paschasius:* We have learned that he was carried to the joys of eternal life by bands of angels. In fact the venerable Queen Irmingard related it.[140] With a fondness for pious recollection, she often said that, at the departure of the great man, in the very hour of his death, she sent throughout the different places of Italy for each person to commend with prayers the soul of the blessed man to the Lord. Among them she sent to her own illustrious convent, below the walls of Brescia [141] about forty miles from Ticino, where a multitude of nuns serve the Lord. She enjoined and implored them to commend with prayers the blessed soul of the man of God to Christ as to God. When her emissaries arrived, they found Christ's handmaidens already concerned about the death of Arsenius and speaking among themselves, foreknowing the hour and time of his departure. When the sacred letters which the queen had sent had been carefully read, they found that everything about him had already been revealed to them by angels.

24:2. There had lived among them two consecrated virgins who testified all these matters to them as they had foretold. They had heard angelic choirs carrying the soul of the blessed man to heaven. At his obsequies they sang among other things the hymn, "We praise you, O God; we acknowledge you to be the Lord," [142] in alternate voice in the ecclesiastical manner. In harmony they commended the obsequies of the blessed man to the holy Lord. The two listened to these praises for a very long time. Then they summoned all the rest that they too might listen. To none, however, was it granted except to those two alone, that they might be witnesses of the truth.

24:3. While they were talking thus, the sacred letters which the aforesaid couriers had brought were read. They discovered then that he had died in the same hour and day when the angels had carried him away with praises. What Scripture testifies is certain, "Blessed is the man who endures temptation, for when he has been proven, he will receive the crown of life." [143] That these matters might become public knowledge, the community ordered prepared for the queen a true account of such things as the two had heard together with other matters not to be uttered.

24:4. But perhaps a certain unbelieving slanderer will say that a man exposed to great temptations and cast down by pressures did not merit such attention. We believe, however, that Christ himself, the Judge who presented and approved, also rewarded the one whom He had approved, as He promised in the Gospel, "Well done, good and faithful one, because you have been faithful in a few things, I will put you over many things; enter into the joy of your Lord." [144] Make what I say false, although it is true . . . what I say has already been related. With his own just ones therefore . . . is from God, to have received the rewards of life eternal . . . saying for him from the Gospel, "Friend, I do you no injury: I grant freely. Have you not also agreed with me for the coin of life eternal? Am I not permitted to do what I will? Freely only do I pay anyone in the same weight some merchandise. Is your eye worthless because I am good?" [145] Because I weigh out freely . . . to no one except who is [received by grace, not] by work for God. I therefore beg, let us thank God, brothers, who has granted such things to us and promised Himself to us, that such things have surpassed him . . . that we may rejoice much. . . .[146]

Notes

INTRODUCTION

1. Henri Peltier, *Pascase Radbert* (Amiens: Duthoit, 1938). Other easily accessible material on the life of Paschasius Radbertus: by Jacques Mabillon, reprinted in PL, cxx, 9A—24D; by Ludwig Traube (see next note); by Engelmodus, see PLAC, III, 62–66. Peltier presents a convenient summary of the available evidence. More briefly, see George E. McCracken and Allen Cabaniss, *Early Medieval Theology* (Library of Christian Classics, IX) (Philadelphia: Westminster, 1957), 90–93. For excellent treatment, consult Max Manitius, *Geschichte der lateinischen Literatur des Mittelalters*, I (Munich: Beck, 1911), 401–11. See also Adolf Ebert, *Allgemeine Geschichte der Literatur des Mittelalters im Abendlande*, II (Leipzig: Vogel, 1880), 230–44; Ernst Dümmler's notes in *Gesellschaft für ältere deutsche Geschichtskunde Archiv* (Hanover), IV, 301–305.

2. Ludwig Traube in PLAC, III, 38, n.1.

3. Paschasius Radbertus, *Expositio in Psalmum XLIV*, III, *ad init.* (PL, cxx, 1040B).

4. *Wala*, I, 14:2; 15:3 (as translated below).

5. He is listed as a saint, although his canonization rests only on historical evidence of veneration.

6. PL, cxx, 31B—994C.

7. PL, cxx, 1387C—1436A. The acrostic *invocatio* is also given in PLAC, III, 51.

8. PL, cxx, 1435B—1458B.   9. PL, cxx, 1458C—1490A.

10. PLAC, III, 62–66 (esp. lines 142–47).

11. PL, cxx, 1507C—1556C. Extensive selections of the *Vita* are given in MGH, Scriptores, II, 524–32. The *Ecloga* is beautifully edited by Traube in PLAC, III, 42–51; see also Dümmler's notes cited in Note 1 above.

12. PL, cxx, 1259B—1350D; partially translated by McCracken in McCracken and Cabaniss, *op. cit.*, 94–108.

13. Translated in full by McCracken in McCracken and Cabaniss, *op. cit.*, 118-47.

14. PL, cxx, 1351A—1366A.   15. PL, cxx, 1059C—1256B.

16. PL, cxx, 1367B—1386D, reconstituted from the doubtful works of St. Ildefonsus, PL, xcvi, 207A—236C.

17. PL, cxx, 1489B—1508C.   18. PL, cxx, 993D—1060B.

19. PL cxx, 1559D—1650B. There is an excellent edition by Ernst Dümmler in *Philosophische and historische Abhandlungen der königlichen Akademie der Wissenschaften zu Berlin*, II (1900), 18–98. The ensuing translation is based on this edition as well as the version in PL.

20. Among the doubtful works of St. Jerome, PL, xxx, 297D—305B.

21. "Cogitis me," among the doubtful works of St. Jerome, PL, xxx, 122C—142D; "Hodie dilectissimi," among the doubtful works of St. Ildefonsus, PL, xcvi, 239A—250C, with which is to be included the fragment, "Quotiescumque dilectissimi," PL, xcvi, 235B—236C; "Inter praecipuas," as in the foregoing, PL, xcvi, 254C—257D; "Adest nobis," as in the foregoing, PL, xcvi, 254C—257D.

22. The "Bibliographical Notes" below in this introduction set forth the titles of several treatises employed here. The latest and best is Lorenz Weinrich, *Wala—Graf, Mönch and Rebell: Die Biographie eines Karolingers* (Lübeck and Hamburg: Matthiesen Verlag, 1963), being Vol. 386 of *Historische Studien*.

23. See the genealogical chart in Weinrich, *op. cit.*, 107.

24. *Ibid.*, and Joseph Calmette, *De Bernardo s. Guillelmi filio (?-844)* (Toulouse: Privat, 1902).

25. *Adalard*, ch. 7 (as translated below).

26. Notker, *Gesta Karoli*, II, 17, in Reinhold Rau, ed., *Fontes ad historiam regni Francorum aevi Karolini illustrandam*, Part III (Berlin: Rütten und Loening, 1960), 412, being Rudolf Buchner, ed., *Ausgewählte Quellen zur Deutschen Geschichte des Mittelalters*, VII.

27. Einhard, *Vita Karoli*, 18, in Rau, ed., *op. cit.*, II (1956), 188, being Buchner, ed., *op. cit.*, V.

28. *Adalard*, 8:2.   29. *Ibid.*, 9:1.   30. *Ibid.*, 9:2.

31. *Ibid.*, 11:2—13:1.   32. *Ibid.*, 14.

33. *Annales regni Francorum*, anno 809.

34. Charlemagne had an older son (illegitimate) named Pepin and called "the Hunchback." The Pepin mentioned in the text was a son of Charlemagne's second wife Hildegard and was originally named Carloman. See Einhard, *op. cit.*, 20.

35. *Adalard*, 16:1.   36. *Ibid.*, 16:2.

37. *Translatio s. Viti*, 3, ed. F. Stentrup in *Abhandlungen der Corveyer Geschichtschreibung* (Münster: Commission der Aschendorffschen Buchhandlung, 1906), 79.

38. *Adalard*, 17.   39. *Ibid.*, 29.   40. *Translatio s. Viti*, 3.

41. *Annales regni Francorum*, anno 811.   42. Einhard, *op, cit.*, 33.

43. *Annales regni Francorum, anno* 812.   44. *Wala,* I, 6:2.

45. Weinrich, *op. cit.,* 17.   46. *Wala,* I, 6:3.

47. Weinrich, *op. cit.,* 18.   48. *Wala,* II, 8:4.

49. *Adalard,* 32:2; *Wala,* I, 6:5.   50. *Wala,* I, 6:5f.; 11:12.

51. *Adalard,* 32:1—35:2.   52. *Ibid.,* 32:1.   53. *Ibid.,* 33:1.

54. Alcuin, *Epistola* 125, as numbered in PL, c, 360C—362A.

55. The letter to a beloved "daughter" on the errors of Felicianism in PL, ci, 299D—304B; *De animae ratione liber ad Eulaliam virginem,* PL, ci, 639A—647B.

56. PLAC, I, 396.   57. *Adalard,* 33:2; Weinrich, *op. cit.,* 20.

58. Peltier, *op. cit.,* 30f.   59. *Adalard,* 35:2.

60. *Translatio s. Viti,* 3.

61. Allen Cabaniss, trans., *Son of Charlemagne,* (Syracuse: Syracuse University Press, 1961), 54.

62. *Adalard,* 32:1.   63. *Ibid.,* 35:2.   64. Cabaniss, *op. cit.,* 72.

65. *Adalard,* 35:2.   66. *Ibid.*   67. *Ibid.*   68. *Wala,* I, 7:8.

69. *Wala,* I, 9:1—12:6.   70. *Adalard,* 41.

71. *Annales regni Francorum, anno* 821; cf. Cabaniss, *op. cit.,* 72.

72. *Adalard,* 49, 50.   73. *Ibid.,* 50.

74. *Annales regni Francorum, anno* 822.

75. The two preceding paragraphs have been summarized from Allen Cabaniss, *Agobard of Lyons: Churchman and Critic* (Syracuse: Syracuse University Press, 1953), 39–47.

76. Agobard, *De dispensatione,* 3; cf. Cabaniss, *op. cit.,* 46.

77. *Adalard,* 52.

78. In Adalard's case, cf. Agobard, *Consultatio et supplicatio* (PL, civ, 101A) and *De dispensatione* (PL, civ, 230C); cf. Cabaniss, *op. cit.,* 46.

79. *Adalard,* 54, 59.

80. See his statutes for the government of a monastery in PL, cv, 535C—550C, dated *ca.* 822.

81. Hincmar, *Pro institutione Carolomanni regis et de ordine palatii,* XII (PL, cxxv, 998BC): "In my youth I saw the wise old man, Adalard, kinsman of Emperor Charles the Great, abbot of the monastery of Corbie, first among the first councilors. His booklet, *De ordine palatii,* I read and copied." And no doubt incorporated large segments of it into his own book. Otherwise the work is not extant. See J. M. Wallace-Hadrill, *The Long-Haired Kings* (New York: Barnes and Noble, 1962), 119f.

82. Edmund Bishop, *Liturgica Historica* (Oxford: Clarendon Press, 1918), 333–48.

83. Agobard, *Consultatio et supplicatio, ad init.,* and *De dispensatione, ad fin.* (see Note 78 above).

84. *Translatio s. Viti,* 3.   85. *Wala,* I, 12:6—13:2.

86. *Translatio s. Viti,* 3.   87. *Ibid,* 3.

88. *Ibid.; Adalard,* 66; 67:2; 69.

89. *Translatio s. Viti,* 3; *Wala,* I, 20:1f.   90. *Adalard,* 67:2.

91. *Wala*, I, 12:6; 15:1, 4.   92. *Ibid.*, I, 13:2.

93. *Ibid; Translatio s. Viti*, 3.

94. *Wala*, I, 7:2.   95. *Ibid*, I, 16:3.

96. *Ibid.*, I, 20:2; *Translatio s. Viti*, 4.

97. *Annales regni Francorum, anno* 822; Cabaniss, *Son of Charlemagne*, 74.

98. *Wala*, I, 25:4; 29:2.   99. *Ibid.*, I, 26:1–12; 27:2.

100. Amalarius, *Prologus antiphonarii*, 2, in J. M. Hanssens, *Amalarii episcopi opera liturgica omnia*, I (Studi e Testi, 138; Città del Vaticano: Biblioteca Apostolica Vaticana, 1948), 361; cf. Allen Cabaniss, *Amalarius of Metz* (Amsterdam: North Holland Publishing Co., 1954), 76.

101. Agobard, *Consultatio et supplicatio* (see Note 78 above).

102. Agobard, *De dispensatione* (see Note 78 above).

103. *Annales regni Francorum, anno* 825; Weinrich, *op. cit.*, 51; *Wala*, I, 28:1.

104. *Wala*, I, 29:3, 5.   105. *Adalard*, 78.   106. *Ibid.*, 79.

107. *Ibid.*, 81:1; 82.   108. *Ibid.*, 79, 87.   109. *Ibid*, 77.

110. *Wala*, I, 11:6.   111. *Ibid.*, I, 20:2; *Translatio s. Viti*, 4.

112. *Wala*, I, 11:6.   113. *Ibid.*, I, 11:7.

114. Agobard, *Contra preceptum impium, ad init.* (PL, civ, 175A); Cabaniss, *Agobard*, 57f.

115. Rimbert, *Vita s. Anscharii* (PL, cxviii, 967B); Weinrich, *op. cit.*, 56f.

116. *Wala*, I, 4:1.   117. *Ibid.*, I, 4:2f.; II, 15:2.   118. *Ibid.*, I, 4:5.

119. *Ibid., passim*, esp. I, 9:8; 21:1f.   120. *Ibid.*, II, 7:3—8:3.

121. *Ibid.*, II, 8:4.   122. *Ibid.*, II, 6:3; 8:2.   123. *Ibid.*, II, 8:5, 7.

124. *Ibid.*, II, 8:8—10:2.   125. *Ibid.*, II, 1:3.   126. *Ibid.*, II, 10:1.

127. *Ibid.*, II, 10:4.   128. Cabaniss, *Agobard*, 79f.

129. *Wala*, II, 10:1f.   130. *Ibid.*, II, 10:2, 10.   131. *Ibid.*, II, 10:4.

132. *Ibid.*, II, 10:14; 12:1.   133. *Ibid.*, II, 12:2, 7.

134. *Ibid.*, II, 13:2f.

135. *Ibid.*, II, 14:1; Cabaniss, *Son of Charlemagne*, 91.

136. Cabaniss, *Agobard*, 83–87.   137. *Wala*, II, 14:2.   138. *Ibid.*

139. *Ibid.*, II, 15:8.   140. *Ibid.*, II, 16:1.   141. *Ibid.*, II, 16:2—18:3.

142. *Ibid.*, II, 19:1–4.   143. Cabaniss, *Agobard*, 88.

144. *Wala*, II, 18:3.   145. *Ibid.*, II, 20:1–3.   146. *Ibid.*, II, 20:5.

147. Thegan, *Vita Hludowici, appendix* (p. 250 of vol. cited in Note 27 above); Cabaniss, *Son of Charlemagne*, 108.

148. *Wala*, II, 23:2; 24:1–3.   149. Thegan, *op. cit.*

150. Cabaniss, *Son of Charlemagne*, 110.   151. *Wala*, I, 6:5.

152. *Adalard*, 4:2.   153. *Ibid.*, 85:2.   154. *Wala*, I, (1).

155. Weinrich, *op. cit.*, 7.   156. *Adalard*, 20:1f.; cf. *Wala*, I, (1).

157. *Adalard*, 84.   158. See below, following *Adalard*, 88.

159. *Adalard*, 57.   160. *Wala*, I, 1:2.

161. *Ibid.,* I, 8:3; 21:1–3, 10; etc.   162. *Ibid.,* II, 20:2–4.

163. E.g., *Adalard,* 17; *Wala,* I, 26.2.

164. Wordplays: *Adalard,* 4:2; 5:1; *Wala,* I, (9), (14), (17); alliteration: *Adalard,* (d); *Wala,* II, 2:4; 10:6f.; 12:1.

165. *Wala,* I, 15:2.

166. Horace, *Satirae,* II, 7, 86, in *Adalard,* 15, and *Wala,* I, 9:2; Cicero, *De inventione rhetorica,* II, 1, in *Adalard,* 20:1, and *Wala,* (1); Revelation, *passim,* in *Adalard,* 39, and *Wala,* II, 12:2; II Tim. 2:4, in *Adalard,* 68:2, and *Wala,* II, 2:7 and 3:4; II Macc. 15:14, in *Adalard,* 86, and *Wala,* I, 2:6; John 11:11 (and similar references) in *Adalard,* I, and *Wala,* II, 22:3.

167. *Adalard,* 81:1; *Wala,* II, 24:1–3.   168. *Adalard,* 26:3.

169. *Wala,* I, 29:9.   170. *Ibid.,* I, (15)–(17).

171. *Ibid.,* I, (1); cf. 6:2; 15:2; II, 10:1; 20:5.

172. *Ibid.,* II, 1:3; 2:2–5; 3:1–5.   173. *Ibid.,* II, 16:3.

174. *Ibid.,* II, 17:1–15.   175. *Ibid.,* II, 24:1–3.   176. *Adalard,* 18.

177. *Ibid.,* 33, 61, and elsewhere; *Wala,* I, 1:2, and elsewhere.

178. *Adalard,* 7; 9:2; 11:2; 12:1; 16:1; 29; 30:2; 50; *Wala,* I, 2:2f.; 6:3–6.

179. *Adalard,* 8:2.   180. *Wala,* I, 6:6; 7:2–4; 16–3.

181. *Adalard,* 7; per contra, Peltier, *op. cit.,* 33.   182. *Wala,* I, 5:5.

183. *Adalard,* 23:2f.   184. *Ibid.,* 28.   185. *Adalard,* 47:2.

186. *Wala,* I, 10:5.   187. *Ibid.,* I, 10:6.   188. *Ibid.,* I, 11:4.

189. *Ibid.,* I, 16:5.   190. *Ibid.,* I, 16:6.   191. *Adalard,* 59:2.

192. *Wala,* I, 21:8.   193. *Ibid.,* I, 24:2.

194. Calmette, *op. cit.* (in Note 24 above).

195. Mrs. Bernard Fischer is still at work on a University of Chicago Ph.D. thesis about Judith.

196. *Wala,* II, 7:2f.   197. *Ibid.,* II, 8:4f.   198. *Ibid.,* II, 9:1.

199. *Ibid.,* II, 8:6; 9:6.   200. *Ibid.,* II, 16:1, 4.

201. *Ibid.,* II, 12:2; 21:2.   202. *Ibid.,* II, 23:3.

203. Bernard was executed in 844; Judith died in 843.

204. *Wala,* I, (1).   205. *Adalard,* 85:2.

206. *Adalard* and *Wala, passim.*

207. *Adalard,* 8:3; 30:2; 34; 39; 70.   208. *Ibid.,* 67.

209. *Ibid.,* 55; 63.   210. *Ibid.,* 43.

211. The following verses from the Song of Songs are cited in *Adalard*—1:4, 16, 17; 2:5 (bis), 9, 11, 12, 16; 3:1 (bis), 11; 4:8, 12, 16; 5:8 (tris), 10, 11, 12, 13, 14, 16; 6:2, 3, 10, 11, 13; 7:1, 12; 8:3, 5, 6, (bis). Murray Roston, *Prophet and Poet: The Bible and the Growth of Romanticism* (Evanston: Northwestern University Press, 1965), is very important for the study of the influence of the Song of Songs on the development of romanticism and romantic expression, especially in the eighteenth and nineteenth centuries, but applicable also to much earlier periods. See also J. J. Wilhelm, *The Cruelest Month* (New Haven: Yale University Press, 1965), esp. 98–104.

212. M. L. W. Laistner, *Thought and Letters in Western Europe, A.D. 500 to 900*, 2nd ed. (Ithaca, N.Y.: Cornell University Press, 1957), 278.

213. A convenient and delightful example may be found in Charles H. Beeson, *A Primer of Medieval Latin* (New York: Scott, Foresman and Co., 1925), 169–173.

214. The following lines from Terence's plays are cited in whole or in part in *Wala*, I—*Hecyra*, III, 3, 1–3; V, 4, 39f.; *Andria*, I, 1, 34 (bis); *Adelphi*, IV, 3, 14–16; V, 4, 1–20; *Phormio*, I, 8, 57; IV, 1, 23; IV, 2, 1; V, 4, 23–26; *Eunuchus*, I, 2, 1, 4, 7, 16–19, 22; II, 2, 16–22; *Heautontimorumenos*, I, 1, 91–105. On the tradition of Terence in medieval Latin literature, see M. Manitius' notes in *Philologus: Zeitschrift für das klassische Alterthum*, LII, 546–52 (although there are no references to Paschasius Radbertus). Ernst Curtius, *Europäische Literatur und lateinisches Mittelalter* (Bern: Francke, 1948), and W. T. H. Jackson, *The Literature of the Middle Ages* (New York: Columbia University Press, 1960), contain some similar material, but neither refer to Radbertus.

215. Traube (in PLAC, III, 42) suggests perhaps the influence of Cicero's *Cato maior*, but Terence's influence seems more reasonable, particularly in view of the citations in the preceding Note.

216. Pashhur (Latin, *Phasur*), *Wala*, II, 16:3.

217. *Wala*, I, 9:2.   218. *Ibid.*, I, 9:5.

The Life of St. Adalard

1. Ambrose, *De obitu Valentiniani consolatio, ad init.*, as in PL, xvi, 1357A—1384B.

2. Wisd. 2:1.   3. Cf. Mark 12:27 (Luke 20:38).

4. E.g., John 11:11. On this concept see Oscar Cullmann, *Immortality of the Soul or Resurrection of the Dead?* (New York: Macmillan, 1958), esp. ch. IV, "Those Who Sleep."

5. Cf. I. Thess. 4:13.   6. *Ibid.*   7. Cf. Job 11:33, 35.

8. Note the play on words.   9. Cf. preceding Note.

10. Cf. preceding Notes.   11. The romantic "pathetic fallacy."

12. Venantius Fortunatus, Appendix, I, vii, 3–6 (PL, lxxxviii, 593C). It is interesting that these very lines (plus one) are cited by Peter Dronke, *Medieval Latin and the Rise of European Love-Lyric*, I (Oxford: Clarendon, 1965), 204, to suggest Fortunatus' "almost infantile dependence" on Queen Radegunda!

13. Cf. I. Thess. 4:13, as in Notes 5 and 6 above.

14. Cf. S. of S. 2:11.   15. Cf. S. of S. 2:12.

16. Based on Pss. 48:8 (Vulg. 47:9) and 87:3 (Vulg. 86:3). What I

have translated as "Lord of virtues" is usually rendered "Lord of hosts," but the play on words requires my version.

17. Cf. S. of S. 2:9.   18. Cf. S. of S. 8:6.   19. Cf. S. of S. 3:11.

20. See below, 61.

21. "desideratam Desiderii regis Italorum filiam." This could as well be translated "the beloved daughter of Desiderius, king of the Italians." Cf. Einhard, *Vita Karoli*, 18, and Notker, *Gesta Karoli*, II, 16, where she is not named. See Note 181 to the Introduction.

22. Cf. Mark 6:17f., and parallels.   23. Cf. Heb. 11:24–27.

24. Cf. Ex. 2:15.   25. Cf. Ex. 3:1–6.   26. Luke 14:33.

27. Cf. Mark 10:25 and parallels.

28. "et ideo deposuit asello onera ut facilius arctam atque strictam viam mandatorum Dei curreret." Apparently an allusion to Matt. 7:14, but there is considerable variation of language.

29. Cf. Ps. 42:1 (Vulg. 41:2).   30. Cf. Num. 1:2f.

31. Cf. Josh. 8:1–3.   32. Cf. I Sam. 17:39f., 49.   33. Cf. Eph. 6:12.

34. Corbie on the Somme.   35. Cf. Ps. 118:19 (Vulg. 117:19).

36. Cf. Matt. 7:14.   37. *Ibid.*   38. Cf. Ps. 119:32 (Vulg. 118:32).

39. Cf. John 20:14–16.   40. Cf. John 20:12.

41. S. of S. 4:16 (Vulg. 5:1).   42. S. of S. 8:6.

43. Cf. S. of S. 4:16 (Vulg. 5:1).   44. Cf. S. of S. 6:2 (Vulg. 6:1).

45. Cf. Jerome's commentary on ch. 31 of Ezekiel, X (PL, xxv, 300C).

46. Cf. S. of S. 6:11 (Vulg. 6:10); 7:12. "Punic apples" are, of course, pomegranates.

47. Cf. S. of S. 4:11.   48. *Ibid.*   49. Gen. 12:1.

50. Cf. Mark 10:29f.   51. Gal. 2:20.

52. Cf. Vergil, *Eclogue* I, 3: "patriae fines et dulcia . . . arva . . . ."

53. Matt. 12:50.   54. Matt. 8:22.   55. Cf. Matt. 13:57f.

56. Jerome, *Ad Heliodorum* (on the death of his nephew Nepotianus), LX, 11, as numbered in PL, xxii, 596BC.

57. The phrase, "latter rain," appears in Deut. 11:14; Job 29:23; Prov. 16:15; Jer. 5:24; Dan. 11:29; Hos. 6:3; Joel 2:23; Zech. 10:1.

58. Horace, *Satirae*, II, 7, 86; see also *Wala*, I, 9:2.

59. Cf. I Cor. 9:22.

60. The four cardinal virtues; see Wisd. 8:7.

61. See Note 34 to the Introduction.

62. "neque iuxta proverbium vulgi, aureo pugno sit murus eius animi fractus." I have not succeeded in tracing this quotation.

63. Vergil, *Georgics*, II, 492: "Acherontis avari."

64. Since "who" and "were plundering" are plural, I have repeated the word "power" in the plural.

65. "sua cuique," a Ciceronian phrase describing justice; cf. Cicero, *De officiis*, I, 31, 110; *De finibus*, V, 23, 67; *De legibus*, I, 6, 19.

66. *Nuper* ("recently") seems inappropriate here.

67. Cf. S. of S. 4:12.   68. Isa. 66:2.

69. Cicero, *De inventione rhetorica*, II, 1: see also *Wala*, (1).

70. Reading *demum* for *domum*.   71. Cf. Matt. 25:2–10.

72. Cf. Matt. 24:43.   73. Cf. I Cor. 15:28.

74. Alcuin, *Epistolae* 189–93, as numbered in PL, c, 461B—467A.

75. In PL, viii, 795D—812D.   76. Gen. 22:8.   77. S. of S. 2:5; 5:8.

78. Cf. Lev. 1:8f.

79. Here one cannot resist mentioning the learned and delightful work of Leo Spitzer, *Classical and Christian Ideas of World Harmony* (Baltimore: Johns Hopkins Press, 1963), edited posthumously by Anna Granville Hicks.

80. Cf. I Cor. 6:19.   81. Ps. 42:2 (Vulg. 41:3).   82. S. of S. 5:8.

83. Possibly an indication that the book was intended to be read aloud on some occasions.

84. Cf. John 4:21, 23.   85. Cf. I Cor. 6:19.   86. I John 3:15.

87. Jan. 28, 814.

88. Plato, *Republic*, V, 473, as cited in Boethius, *De consolatione philosophiae*, I, 4 (prose), *ad init.*

89. Dan. 6:4.   90. Cf. Luke 14:10.   91. Cf. Matt. 5:3–9.

92. Cf. Matt. 5:10.   93. *Ibid.*

94. It is not clear why Adalard was banished.   95. Rom. 8:31.

96. Cf. Matt. 6:20.   97. Cf. Rev. 6:10.

98. Rom. 12:19 (Deut. 32:35).   99. Vergil, *Eclogue* VIII, 35.

100. See below, 65.   101. Ezek. 1:15–21?

102. "super quos Jesus lorica virtutum succinctus decentissime praesidebat." *Jesus* here may possibly be translated as *Joshua*.

103. Note the phrase, "Francorum imperium."

104. Hab. 3:8 (inexact).

105. "ut beatus Hieronymus ait, iidem in hoc opere unum aurigae jugum trahunt aequa cervice et proposito pares." I have failed in my efforts to trace this citation.

106. Tertullian, *De pudicitia*, 1, *ad init.*   107. Cf. Luke 10:39.

108. Cf. Phil. 3:14.   109. Cf. Luke 10:40.

110. "conceleres." The emendation *concolores* has been suggested, but it does not seem necessary.

111. Perhaps a confused allusion to Gen. 43:34.

112. Cf. II Chron. 16:9; Zech. 4:10.

113. Wisd. 8:1. This phrase occurs also in one of the Great Advent (or "O") Antiphons; see Cabaniss, "A Note on the Date of the Great Advent Antiphons," *Speculum*, XXIII, No. 3 (July, 1947), 440–42.

114. Later, on the eve of his restoration, he was found to be at Fleury; cf. Cabaniss, *Son of Charlemagne*, 72.

115. Cf. Acts 5:41.

116. "doluit se fecisse, quod iam ruboris erat inhibere." I have inserted *nihil* to complete the apparent meaning.

117. Cf. Job 23:14.   118. Cf. I Sam. 26:19.

119. "saxeum pectus." See Ezek. 11:19; 36:26, "lapideum pectus."

120. The Book of Revelation, *passim*.

121. I.e., *ca.* 815–22.   122. Cf. Isa. 11:2.

123. Cf. Song of Three Children (Apocrypha), 27 (Vulg. Dan. 3:50).

124. Cf. Rom. 8:35.   125. Cf. Matt. 7:25.

126. Cf. Ps. 34:8 (Vulg. 33:9).   127. Cf. Gen. 1–3.

128. Cf. Gen. 3:7, 10, 23f.   129. Vergil, *Georgics*, II, 467f.

130. Bede, *Homiliae*, I, 8 (on the feast of St. John, 27 Dec.), as in PL, xciv, 44C—49D, esp. 47B.

131. Cf. Rev. 2:20. "Jezebel" is obviously an allusion to the Empress Judith.

132. Two of the so-called seven deadly sins.

133. Vergil, *Eclogue* III, 92f.   134. Cf. Phil. 3:20.

135. Cf. Col. 3:2.   136. Cf. Col. 3:3f.   137. Cf. I Cor. 10:4.

138. Perhaps a reference to an art form.

139. The foregoing seems to be in some way related to Cicero, *Pro Sestio*, 65. The word *struma* (tumor) appears in both places.

140. *Annales regni Francorum, anno* 821; Cabaniss, *Son of Charlemagne*, 72.

141. Abbot when the relics of St. Filibert were brought to the monastery.

142. "ubi cum introisset, velut quidam ait, virtutum radiis illustratus, quia venit Titan, marcescunt sidera." I have not traced this citation.

143. *Annales regni Francorum, anno* 822; Cabaniss, *Son of Charlemagne*, 73, and *Agobard of Lyons*, 45.

144. Note the ambiguity; see the references in the preceding Note.

145. See Note 65 above.   146. Cf. I Tim. 6:4.

147. Cabaniss, *Agobard of Lyons*, 48.

148. "videtur demum novus renasci Francorum ordo et aurora iustitiae quasi ab ortu surgere."

149. Vergil, *Eclogue* IX, 58.

150. Cf. Vergil, *Eclogue* IV, 6f. (a free paraphrase).

151. S. of S. 5:10.   152. Cf. Isa. 40:6.

153. The Greek word means "a characterization."

154. Cf. Heb. 12:22.   155. Cf. Tit. 3:7.   156. Cf. Eph. 2:6.

157. Reading *gratiam* for *patriam*.

158. "propter quod ut credimus, ut optamus, supra multa constitutus iam ei vitae gaudia famulantur." Probably an allusion to Matt. 25:21.

159. From this point to the next annotation the quotations are from S. of S. 5:11–14, 16.

160. Cf. S. of S. 6:3 (Vulg. 6:2).   161. Cf. *ibid.*, 3:1.

162. Cf. Acts 7:22.   163. Ps. 132:8 (Vulg. 131:9).

164. Cf. Matt. 22:11–13.   165. Cf. Gen. 3:7.   166. Cf. Luke 10:31.

167. Based on Rev. 3:5.   168. Matt. 19:21.   169. Cf. Acts 20:35.

170. Cf. Heb. 9:4.   171. Cf. I Kings 6:20.

172. "illud beati Antonii quod sensus adinvenerit artem, et qui sensu fit integer eum arte non indigere." I have not succeeded in tracing this citation.

173. Cf. Rom. 10:12.   174. Cf. S. of S. 7:1.

175. "voce quidem canorius cygno mulcebat auditum." Probably related to some such sentiment as in Ovid, *Metamorphoses*, XIV, 430, "ut olim / carmina iam moriens canit exequialia cygnus . . . ."

176. Cf. Phil. 1:23.   177. *Translatio s. Viti*, 3.   178. Acts 20:35.

179. Paderborn.

180. Latin, *Corbeia*, designated as "new" to distinguish it from the older foundation and commonly spelled in English *Corvey* to differentiate it from *Corbie*.

181. Cf. I Cor. 13:13.   182. II Tim. 2:4; cf. *Wala*, II, 2:7; 3:5.

183. Cf. Matt. 5:3.

184. Augustine, *De quantitate animae*, XXXIII (PL, xxxii, 1073D—1077C).

185. Ps. 42:2 (Vulg. 41:3).

186. Cf. I Pet. 1:12; here cited out of context.

187. II Kings (Vulg. IV Kings) 2:12.   188. Cf. S. of S. 5:8.

189. "qui vestiebat nos charitatis coccini desuper totum deliciis intextum." Cf. II Sam. (Vulg. II Kings) 1:24.

190. Cf. Ps. 42:3, 9 (Vulg. 41:4,7).   191. Cf. S. of S. 3:1.

192. Note the play on words.   193. Cf. S. of S. 6:13 (Vulg. 6:12).

194. Cf. S. of S. 6:10 (Vulg. 6:9); 8:5.   195. Cf. Matt. 25:20–27.

196. Cf. Eph. 6:12.   197. Cf. Luke 19:41.

198. "Teutiscam"; see *Wala*, I, 1:2.   199. Cf. Lam. 1:12.

200. Cf. Luke 2:25.   201. Cf. Matt. 25:1.

202. Cf. Ps. 19:5 (Vulg. 18:6).   203. I.e., Dec. 23 [825].

204. S. of S. 2:5.   205. Cf. James 5:14.   206. Cf. Luke 2:29.

207. Cf. Mark 14:36.   208. Cf. Matt. 6:10.   209. Rom. 13:12.

210. Jan. 1 [826].   211. Cf. I Cor. 2:9.   212. II Tim. 4:7f.

213. I.e., about 3:00 P.M., Jan. 2, 826.

214. "quoniam, sicut alibi dictum est, et pium erat tanto viro congaudere et pium erat ab eius abscenssu flere." I have not traced this cliché.

215. Gen. 3:19.   216. Cf. Jer. 31:21.

217. Cf. Ps. 19:7 (Vulg. 18:8) or 23:3 (Vulg. 22:3).

218. Cf. Ps. 22:14 (Vulg. 21:15).   219. Cf. Ps. 137:6 (Vulg 136:6).

220. Cf. S. of S. 1:4.

221. As, e.g., in Ovid, *Metamorphoses*, XI, 1–66. See the interesting treatment, not of this, but of other pagan legends by Hugo Rahner, *Greek Myths and Christian Mystery*, trans. Brian Battershaw (New York and Evanston: Harper and Row, 1963).

222. Cf. S. of S. 4:8.   223. Cf. *ibid.*, 8:3.

224. Cf. *ibid.*, 1:16f. (Vulg. 1:15f.).   225. Cf. Luke 15:8f.

226. Cf. Prov. 22:1.   227. Cf. Vergil, *Eclogue* II, 47f., 50.

228. Cf. Rev. 3:12.   229. Cf. Ex. 17:8–13.

230. This and the quotation immediately preceding are from II Macc. 15:14.

231. "iuxta beati Ambrosii vocem, quia nemo habet quod aliis plus deferat quam quod sibi optat." I have not traced this allusion.

232. Note the alliteration, "sed nescis misera miseris miserans misereri."

233. Adalard was probably about seventy-five years old when he died.

234. The opening words of the great Palm Sunday hymn often attributed to Theodulf of Orléans (d. 821).

235. See Allen Cabaniss, "Alleluia: A Word and Its Effect," *University of Mississippi Studies in English*, V (1964), 67–74.

The Life of Wala, BOOK I

1. Cf. Cicero, *De inventione rhetorica*, I, 1, 1.

2. Cf. Vergil, *Aeneid*, II, 3.

3. Cf. Cicero, *op. cit.*, II, 1, and *Adalard*, 20:1.

4. Terence, *Hecyra*, III, 3, 1–3.   5. Wisd. 5:14.   6. John 11:26.

7. Jer. 15:10.   8. Rev. 8:8.   9. Cf. Rev. 8:11.

10. Cf. Seneca, *De beneficiis*, I, 3, "Chrysippus quoque penes quem subtile illud acumen est et in imam penetrans veritatem, qui rei agendae causa loquitur et verbis non ultra, quam ad intellectum satis est, utitur . . . ."

11. Note the conscious play on words.

12. Cf. Ps. 25:9 (Vulg. 24:9)?   13. Cf. I Tim. 4:8.

14. Seneca, *Ludus de morte Claudii*, 1.

15. "nonne legisti quod inefficacem petat studium res quae caret effectu?" I have not identified this allusion.

16. "lacrimis."   17. "fletibus."

18. "sed si proverbium illud antiquius verum esset, quod sola miseria invidia caret . . . ." The source of this proverb is unknown to me.

19. "fabula."   20. "fabulam."   21. "historiam."

22. Cf. Seneca, *op. cit.*, 1.   23. Prov. 27:17.

24. *Acta s. Sebastiani*, 1 (*Acta SS.*, ed. Bolland, Januar., II, 265), "Erat enim vir totius prudentiae, in sermone verax, in judicio justus, in consilio providus, in commisso fidelis." (I owe this reference to Dümmler's ed. of *Vita Walae;* see Bibliographical Notes.) Cf. *Annales regni Francorum, anno* 826.

25. *Ibid.*   26. Cf. Cicero, *op. cit.*, I, 4, 5.

27. Presumably Germanic and Latin; see *Adalard*, 77.   28. Jer. 15:10.

29. Cf. Jer. 15:17.

30. Cf. Ennius, *Annales* (*apud Charisium*, 251), a fragment of uncertain location, "Marsa manus, Peligna cohors, Vestina virum vis."

31. Corbie on the Somme; see *Adalard*, 8:1; Cabaniss, *Son of Charlemagne*, 91; *Annales regni Francorum, anno* 826.

32. Rom. 8:14.   33. Jer. 9:1; see 2:5 below.

34. Ps. 19:7; 23:3 (Vulg. 18:8; 22:3); cf. also Lam. 1:16.

35. Jer. 18:18.

36. Bobbio? Cf. II, 23:2 below. For the biblical allusion, see Ps. 91:1 (Vulg. 90:1).

37. Lam. 2:11.   38. Cf. Lam. 1:2.

39. Cf. Jer. 9:1; Bede, *De die judicii*, 13 (see 2:4 above).

40. Cf. Jer. 38:6, 13.   41. Jer. 7:16; 11:14; 14:11.

42. II Macc. 15:14.   43. Terence, *Andria*, I, 1, 34.

44. Terence, *Adelphi*, IV, 3, 14–16.   45. Gal. 5:6.   46. Cf. *Ibid.*

47. See Mark 6:26 (Matt. 14:9).   48. Cf. Rom. 13:8.

49. Cf. Gal. 5:6.

50. The text has *mentes* as here translated, but it appears that *montes* would be far more apt.

51. Terence, *Phormio*, I, 8, 57.   52. Cf. Terence, *Phormio*, IV, 1, 23.

53. Statius, *Thebaid*, X, 896.   54. Cf. Gal. 5:6.   55. Eccl. 12:11.

56. "putantne contra Apostolum, quod a Domino ulterius iustorum extorris a consilio iudicetur?" By no means an exact quotation, but perhaps a reflection of Luke 1:17.

57. Ps. 91:3 (Vulg. 90:3).   58. Wisd. 3:3.

59. A free paraphrase of Seneca, *Epistola ad Lucilium*, 63 (VII, 1), "Nam, ut dicere solebat Attalus noster, 'sic amicorum defunctorum memoria iucunda est, quomodo poma quaedam sunt suaviter aspera . . . .'"

60. Cf. John 16:7.

61. E.g., Ps. 13:3 (Vulg. 12:4); John 11:11; etc.

62. "spectant, ut quidam sanctorum ait, iam puro etherioque sensu." No commentator appears to know the source of this citation.

63. Cf. I Cor. 15:54.   64. Cf. Acts 17:28.

65. First reference to this interlocutor (with a Terentian name) who plays only a minor part in the conversation.

66. Cf. I Cor. 12:6 (not very apt).   67. Cf. Wisd. 3:6.

68. Accepting an emendation suggested by Weinrich, *op. cit.*, 16 and n. 49.

69. II Sam. 6:22.

70. "et cum sibi magnus sufficiensque, utique, sicut legitur, parvulus estimatur." This seems to be made up of tags from such Scriptures as I Cor. 6:4; II Cor. 3:5; 12:9; I Sam. 15:17; II Sam. 7:19.

71. Cf. Gen. 41:38–43; *Adalard*, 32:2; *Annales regni Francorum, anno* 812; Cabaniss, *Son of Charlemagne*, 54.

72. Against the Abitrices (Abotrites?); see 11:11 below; *Annales regni Francorum, anno* 811.

73. New Corvey on the Weser; see *Adalard*, 65–67.

74. "an ignoras quod qui mundum colit preciosa perdit?" Cf. Mark 8:35–37.

75. Traube suggests a relationship between this sentence and Cicero, *Somnium Scipionis*. If so, it may be to *Somnium*, III, 1 and 6.

76. Cato, *Disticha*, I, 13, 2 (inverted); surely not II, 20, 2, as given in Dümmler's ed. of the *Vita Walae*, 31. An interesting edition of Cato's *Disticha* is Halldór Hermannsson, ed., *The Hólar Cato* (Islandica, XXXIX; Ithaca, N.Y.: Cornell University Press, 1958); the distich here referred to occurs on p. 10. Cf. Richard Hazelton, "The Christianization of 'Cato': the *Disticha Catonis* in the Light of Late Medieval Commentaries," *Mediaeval Studies* (Toronto), XIX (1957), 157–73.

77. E.g., Luke 24:22–43; John 20:24–28.   78. Heb. 11:5.

79. See *Butler's Lives of the Saints*, ed. Herbert Thurston and Donald Attwater (New York: P. J. Kenedy and Sons, 1956), IV, 509–16.

80. *Ibid.*, I, 77–80.   81. II Tim. 2:21.

82. Second reference to Chremes.

83. First reference to Allabigus, who figures briefly in the conversation.

84. The first time Chremes speaks; see 26:1–11; 27:2.

85. The only time Allabigus speaks.

86. II Kings (Vulg. IV Kings) 2:23.

87. Terence, *Eunuchus*, II, 16–22.

88. II Kings (Vulg. IV Kings) 2:10.

89. "In the middle" implies an awareness that there is a distinct break between Isa. 39 and 40.

90. Isa. 19:2f.   91. See Note 39 above.

92. Not quoted by Vergil, but by Ausonius in his *De viro bono*, 5. See Bernard Simson, "Zum Gedicht de viro bono," *Rheinisches Museum für Philologie*, XLI, 638f.

93. Horace, *Satirae*, II, 7, 86; see also *Adalard*, 15.

94. Again, not Vergil, but Ausonius, *Eclogue* VII, 3, 1–3; see the two preceding Notes.

95. Cf. Rev. 4:3.   96. Ps. 84:5 (Vulg. 83:6).

97. Ps. 84:7 (Vulg. 83:8).   98. Rom. 8:28.

99. Ps. 17:4 (Vulg. 16:4).

100. This is a statement attributed to St. Anthony in St. Jerome, *Vita s. Pauli*, 13 (PL, xxiii, 26C).

101. *Regula s. Benedicti*, 64, "prodesse magis quam praeesse."

102. I Cor. 13:8.   103. Cf. Mark 9:6.   104. Cf. Luke 10:39.

105. Ps. 119:82 (Vulg. 118:82).   106. Luke 10:41f.

107. "illud Catonis: Si velim, aut nolim, et si possim, aut non possim." Not in Cato's *Disticha*; is this perhaps a variation on the quotation from Terence, *Phormio*, I, 8, 57, in 3:4? See Note 51 above.

108. Prov. 8:34?

109. "ne comicorum notam incurras." The quotations following are from Terence, *Heautontimorumenos*, I, 1, 91–105.

110. Cf. Heb. 11:1.   111. Cf. Wisd. 3:6.

112. Jan. 2, 826; see *Adalard*, 81:2; 82; 87.   113. See *Adalard*, 86.

114. Cf. Deut. 28:13.   115. Terence, *Andria*, I, 1, 34; cf. 2:8 above.
116. John 11:25.   117. Gal. 5:6.   118. Cf. II Cor. 4:10.
119. See 6:6 above.   120. Cf. 13:2 below.   121. Cf. Gal. 6:2.
122. New Corvey for men and Herford for women; see 15:1, 4 below.
123. See *Adalard*, 65.   124. Cf. Tob. 5:23; 10:4.
125. Exact phrase not in the New Testament, but familiar today from its use in the Dead Sea Scrolls.
126. Luke 6:40.   127. Vergil, *Aeneid*, X, 535f.
128. "perciperem."   129. "exciperem."
130. "excipere." Observe the rhyme in this and the two preceding Notes.
131. Cf. Matt. 10:16?
132. Cf. Ezek. 40:2. The Hebrew text reads, "to the south"; the Greek LXX, "opposite me"; and the Vulgate, "to the south."
133. Cf. John 20:24–29. Or this may perhaps be an allusion to the apocryphal *Acta Thomae*.
134. Based on Rev. 21:2 and Isa. 61:10.
135. Cf. 13:2 above and *Translatio s. Viti*, 3.
136. Boethius, *De consolatione philosophiae*, II, metrum V, line 10. In Dümmler's ed. of *Vita Walae*, 46, n. 2, there is a reference to Vergil, *Georgics*, III, 530, but the similarity is not as precise as in Boethius.
137. Cf. Gen. 28:11.   138. Cf. Mark 6:8.
139. Cf. Vergil, *Aeneid*, II, 368f.
140. Reminiscent of St. Augustine, *De civitate Dei*.
141. Note play on words.   142. See Note 132 above.
143. Cf. Matt. 5:3, 5–7.   144. Cf. *Adalard*, 68.   145. Cf. Isa. 5:8.
146. Warinus, Adalard's successor at New Corvey, ruled thirty years, 826–56; see *Translatio s. Viti*, 4.
147. See Note 132 above.   148. Matt. 19:29.
149. Cf. Ps. 102:4f. (Vulg. 101:4f.).
150. Terence, *Eunuchus*, I, 2, 22.
151. *Ibid.*, II, 2, 16–19; cf. 8:3 above.
152. *Ibid.*, II, 2, 1. Paschasius Radbertus has substituted "bone Jesu" for the Terentian "di immortales."
153. *Ibid.*, II, 2, 7.   154. *Ibid.*, II, 2, 4.   155. E.g., Jer. 43:1f.
156. II. Tim. 4:2.   157. Terence, *Phormio*, IV, 2, 1.
158. Isa. 48:9.   159. Eccl. 12:11.
160. *Regula s. Benedicti*, 36, "ante omnia et super omnia."
161. Cf. Ps. 23:2 (Vulg. 22:2).
162. Based on Terence, *Adelphi*, V. 4, 1–20.
163. Not in Prov., but in Eccl. 2:24 and 3:12.
164. Severus was one of Adalard's successors as abbot of Corbie.
165. Based on Terence, *Adelphi*, V, 4, 1–20; see Note 162 above.
166. Terence, *Adelphi*, V, 4, 23–26.   167. Cf. Luke 15:20, 22.
168. Based on Matt. 25:18, 24–27.   169. *Ibid.*

170. Is this not rather an allusion to Ezek. 3:8?

171. Ps. 111:10 (Vulg. 110:10).   172. Cf. Luke 15:20.

173. "et tamen recidivi surgebant casus," an interesting play on words.

174. Cf. John 13:3.   175. Rom. 12:2.   176. Vergil, *Aeneid,* I, 118.

177. Job 29:24.   178. *Ibid.*   179. Job 29:21   180. Job 29:14.

181. Job 29:16.   182. *Annales regni Francorum, anno* 822.

183. "unum e pluribus"! Cf. Augustine, *Confessions,* IV, 8, "ex pluribus unum facere."

184. "et bene (ut aiunt iocose) omnia defendit, qui possessori nihil relinquit." Apparently a popular remark current at that time.

185. Cf. Isa. 1:23; 56:11.   186. Isa. 1:23.   187. Cf. Gen. 4:10.

188. Ps. 7:9 (Vulg. 7:10).   189. Cf. Gen. 4:10.   190. Cf. Isa. 1:23.

191. Cf. Ecclus. 35:18f.   192. Cf. Gen. 4:10.   193. Isa. 1:23.

194. Cf. Isa. 1:23; 59:14f.   195. Cf. Terence, *Hecyra,* V, 4, 39f.

196. Vergil, *Eclogue* IV, 6; VI, 41; *Aeneid,* XI, 253.

197. Eugenius II, 824–27. The name of this pope and that of Queen Irmingard (see below, II, 24:1) are the only real names employed in *Wala;* all the others are pseudonyms.

198. Cf. Acts 14:16.

The Life of Wala, BOOK II

1. "alioquin honestius non inchoasse quam inchoata non explere." This statement may be a quotation, but if so I do not know the source.

2. Note the play on words.

3. I Kings (Vulg. III Kings) 2:2.

4. I.e., amid the disorders that happened at Corbie while Radbertus was abbot; see Englemodus, *Carmina,* III, in PLAC, III, 62–66.

5. Cf. II Cor. 13:1.   6. Isa. 28:19.   7. Held in 829.

8. Cf. Sulpicius Severus, *Vita s. Martini,* 20 (*Corpus Scriptorum Ecclesiaticorum Latinorum,* I, 128f.).

9. *Annales regni Francorum, anno* 810; see also Cabaniss, *Agobard of Lyons,* 21, and "Agobard of Lyons: Rumour, Propaganda and Freedom of Thought in the Ninth Century," *History Today,* III, No. 2 (Feb., 1953), 128–34. The latter was reprinted as "Agobard of Lyons" in *Diversions of History,* ed. Peter Quennell (London: Allen Wingate, 1954), 41–51 (illustrated). The incident was a very curious one, arousing much interesting speculation.

10. There was indeed an unusual number of miracle stories and miracle-filled lives of saints in the ninth century. Consult Edward P. Colbert, *The Martyrs of Córdoba (850–859): A Study of the Sources* (Washington, D.C.: Catholic University of America Press, 1962).

11. A conceit that the late Leo Spitzer would have enjoyed. See his *Classical and Christian Ideas of World Harmony*.

12. "ut daretur intelligi, quod nostra infidelitas iuxta apostolum id exigeret, quia signa non fidelibus, sed infidelibus, ipso teste, verissime dantur." Cf. I Cor. 14:22.

13. Cf. John 1:9.   14. Wisd. 6:24 (Vulg. 6:26).

15. "quando *honores* ecclesiarum, immo, ut sentio, *onera*." Note the play on words, indicating disappearance of the aspirate.

16. "ne aut tu tibi tua eligas, tibique." Note alliteration.

17. Cf. I Cor. 6:8f.   18. Prov. 9:17.

19. Cf. Ps. 107:40 (Vulg. 106:40).

20. II Tim. 2:4; cf. Note 22 below and *Adalard*, 68:2.

21. Cf. Matt. 16:19.

22. II Tim. 2:4; cf. Note 20 above and *Adalard*, 68:2.

23. Charles the Bald, son of Louis the Pious and Judith.

24. Actually at four places: Mainz, Paris, Lyons, Toulouse.

25. Cf. Rom. 8:38f.

26. Cf. Walafrid Strabo, *Visio Wettini*, 327–38 (PL, cxiv, 1070C—1071A); Lupus Ferrariensis, *Epistola* 25 (PL, cxix, 474B—475B); Cabaniss, *Agobard of Lyons*, 61.

27. Cf. Matt. 6:33.

28. Cf. Jer. 49:7. Dümmler, in his ed. of *Vita Walae*, cites Ps. 107:27 (Vulg. 106:27), but, despite similarities, the reference to the prophet suggests that the allusion is to Jeremiah.

29. Cf. II Cor. 12:9?

30. Cf. Lucan, *De bello civile*, I, 1. Radbertus makes the same allusion in his commentary on Matthew XI, 24, and on Lamentations, IV.

31. By his father, St. William of Gellone.

32. The four cardinal virtues; see Wisd. 8:7.   33. Cf. Zeph. 1:15.

34. Cf. Num. 24:15f.   35. Cf. Isa. 10:5.   36. Probably Rothlindis.

37. Cf. Ex. 14:13.

38. Cf. Cicero, *Pro Sestio*, VII, 15, "ex omnium scelerum colluvione natus."

39. Phrase repeated in 9:3 below.

40. "deceptus a qua eum Salomon cavere monuerat, immo lenonis eiusdem insidiis." Cf. Eccl. 7:26?

41. Phrase employed also in 9:2 above.

42. Surely Louis did speak ambivalently.

43. See Cabaniss, *Son of Charlemagne*, 90.   44. *Ibid.*   45. *Ibid.*, 91.

46. Near Lake Leman; see 12:1 below.   47. "excessisse."

48. "excessus." See preceding Note. Is this a play on words?

49. Cf. Phil. 2:21.   50. Cf. Matt. 5:10.   51. Cf. I Tim. 2:2.

52. Matt. 12:25.

53. In 817 and confirmed in 823; see Cabaniss, *Son of Charlemagne*, 75

54. Two of the seven gifts of the Holy Spirit; see Isa. 11:2.

55. Cf. 13:1 below and *Adalard,* 32:1.　　56. Cf. Phil. 4:18.

57. Cf. II Cor. 2:15.　　58. Cf. II Tim. 2:12.

59. "secum semetipsum semper sibi praesentem ferebat." Note the heavy alliteration.

60. Cf. Ps. 93:3f. (Vulg. 92:3f).　　61. Job 38:11.

62. Cf. *Adalard,* 39.　　63. Cf. Matt. 11:2f.; Luke 7:19.

64. Cf. 11:2 above and *Adalard,* 22:1.　　65. See *Adalard,* 40, 41.

66. Cf. Mark 6:27; Matt. 14:10.　　67. Perhaps Fulda?

68. Cf. Ps. 126:6 (Vulg. 125:6).　　69. Pope Gregory IV, 827–44.

70. Cf. *Regula s. Benedicti,* 4, "Officina vero, ubi haec omnia diligenter operemur claustra sunt monasterii . . . ."

71. Cf. Matt. 11:11 (Luke 7:28); I Kings 17—II Kings 2 (Vulg. III Kings 17—IV Kings 2); II Kings 2–13 (Vulg. IV Kings 2–13).

72. Cf. Matt. 23:35 (Luke 11:51); Jer. 38:6; Heb. 11:37.

73. The death of Bernard of Barcelona (Naso) is recorded in *Annales Bertiniani, anno* 844, "Bernardus comes marcae Hispanicae, iam dudum grandia moliens summisque inhians, maiestatis reus Francorum iudicio, iussu Karoli [Calvi] in Aquitania capitalem sententiam subiit."

74. Cf. Ex. 32:22.　　75. Cf. Rom. 9:3.

76. "quoniam laudibilius est bene mori vel periclitari cum bonis et optimis quam male vivere aut consentire cum pessimis." This statement has the appearance of being a quotation or an allusion.

77. Eph. 6:5; Phil. 2:12.　　78. I.e., Bernard of Barcelona (Naso).

79. Cabaniss, *Son of Charlemagne,* 96, and *Agobard of Lyons,* 84.

80. Cf. Jer. 20:1 for this name. Pashhur (Latin, *Phasur*) is the only pseudonym here used that has not been penetrated.

81. A familiar concept respecting the papal office: cf., e.g., Alcuin (to Arno), *Epistola* 108 (PL, c, 326). The language goes back to I Cor. 2:15.

82. Cf. II Chron. (Vulg. II Paral.) 18:10; see also Ezek. 34:21 and Ecclus. 5:11.

83. Eph. 6:1, 4; Col. 3:20f.

84. There is no other record of these *capitula.*

85. Cabaniss, *Agobard of Lyons,* 81.　　86. Cf. Isa. 40:4.

87. "hoc legimus in gestis antiquorum."

88. See Cabaniss, *Son of Charlemagne,* 97.　　89. Cf. John 14:27.

90. Cf. Matt. 10:13 (Luke 10:6).　　91. Cf. Gen. 3:6, 12.

92. Matt. 10:40; Luke 10:16.　　93. Cf. Ps. 1:2.

94. Probably in annals of the time.

95. Or more probably with persuasion and urging, perhaps even bribery; see Cabaniss, *Son of Charlemagne,* 97.

96. Cf. Ex. 16:15.　　97. Ps. 118:16 (Vulg. 117:16).

98. "totius monarchiam imperii."

99. Vergil, *Aeneid,* VI, 733, "Hinc metuunt, cupiuntque; dolent, gaudentque . . . ." Radbertus uses the same allusion in his commentary on Jeremiah, III.

100. Cf. Matt. 12:25.   101. Cf. Prov. 11:14.   102. Cf. Job 12:6.

103. Cf. Job 12:13.   104. Cf. Job 12:14.   105. Cf. Job 12:16.

106. Cf. Job 12:17.   107. Cf. Job 12:18.   108. Cf. Job 12:19.

109. Cf. Job 12:20.   110. Cf. Job 12:21.   111. Job 12:24.

112. Job 12:25.   113. Job 23:13.

114. "pennigeroque gressu." *Translatio s. Viti*, 3, relates that a messenger brought news of Charlemagne's death to Italy with winged flight (*penigero volatu*). Heinz Löwe, in Wilhelm Levison and Heinz Löwe, ed. (Wattenbach-Levison) *Deutschlands Geschichtsquellen im Mittelalter: Vorzeit und Karolinger*, II, *Die Karolinger vom Anfang des 8. Jahrhunderts bis zum Tode Karls des Grossen* (Weimar: Hermann Böhlaus Nachfolger, 1953), 235, n. 229, cites an article (which I have not seen) by Henri Peltier, "Nuntius pennigero volatu. Pigeons voyageurs?" *Rev. Moyen Age Lat.*, 3 (1947), 156–58. Although the phrase in *Wala* is used in a different context from the one in *Translatio*, the latter book, depending, as it does, on the former, probably took the idea and one word from it.

115. Bobbio.

116. Cf. Jonas, *Vita s. Columbani*, 33 (PL, ciii, 1030B–D). The reference is to the Visigothic Queen Brunhilda.

117. Cf. Matt. 25:25. One can only agree with Dümmler and Mabillon that the language here is tangled and obscure, that on the surface it may appear to refer to St. Columban, but that on closer inspection it seems to refer to Wala.

118. Cf. the "Eclogue" with which *Adalard* concludes, (a) above.

119. "eiusque memoriae commendatio declarat quod melior est dies mortis quando perpetuam ingressus est vitam quam dies nativitatis eius quando ut vivere coepit mox morti obnoxius fuit." This statement may be a quotation, but if so I have not traced the source of it.

120. Cf. Rom. 5:15.   121. Cf. Ps. 84:10 (Vulg. 83:11).

122. Cabaniss, *Son of Charlemagne*, 108, 110.   123. Cf. Eph. 1:18.

124. Cf. Eccl. 4:12?

125. Aug. 31, 836; Bernard Simson, *Jahrbücher des fränkischen Reichs unter Ludwig dem frommen*, II (Leipzig: Duncker-Humblot, 1876), 156, n. 5.

126. I.e., in Italy.   127. Cf. I Cor. 15:31.

128. "ut philosophi dicunt, sapientis viri vita meditatio mortis est." See Jerome, *Epistola* LX, 14 (as numbered in PL, xxii, 598A), "Platonis sententia est omnem sapientium vitam meditationem esse mortis." Plato's statement occurs in the *Phaedo*.

129. Cf. I Cor. 13:9, 12.   130. Ps. 39:5 (Vulg. 38:6).

131. Ambrose, *De bono mortis*, 2:3, "sed mortis tria sunt genera." See Note 137 below.

132. Cf. Rom. 6:11.   133. Ezek. 18:4.   134. Cf. Rom. 6:7.

135. Gen. 3:17, 19.

136. Based on Gen. 3:18; Mark 4:7 (Matt. 13:7; Luke 8:7); Mark 4:19 (Matt. 13:22; Luke 8:14); John 6:32f.

137. Ambrose, *De bono mortis* in PL, xiv, 539A—568A.

138. Cf. Phil. 1:21.   139. *Ibid.*

140. Irmingard, wife of Emperor Lothair I, d. Mar. 20, 851; see *Annales Bertiniani, anno* 853. Queen Irmingard and Pope Eugenius II (see above, I, 28:1) are the only persons mentioned in *Wala* by their real names, not by pseudonyms.

141. The convent of San Salvatore.   142. The hymn *Te Deum*.

143. James 1:12.   144. Matt. 25:21.

145. Adapted from Matt. 20:13–15.

146. The last two pages of the MS are defective.

Index of Principal Names